Jack & Bill's War

Jack & Bill Fairs

A diary of their experiences
with the RAF in the Middle East

Jack & Bill's War

ISBN 0-9532991-7-1 (paperback)
ISBN 0-9532991-8-X (hardback)
First Published in 2001 by Classfern Limited
2 South Hill Grove, Oxton Village, Wirral, CH43 5SH

Designed and Typeset by Nemo of Liverpool
Printed & Bound by MFP of Stretford, Manchester

to Muriel and Sybil
for patience and encouragement

The Authors

Jack and Bill Fairs were born in Rock Ferry on the Wirral peninsula on 25th August 1918. Identical twins, Jack was the elder by one hour and throughout their childhood, adolescence, teenage years and, indeed, the whole of their adult lives they have remained very close to each other.

Not only are they identical twins, but they also think alike and now, even after more than 80 years, do not like to to be parted from each other for more than a few days.

If there is a difference between the twins, it is in their personalities; Jack is, perhaps, the more serious, whereas Bill has always been the more outspoken and adventurous. And so it is with this account of their 'war'. Most of the book has been written by Jack but it has only been possible with Bill's recollections, assistance and encouragement.

After leaving school in the thirties, Jack and Bill followed different routes into their eventual chosen career – photography. Just before the outbreak of war in 1939 they had established their own small photograhic studio. As a result, when they were called up to serve their King, they applied to join the RAF and were posted into the photo reconnaissance section.

Today, Jack and Bill and their wives, Muriel and Sybil, still live close to each other in Bebington and close, also, to the business they have built up in the years since the war.

Jack and Bill with equipment used in their childrens' photographic studio

Jack and Bill Fairs in 1939

Foreword

I have known Jack and Bill Fairs, personally, for only a few years but, like many others, I have been swept along by their enthusiasm for life. Now well into their eighties these identical twins, who are gradually becoming easier to tell apart, still retain a youthful vigour and a refreshing sense of fun. They remain very closely involved with the highly successful business which they have built up over long years of hard work and good service.

There is no doubt that they are both very successful businessmen and they enjoy fully the fruits of their long working life, but, nevertheless, they still retain a 'down to earth' simplicity in all they do. Jack, for example, has always been a bit of an inventor – coming up with novel ideas to solve simple problems. He designed a tool for picking up litter which is now used almost universally by cleansing departments throughout the country, and indeed, across the world.

But it is their sense of fun sprinkled with a bit of 'mischief' that oozes out of these pages. Their accident of birth – being identical twins – gave them a base from which much of this fun emanates. Their charm and charisma, particularly with the young ladies they often 'shared', knowingly or, in some cases, unknowingly, ensured that they were always the centre of attention. Their sense of adventure and natural curiosity often led them into very interesting situations, many of which are recounted in the pages of this book.

But, perhaps more than anything else, their sense of giving and helping their fellow man has been part of their lives since their youngest days, when, only in their early teens, they formed their own boys' club in Birkenhead. Later they were to become involved with the Toc-H organisation and later still, the Salvation Army.

They had a 'good war', they are the first to admit. They appreciate that many were much less fortunate, and many, indeed, paid the ultimate price. However, Jack and Bill played their part, and a very vital part at that. They were always where the action was about to happen and often got caught up in it. But, wherever they were, whatever they were doing, they managed to find time to explore and enjoy the world, its places and its people.

Join these two remarkable men in 'their war' and enjoy these stories and their amazing photographs, I did.

John Birtwistle, Editor/Publisher, Wirral Champion Magazine

Introduction

This book recounts the amazing experiences of Jack and Bill Fairs covering the period from the late 1930s to the late 1940s including, particularly, their remarkable period of war service, from 1939 to 1945. This was mainly in the Middle East where they moved around extensively, but they also saw service in England, Scotland and across Europe. The book also includes an introduction to their careers in photography, careers which intrinsically led to these wartime experiences.

Follow them to Egypt, Greece, Crete, Palestine, Iraq, then back to Egypt and the Western Desert. Meet the many fascinating people they encountered on their travels and, particularly, the many young ladies they had the pleasure, and opportunity, to escort. Read also much background information on the development of photo-reconnaissance and on other aspects of many wartime operations.

At the end of the war they returned home to their fledgling photographic studio. Then, after a short stay in Canada in 1947, when they had considered emigration, Jack returned to join his brother Bill in 'William Fairs, Photographer of Children'. Over the subsequent years they have built this small studio into one of the most successful private businesses on Wirral. Fairs Cameras of Dacre Hill is now a major and much respected retailer of photographic, audio-visual and related equipment and, now in their eighties, Jack and Bill still 'go to the office' each day, overseeing the business they have lovingly built up over more than fifty five years.

The book is based on the numerous letters home which Jack wrote over a period of six years to their Mother and Father and sister Gladys in Rock Ferry. Every few days he would meticulously recount the events of the previous days and, when possible, would include photographs of the people they had met and the places they had seen and visited.

Thanks to this steady flow of letters from Jack together with their sister's careful preservation of all the material, an 'archive' of their war gradually built up. It is this 'archive' together with the many friendships made during those difficult years, which now form the basis for this fascinating book.

Index

Chapter		Page N°
1	The Cruise	1
2	Slow Boat to Egypt 1940	5
3	Arrival in Egypt	11
4	Photography – The Beginning	15
5	In the RAF – The Beginning	19
6	Greece – Beauty and Horrors	23
7	Greece – Bombers and Brothels	29
8	Greece – A Village Visit	33
9	Greece – Tremors and Teeth	37
10	Retreat from Larissa	43
11	To Corinth	47
12	To Nauplian	51
13	Crete	55
14	Letter from Israel	59
15	A Day in the Life of Jack & Bill Fairs	63
16	The Enchanted Garden	67
17	The Zelcers	69
18	Goodbye Tel Aviv	73
19	Crossing the Desert	77
20	Habbaniya, Iraq	81
21	Habbaniya Memories	85
22	The Western Desert	89
23	Letter from the Desert	93
24	A Momentous Decision	97
25	Posted to Heliopolis	99
26	Another World	103
27	The Cotton Story	107
28	Is Jack Guilty?	111
29	Letter from Heliopolis	115
30	One of Our Planes is Missing	117
31	Letter to the CO	121
32	The Stirling Story	123
33	Suda Bay	127
34	Heliopolis Bombed	129
35	Toc-H	135
36	We Join the Army	139
37	Tea Sar	141

Chapter		Page N°
38	Twenty Four Hours	145
39	First Priority	151
40	The Magicians	155
41	The Battle Begins	157
42	The Dead City	161
43	Jack Joins the Navy	165
44	The Three Palaces	169
45	The Tura Caves	173
46	Some Very Interesting People	177
47	The Birthday	181
48	Night of the Big Fish	187
49	The WAAFs	189
50	Kan el Khalili	193
51	The Mosquito	197
52	Cleo and Alexandria	201
53	Most Secret	205
54	Tented Camp	209
55	Ali Shaltoot	213
56	Dishforth	215
57	Eyes in the Sky	221
58	The Last Letter	225
59	Goodbye Cairo!	227
60	The Boat	235
61	Home and Tain	239
62	Benson	243
63	London and the BBSU	247
64	Bad Nenndorf	251
65	The Teams	255
66	Berchtesgaden	259
67	Hitler's Chalet	265
68	Demob' Centre	269
69	The Studio	273
70	Emigration	277
71	Halifax and the USA	279
72	Vancouver	283
73	Back Home	289

Illustrations

page	
vii	Jack & Bill with photo equipment in studio
viii	Jack & Bill in 1939
2	'Cruise Ship' life around pool
2	'Empress of Canada'
4	Crew of 'Empress of Canada'
4	Church service on ship
7	'True Sons of the Sea' thrown into pool
7	'Father Neptune' and his 'Queen'
8	Durban
8	Men in rickshaw in Durban
9	'Barbers' lathering novices
10	Sitting in the 'Dr Zhivago' cattle truck
10	Boy with two laden camels
12	Jack & Bill with El Gindi family in the garden
12	Group of 15 ACIs with Jack & Bill
14	Jack & Bill and friends with empty bottles
14	Empty factory
17	Commercial Solvents Bromborough factory
17	Jack & Bill in the 30s
18	Bell tents on the farm at Tafarn-y-Gelyn
18	Jack & Bill in uniform
21	Aircrew at Debden
21	Fairey Battle
24	Large Greek railway locomotive
24	Larissa
24	Washing our gumboots
26	Bill sitting on 250lb bombs
27	Visiting Greek soldiers in hospital
27	Group of nurses and patients outside hospital
28	Jack and Dunmore loading the camera
28	Old Greek shepherd in sheepskin coat
28	Bill and Tommy in the irrigation channel
31	Bill shaving in cold water
31	Bill at his 'desk' writing home
32	The whole village turned out
32	Drinking coffee round a table
32	Group of ladies making scarves
34	Little church in Larissa
35	Basket-maker
35	Tapping tree to make Retsina
35	The postman with the villagers
36	Jack and Greek soldier reading newspaper
37	Greek trumpeter
38	Remains of the cookhouse
38	Clockface in the earthquake rubble
38	Italian prisoners digging in rubble
39	Mount Olympus and our tents
40	The dentist's premises in Athens
40	Filling petrol drums with soil
40	Jack with aeroplane and villagers
42	View from the Acropolis
42	Jack with the palace guard

page	
42	Pretty little Greek girl
44	Soldiers shaving at the roadside
44	Tent camouflaged with branches
46	Smoke rising from crashed Blenheim
46	View from the camp at Tatoi
48	Paddy Duff with machine gun
48	Jack & Bill outside 'Dapper Dan's Cabin'
49	Bill crouching in the slit trench
50	Waiting at Menidi airfield
50	Troops welcomed in Athens
50	Hypo, our pet pooch
52	Jack and Paddy Boreland and village girls
52	Pretty girl cooking eggs for Bill
52	On our way to the Corinth Canal
54	On board the 'Glenern'
54	Jack in a hole in the ground
56	The pretty secretary at Commercial Solvents
56	Sunderland flying boat at Suda Bay
58	Jack & Bill in standard iron beds
60	The convoy kicking up dust
60	Lads waking up next to truck
62	The beach at Tel Aviv
62	Jack and Tommy at the Sieff Research Institute
64	Jack & Bill checking film with pilot
64	Jack with Miriam and Etti
65	The Ben Yehuda Cafe in Tel Aviv
66	Miriam and Etti on the beach
67	Ilsa, the waitress at the Ben Yehuda Cafe
68	The Kibbutz of Ramat Gann
69	Frank Sheepwash and colleague Bob
70	Jack and Tommy on the Zelcer's balcony
70	The Mograbi Cinema in Tel Aviv
72	Etti with her mother
72	The beautiful beach at Tel Aviv
74	Jack and George on the promenade at Tel Aviv
74	The Brock girls on Jack's back
74	Jack, Tommy and Mr Dixon at Ben Yehuda
76	Bill climbing the date palm
79	Hard tack biscuits and tins of pilchards
79	Corned beef turns to fat!
79	Rolls Royce armoured cars
80	Habbaniya Camp sign
80	The tented village known as 'Hell's Villas'
83	The articulated Mercedes Benz coach
83	Swimming pool at Habbinaya Camp
84	Mounted policeman at Habbinaya
84	English style church at Habbinaya
85	Shaving with a piece of broken glass
87	Mountains of lemonade bottles at cinema
87	Open air cinema at Habbinaya
88	Group of men on truck leaving Habbinaya
90	Winter uniform at Dishforth

page	
90	Summer uniform in the Western Desert
91	Bill 'thinking' on the beach
91	MT Section coming to the rescue
92	Some of the lads dressed as Arabs
94	Jack & Bill in portable darkroom
95	Jack reading the newspaper
95	Etti standing on the beach
95	Jack having a haircut
96	Group standing beside finished trench
96	Drinking tea around the cans
96	'Desert Lillies' found in many camps!
96	Medical Section's sign – skull and crossbones
98	Jack's application for a posting
99	Cartoon of old lady
100	Paddy field and Pyramids
102	Tram in Heliopolis main street
102	Girls carrying water jugs on their heads
103	Cartoon of pig
104	Servicemens' club in Heliopolis
104	Heliopolis open-air cinema
105	Metro tram in Heliopolis
108	Stanley Cotton's Lockheed 12A
109	Wing Commander F Sidney Cotton
110	Gordon Turvey and Matron at Cairo Toc-H
110	Cairo's modern buildings
113	Young girls tending goats
113	Conductor on tram
114	Jack & Bill in the El Gindi home
114	Wedding party for Greek girl
116	Alice, a redhead with sparkling eyes
117	German pilot, Heinze Knoke
118	Spitfire leaving vapour trail
119	Irene Blodwyn Jones
120	Modern villa in central Cairo
120	Separating grain from husks
122	Two shy maidens
124	Making a photographic mosaic
124	Town and port of Rhodes
124	SAS in action behind enemy lines
126	PRU Secret Daily Operation Record
126	The Gezira Sporting Club in Cairo
127	Working with enlargers in the darkroom
128	Bill's friend, Anna
129	One of the hangars on fire
130	Being chauffeured to the opera
130	Our palatial headquarters in Heliopolis
132	Crippled children's party
132	Toc-H in Soliman Pasha Street, Cairo
132	Nubian servant in fez
135	In the lounge of the Toc-H club
136	Chatting round the table at the Gezira Club
136	Major Pearson with Jack and mobile canteen

page	
138	Captain Wilcox of the Salvation Army
140	The Puritan Houseboat at the Gezira Club
140	Servant bringing tea in morning
140	The charming Tatiana
142	Impressive approach to the Gezira Club
143	Interpreters working at desks
144	Our plush new apartment block in Heliopolis
145	Fl/t Lieutenant Lamboit
146	Jack & Bill with guard, Hussein Sunheil
146	The 'Baron's Folly' in Heliopolis
148	St Andrew's Church, Heliopolis
148	Mosaic of Tobruk harbour
151	Whole unit on parade
152	Men carrying 'tank'
152	Sherman tank disguised as a lorry
152	The Steffell family
154	'Maid of the Mountains' at the Opera House
156	The huge F52 camera
157	Jack & Bill's friend Romeo
157	Jack & Bill with the Mather girls
158	Monastery of the Whirling Dervishes
158	Priest calling faithful to prayer
161	City of the Dead
161	Roy silhouetted in window
162	A bat from the hall
162	The Citadel
162	Vaulted ceiling of bats
163	Jack with the F24 aircraft camera
164	Our HQ, a lovely villa
165	Part group by pool
166	King Farouk's Ras El Tin Palace, Alexandria
166	The United Forces Club, Alexandria
169	Queen Farida's Palace, Heliopolis
169	Jack and Elsie on the balcony
170	Loving chair from the palace
171	The Pyramids
172	View from the Tura Caves
172	Airmen with repaired propellor
174	Girls on balcony
174	Bill whistling
174	Ethelwyn, Sylvia and Jack in Zamalek flat
177	Norman Shirley DFM
178	Ruby, Jack, Doris, Sydney and Iona; a picnic
179	Jack & Bill as babies
181	Flt/Lt J Telles with two pretty girls
181	Two pretty girls at the Pyramids and Sphinx
182	Mena House Hotel by the Pyramids
183	Little ragged girl
184	Jack and friends on a truck
184	Canada House, Alexandria
184	Sea front at Alexandria
184	Natives ironing with feet

page	
186	Unit photograph of MEIU
188	Four lads and four WAAFs
189	Cairo Zoo
190	Yausef's Well in Cairo
192	Craftsman working on plate
192	Market street scene
192	Little boy carving
194	The Mosquito
196	A cottage industry
196	Mrs Hale and friends
197	Mosquito – wooden wonder
198	Seaside villas, Alexandria
198	Three lads on truck
199	German ploughing
200	Cleo in nurse's uniform
201	Cleo outside Beau Rivage Hotel
202	Model of Amiens Prison
202	Reconnaissance photo of prison
206	Palm trees at camp
206	Bill and companions in tent
209	Group outside Corporals' Bar
210	Buffalo ploughing
210	Women carrying water
213	Ali Shaltoot and village elders
213	Jack on small horse
214	With two Egyptian girls
215	Bill thumbing a lift
216	Vera, a lovely girl
217	Jack & Bill's postcard home
219	Hut 11 at Dishforth
220	Fl/Sgt Waring working on model
220	Model of Palermo, Italy
221	Pigeon with camera
224	With the WAAFs on the bridge
224	Jack, Doris, Bill and Evaline dancing
226	Jack & Bill in tent
227	Colonel Steffell
227	Mrs Steffell
228	Major Pearson and wife
228	Captain Wilcox
229	Tatiana
229	Georgette Mather
230	Farid el Gindi
230	Cyril Ritchard on stage
231	The Royal Opera House, Cairo
231	Flt/Lt Langdon
233	Centre of Heliopolis, 1943
234	Bill and two rabbits
234	The YMCA in Cairo
236	The American Roof Garden, Cairo
238	The Stirling Castle
239	Mum, Dad and sister Gladys

page	
240	Cooking an egg
241	The huge Liberator
243	Three cameras under Spitfire
245	Girls with the large film cans
246	Betty
246	Bill and Hazel in rowing boat
247	WAAF personnel working at Medmenham
248	Danesfield at Medmenham
248	The BBSU's own Avro Anson
250	WAAF interpreter at Medmenham
251	The Kassel Hotel west of Hannover
252	Attractive path near HQ
252	The Shooting Lodge
254	Complete devastation
254	German engineer with RAF personnel
255	Bill with four companions
257	Tangled pipework at factory
257	Noticeboard on side of shed
258	Fraulein Rita
258	Large modern building
260	German military postcard
260	Vandalised house
262	Damaged railway locomotives
263	Relaxing in the Sergeants' Mess
264	Artificial trees at Berchtesgaden
264	Film projectors in Hitler's chalet
267	Hitler's dining room pre-war
267	The beautiful village of Berchtesgaden
268	Destroyed autobahn bridge
270	Regal Cinema, Bebington Road
271	Martins Bank Building, Dacre Hill
272	Martins Bank, Water Street, Liverpool
275	Home of Frank Sheepwash in Vancouver
276	SS Aquitania
276	First Class Restaurant, SS Aquitania pre-war
280	Aunt Maggie, Uncle Bert and cousin Charles
284	Drawing of the Sheepwash home
285	Little house on Grouse Mountain
286	Roger, friend and dead moose
287	Two-seater Ford with 'dickie seat'
287	Roger chopping logs
288	Roger, Diane, Sheri and their dog, Spot
289	Surprise Creek Bridge, British Columbia
290	Banff Springs Hotel
292	The original Horseshoe Trestle
292	Red River Bridge into Winnipeg
293	Passengers boarding train
293	Hudson 4-6-4 locomotive
294	Aerial view of Halifax, Nova Scotia
295	First Class Smoking Room, SS Aquitania
296	Drawing; Aquitania in the Mersey
300	Fairs Cameras, Dacre Hill, today

A Smile

A smile costs nothing, but gives so much.
It enriches those who receive, without
making poorer those who give. It takes
but a moment, but the memory of it
sometimes lasts forever.

None is so rich or mighty that he can get
along without it, and none so poor but that
he can be made rich by it.

A smile creates happiness in the home,
fosters goodwill in business and is the
countersign of friendship. It brings rest to
the weary, cheer to the discouraged,
sunshine to the sad and is nature's best
antidote for trouble.

Yet it cannot be bought, begged, borrowed
or stolen, for it is something that is of no
value to anyone until it is given away.

Some people are too tired to give you a
smile. Give them one of yours, as none
needs a smile so much as he who has no
more to give.

anon

1: The Cruise

It was 15th November 1940 and we were about to embark upon a cruise. We had promised ourselves a special holiday some fifteen months earlier when we had celebrated our twenty first birthdays. The day following our birthday, His Majesty had called us up to serve him, and the nation of course, and as a reward, seemingly, we were given this lovely cruise. It was not to be a world cruise, it is wartime, of course, not really the time to take an extended holiday, so we would just take a few weeks, courtesy of His Majesty. Our 'cruise' was actually our RAF posting!

So, off we go to our 'hotel' – well, not exactly a hotel – more of a hut at RAF Padgate, an embarkation station. It has been raining for three whole days and, when we arrive at Warrington station, we find that the 'hotel' have forgotten to send our taxi, or rather, RAF Transport Section have not sent that little truck with canvas sides and wooden seats to collect us and our kit bags. What is more, they say, "Sorry, you'll have to find your own way here." So, we phone for a taxi. Guess what arrives? – A Rolls Royce! Not a black cab – a real Rolls Royce! Unbelievable but true. And the cost? Just four shillings. This piece of good fortune at the very start was to be a portent for our 'war' – a 'bright star shining'.

We didn't know the destination of our 'cruise', but, as we've all been issued with khaki shorts and pith helmets, there were suggestions that it would probably be Iceland! – you get the picture? We travel up to Gourock in Scotland and are delighted to see that we are to embark on that luxury liner, the 'Empress of Canada', a twenty thousand tonner. Now Jack, he's the twin writing this, is quite used to liners, having worked for Kodak before the war – he delivered packages of films to the shop on the Cunard liners in Gladstone Dock – so he's not over-awed by any of this! We are over-awed, however, when shown to our cabin, way, way down below decks. It is a massive metal hold filled with dozens of hammocks hanging from the ceiling, (sorry – deck – not got used to shipboard life yet!), and beneath these are the mess tables. We now see why it is called a 'mess'!

Our immediate reaction is, "Oh dear, this will never do. We'll have to see the captain. Here we are, reduced to 'steerage', and to think – we came here by Rolls Royce!" However, glancing at the propeller symbols emblazonned on our sleeves, we conclude that the Royal Navy captain is unlikely to appreciate our concern.

So, we decide to walk the deck and cool off a bit, still feeling very hurt that the 'cruise company' could not give us any better accommodation. We wonder, idly, if we might have

above, 'cruise ship' life revolved around the pool – lazy, self-indulgent decadence in congenial company with the cares of the world so far away!

below, the 'cruise liner' was the 'Empress of Canada'

fared better had we been of 'officer' class.

On our 'walk', naturally, we get into conversation with other 'passengers' including a group of Australians, to whom we explain our disappointment. Sociably, they invite us to their cabin, which has four bunks and is spacious and extremely well fitted. We are very envious which obviously showed since, out of the blue, Johnny Blincoe, one of the Aussies, says, "There's plenty of room, you can sleep on our cabin floor if you wish..."

Heaven be praised, do we wish! "Thank you very much, it is very kind of you to put up with such inconvenience". "Don't think of it," they say, "we've had such a good time with your 'Sheilas', that this is a way to say, Thank You, England!" ..... We thought, "Thank you girls!" – I'll bet they little thought when they were 'entertaining' these Aussies that it would result in two young Wirral airmen having such splendid accommodation. Then, to make things even better, the Aussies went below and 'borrowed', from somewhere, a couple of mattresses. We can just imagine some poor soul saying, "This bunk is b......... hard!"

So, for six and a half weeks, the duration of the 'cruise', we sleep on the floor of their cabin. Yes – despite daily inspections! We are never troubled – our mattresses are kept hidden on the other bunks until bedtime.

Oh, bright star that shines on us!

There are one or two other 'cruise' liners about and, lest our 'holiday' be interrupted by submarines shooting unwelcome 'torpedoes' at us, we have a couple of destroyers keeping us company. We are sailing so far west though, out deep into the Atlantic, that we begin to think our destination might actually be the USA – but it turns out that we are just avoiding submarines.

On one of our regular morning 'walks' we come across a ship's officer taking a group photograph of the crew, and casually mention to him that we are professional photographers. Frank Sheepwash, the ship's radio officer, is a charming person and invites us to tea in his cabin, and the three of us soon become great friends. He tells us that we can use his cabin whenever we wish, and, that it can be turned into a darkroom! And, he also has an enlarger!

Thank you bright star!

Part of the ship's routine is the parade held each morning when some of the 'passengers' are allocated duties. This seems only fair because, after all, it is a FREE cruise! We all parade and a warrant officer details those for the various duties, "You six in the galley. You four on fire picket. And you," pointing at Bill and I, "get on with the photography!"

Thank you, again, bright star!

We rise early each morning and enjoy our strolls – safer being on deck in case of sub' attack. Food on the 'cruise' is excellent – we have the most lovely hot bread rolls and are called to breakfast at 7.00am by bugle – a tune reminiscent of 'At the Cookhouse Door'. Dinner in the evening is a full three-course affair and we marvel at the quality of the cuisine. It seems that many of the original galley staff from pre-war luxury liner days are still working on board!

And so, this 'cruise of a lifetime' continues.

The crew of the Empress of Canada were photographed by Frank Sheepwash, the ship's radio officer

below, Church services aboard our liner were most impressive

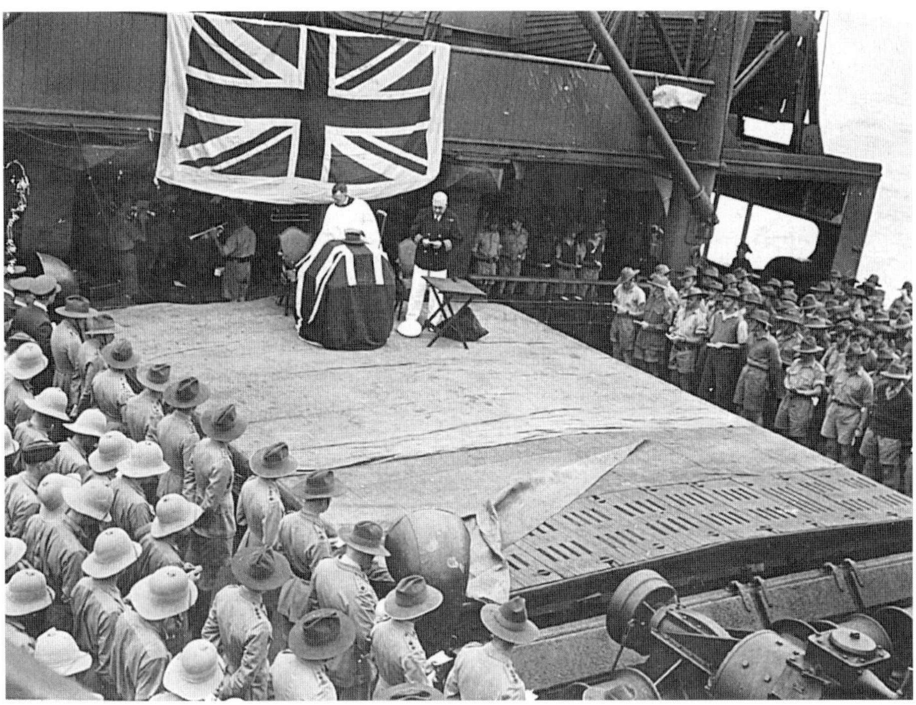

2: Slow Boat to Egypt 1940

The 'Empress of Canada' eventually turns south and then east towards the West Coast of Africa:

Well, there we were, well into our epic voyage. For the first three days we were both seasick and our arms were still painful after the vaccination. Altogether, though, we were not too bad – just off our food. By the fourth day, however, we had become hardened sailors, thoroughly enjoying ourselves. Life was proving to be so different from back home. Blue skies and sunshine abounded every day, but no sight of land for a week. We saw flying fish leaping and skimming the water, and the dolphins just ahead of the ship seemed to be leading us on our course to more adventures.

Now, looking back from so many years later, we wonder whether the days were so carefree. We remember always having to carry our kapok-filled life jackets with us. They were made of two little kapok-filled 'pillow cases' taped together to keep one's head above water. Kapok is a wonderful, natural soft fibre, like cotton wool, five times as bouyant as cork and capable of keeping afloat twenty five times its own weight.

As happens on all cruises, we chatted with the other passengers. Our four Australian cabinmates entertained us with tales of their lives down under. One was a fireman, another erected fences, the third was a farmer while the fourth worked in his father's sawmill when he wasn't going 'walkabout' for three months at a time!

And so we reach the West Coast of Africa – Freetown. Phew! Wasn't it hot here? Swarms of 'bumboats' came alongside. From some boats the Africans sold fish, fruit, necklaces and even monkeys. From others they dived for money, singing out "How about a Scotch sixpence or a Liverpool shilling?" For a joke, the troops dropped pennies wrapped in silver paper and deservedly received some bad language, in English, by return. But, in case we caught disease, troops were not allowed to buy any of the fruit. The Africans would throw a line up on deck so that the men could haul up a basket with their purchases in.

There was no shore leave at Freetown, of course, so we spent three days there with little to see other than the people, palm trees and single storey buildings. Up till then the only 'abroad' in our lives had been the Isle of Man! Yet now we were actually in Africa, paradoxically, we felt more aboard than abroad!

However, the days passed very pleasantly, if somewhat monotonously. We rose at 6am, breakfasted at 7am and retired at 9pm. To amuse ourselves we read, lounged about and pursued our hobby of photography, taking shots of the deck rugby, the boxing, the housey-housey – bingo to you now!

One afternoon whilst taking tea in the cabin of our Canadian friend, Frank, who was a member of the crew, he handed us each half a dollar, saying jokingly, "When you come to Vancouver after the war, you can spend that!" I wonder how many times people say "You must come to see us." Of course, it rarely happens. At that time we thought, "6,000 miles sure is a long way!"

In fact, 7 years later, in 1947, I DID actually visit Frank at his home at 2831 West 32nd Street, Vancouver, and I DID spend his half a dollar!

Then we were on our way again – south and so we crossed the equator – 'the line'. Bill was approached by a naval photographer who had been asked to cover the 'Crossing the Line Ceremony'. We had brought with us a pocket camera, little bigger than a packet of cigarettes. The naval photographer wanted us to take some pictures just in case his didn't turn out well. In fact, they didn't, but Bill's were fine.

The ceremony was quite a show! Father Neptune, with seaweed beard and trident, along with his retinue, was dressed in full regalia. A couple of 'barbers' lathered the novices (people who have never crossed the equator before) from ear to ear and then anointed them with a highly perfumed mixture. The unfortunate 'customers' were then shaved with a huge wooden razor. Finally, after being declared 'true sons of the sea', they were tossed into the swimming pool to howls of delight from the onlookers! When all had been dealt with, Father Neptune and his attendants were invited to the poop to 'splice the mainbrace' – drink a lot of rum!

Then it was on round the Cape and into the harbour at Durban. After four weeks at sea it was truly magical to be able to disembark. We were taken for a day to the city itself just a few miles from the port and we were astonished at the sparkling beauty of the place, by its cleanliness, its palm trees and its difference from any other place we'd ever seen – our idea of heaven! And, after our four week all-male cruise, it was more than just nice to catch a glimpse of lovely girls strolling about. We wandered for hours enjoying the scene, the people, the atmosphere, the ice cream and the solid earth beneath our feet.

When dusk fell, we noted, with delight and almost surprise, the absence of the 'black-out', that terrible but necessary pall imposed on war-time Britain. In the evening, on our trip to the out-of-town Pleasure Gardens, grown-up though we were, we were captivated by the glorious sight of the myriad twinkling fairy lights. The kindness shown to servicemen was apparant everywhere – no fares were ever taken for train, bus or even taxi!

Next day we visited the suburbs. This was to get away from all the troops in the city but also to feast our eyes on the splendid homes of the wealthy. Shades of Hollywood, we thought, as we gazed and wondered who could inhabit such houses. We were soon to find out! A chauffeur driven car drew up; a lady leaned out, "Would you boys like to have a look at Durban's sights?" "Yes, indeed we would. Thank you."

After an hour's tour we were driven up the drive of one of those magnificent houses and were invited in for a meal. All was so opulent with servants gliding around just like in a film. After enjoying a wonderful meal we were driven back to our 'cruise liner', feeling ready for more adventures. Our lucky star was still shining!

However, it was off again. Printing the photos of the 'Crossing the Line' ceremony was now no problem as in Durban we had bought wholesale 700 sheets of Kodak photographic paper. So we spent the next few days enlarging the photos in Frank's cabin and then drying

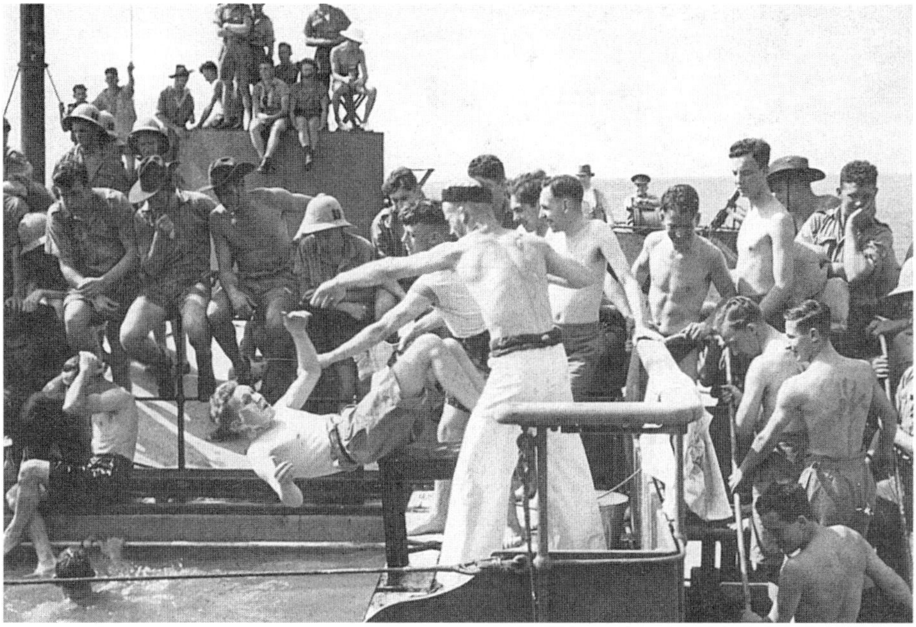

above, Finally, after being declared 'true sons of the sea', they were tossed into the swimming pool to howls of delight from the onlookers!

below, The ceremony was quite a show! Father Neptune, with seaweed beard and trident, along with his retinue, was dressed in full regalia

above, After four weeks at sea it was magical to disembark at Durban, it was different from any other place we'd ever seen – heaven!

below, Some of our pals enjoyed a rickshaw ride in Durban

and pressing them flat with a household iron in the ship's laundry. We smile as we recall how we persuaded the ship's printer to put our name and address on the back of each photo. And so, we sailed on northward up the East Coast of Africa and round into the Red Sea and through the Suez Canal to our destination – North Africa.

Sadly, just over two years later our 'cruise liner' the Empress of Canada was torpedoed but, thanks to the kapok-filled life jackets, 1,546 lives were saved.

above, A couple of 'barbers' lathered the novices from ear to ear and then anointed them with a highly perfumed mixture. The unfortunate 'customers' were then shaved with a huge wooden razor

left, We travel by goods wagon to Cairo. It is the type you will have seen in the Dr Zhivago film – but more comfortable, with feet dangling in passing Egyptian air

below, We saw a young boy, about ten, leading two heavily laden camels, with panniers each side loaded with maize

3: Arrival in Egypt 1941

It was New Year's Day in 1941 when we finally arrived in Egypt, saying goodbye to our cruise ship the 'Empress of Canada'.

With kit bags on our shoulders we make our way down the gangway wondering what adventures lie ahead. We travel by goods wagon to Cairo. It is the type of wagon you will have seen in the Dr Zhivago film – but a lot more comfortable. What scenes met our eyes as we travelled towards Cairo. A young boy of about ten leading two heavily laden camels, with huge panniers on each side loaded with maize. A peasant with his wooden plough pulled by two buffalo – just as it was thousands of years ago. The Egyptians are seemingly ignorant of, or not interested in, progress. These were just two of the fascinating pictures we saw, and took, as we journeyed to Cairo, not looking from the carriage window, but seated in the open doorway of the 'Zhivago' wagon with our feet dangling in the passing Egyptian air.

Upon arrival in Cairo we board a 3-ton lorry and travel to an Army camp, 'Beni Yusef', situated just half a mile from the pyramids at Giza. Are we lucky? Our first day in Egypt and we get to see one of the wonders of the World! The camp had rows of tents, concrete ablution slabs, and corrugated iron latrines and a rough stone Orderly Room. It is situated on slopes of very soft sand which makes walking surprisingly strenuous. We find that we are a party of 17 in total, 15 ACIs and Bill and I, leading aircraftsmen, just a rank below corporal. Nevertheless, as there aren't any sergeants or officers, we decide as leaders that Bill and I had better take command. Kidding actually – we demote ourselves to cooks and decide to make breakfast. The army had provided us with rations – memories of cooking at camp pre-war – but not in such quantities! We have a basket of what appear to be pigeon eggs, being about half the size of eggs back home! We make porridge and together with bread, margarine and a couple of tins of marmalade we have a satisfying breakfast.

Meal over we consider our duty done for the day – no fences – no guardhouse – no signing out. We decide to set off for Cairo, we are told it is seven miles down the Giza road. So we decide to hitch-hike. We like hitching, it is usually more comfortable than trains or trams, and so it proves as, after only a couple of minutes, along comes a large limousine. He stops and speaks to us in French, we think he must be Lebanese. He smiles at us and beckons us so we climb in. After only a couple of miles we pass a group of buildings with the name 'El Misr Studios'. We tapped our driver on the shoulder and indicated that we wished to stop.

left, Bill and Jack with just a few of the El Gindi family outside their 'grand' house in Cairo. It was evident they were in the home of a very rich man

below, We find we are a party of 17 in total, fifteen ACIs and Bill and I (well 16 actually – Bill is taking the photo)

We got out bid him, "Merci beaucoup", and made our way to the studios.

The door was opened by a native in a galabier, like a long dress, who clearly spoke no English. However, he smiled at us and picked up a telephone. After chatting away for a couple of minutes he motioned to us to follow him and takes us to the managing director who asks us, in perfect English, what is our wish. We tell him that we are photographers and would be interested to look over his studios. He introduces us to one of his producers. His name is Farid El Gindi, who tells us that he was educated in England and that it will be his pleasure to show us around. Farid is as good as his word, and we are shown many of the departments, introduced to the cameramen and the film stars, and we partake of tea and biscuits. We tell Farid that this is our first day in Cairo and he kindly offers to show us the sights. That lucky star is evidently still shining up there!

It is soon lunchtime and we ask Farid if we can take him to lunch, at which he smiles and takes us to a cafe and introduces us to the proprietor. Then we sit down to – guess what? Three of those 'pigeons' eggs, tomatoes, chips and bread and butter! Travelling down the main street, Soliman Pasha, we note with interest that the shops are very high class and all are packed with goods. We pass a large cafe, 'La American', packed with a selection of chocolates and mouth-watering goodies. After the severe rationing this was a great surprise. We pass the YMCA fronted by a lovely garden. Surprisingly, we learn that this building was a gift from the 'People of Birkenhead'! On the other side of the road we see the Toc-H hostel (An organisation from the First World War. like the Rotary or Lions, being helpful and doing good works. In fact Bill and I had been members in Birkenhead – but more of that later.)

Farid then takes us to visit his home and meet his family. He has twelve sisters and brothers and two mothers! One mother lives in the grand house we were visiting and the other one of his father's wives lives in a small adjacent apartment. We were taken aback by the furnishings – large settees with heavy gilding, like you see in stately homes, and huge ornate mirrors on the walls. It was evident we were in the home of a very rich man. Indeed, everything was so very different – his two sisters had unusual names – 'Fun Fun' and 'Muher'. The latter sent us a picture of herself, when we were in the western desert, on which she had written "I hope you still remind me – Muher". We were invited to share their meal. I think it was Ramadan, and we were shown a goat which they kept on the flat roof. This was to become our dinner!

(My wife has just interrupted my writing to say, "Reading this, you would not know there was a war on – you seem to be having too good a time!" I replied, "Just you wait!" Later we will tell of the fear of being bombed, of burning aircraft and dodging machine gun fire. In any case – one tends to remember the happy times.)

Meanwhile, at RAF Headquarters Middle East, a clerk woke up and called across to his Liverpudlian colleague, "Eh, whack, did you know there are 17 'bods' at Beni Yusef – we'd better do something about it!" To which 'Whack' replied, "They've had 12 days' leave, let's post them to 11 Squadron – that'll give them something to think about!" And so, a 3-ton open wagon with slatted wooden seats arrived to collect us and we were taken to Helwan RAF station. We arrived in a severe dust storm – we looked as though a bag of fine dust had been emptied over us! These storms are called 'Haseems' and were not unusual, but we learned to take them in our stride, cleaning our eyes, nose and ears, a shake, a shower, and all was well!

So we joined 11 Squadron, a 'mobile squadron'? We certainly soon find out – the next day we are on parade and the CO tells us that we are off to Greece!

So how had all this come about? We'll take you back to the beginning...

above, The empty 'White Elephant Factory' was used only for storing bottles some of which we are holding here with a couple of friends

below, Inside the factory the strong concrete columns and beams had withstood the ravages of time, and the Fairs brothers!

4: Photography – The Beginning

I think we must have been about twelve years old when we first became interested in photography, or perhaps I should say, in printing negatives. From this very early age it was obvious that we were destined to become photographers. Our introduction was through a school chum of ours, Ken Speakman. He had sensitized some paper by coating the surface with ammonium ferric citrate and potassium ferricyanide, in fact, he was making blueprint paper which in those days was used by architects for copying building plans.

Perhaps, it was unusual that one so young as Ken would be into the making of blue print paper. He was of a serious nature and we were not surprised when, eventually, he became a teacher of science. We used Ken's blue print paper by placing the negative against the glass of a small picture frame, and with the coated paper firmly against it, held the frame up to the sun. Then taking the paper from the frame we soaked it in water, and there we were with a blue photo.

The next step in our vocation occurred when we were crossing Victoria Park on our way to school one day, when an older friend presented us with a box of one hundred sheets of Kodak printing paper and a small guillotine (which we still use today). I think that even in those days our lucky star was shining.

One of our friend's mother, learning of our interest in photography, gave us a Blue Ensign box camera called an E29 which made 3 x 2 snaps. in the 1930s some of the packets of cigarettes contained coupons which, when collected in sufficient quantity could be exchanged for gifts and this camera was one such gift; it was similar to the box Brownie with a slightly smaller negative.

Time was marching on and we must consider where we were heading, so we will take Jack first ...

Jack

Leaving school at fourteen my bright star was shining when, one morning The Liverpool Clerks Association directed my steps towards Kodak Wholesale in Liverpool where I obtained a job as an office boy thus coming into contact with everything to do with photography.

The boss would kindly allow me to have, say, a damaged photo dish or a packet of

above, Farmer Willie Jones had kindly permitted us to pitch our bell tents on his farm at Tafarn-y-Gelyn, close to Loggerheads in North Wales

below, Jack & Bill – what a difference a uniform makes!

5: In the RAF – The Beginning

Early in the year 1939 Bill and I came to the conclusion that we could soon be conscripted to join His Majesty's Forces – for a period of two years. We talked this over, and Bill suggested that we write to the RAF and propose that we join to teach photography – we were a bit naive in those days – in fact, we still are.

We wrote, and were instructed to report to Sealand Aerodrome for a medical examination. We rode out on our tandem and we were passed A1, and enlisted in the Royal Air Force Volunteer Reserve as gunners. Can you imagine being shut in a rear turret for hour after hour, being shot at? Besides, Bill and I wanted to serve together and there wasn't room for two in a turret. The planes sometimes came back with holes in them, and we would probably have been dead by now, and unable to write this book.

We heard nothing further until just a week prior to war breaking out. In those far off days, when a person was 21 they were declared a man, not 18 as it is today. And so it was the day after our 21st birthday that the powers that be decided to call the Fairs brothers up to serve King and Country. It was Saturday 26th August 1939. We had made preparations to spend a weekend at our camp in North Wales. We had formed a small camping club of 10 lads, and we had purchased two World War One bell tents. Farmer Willie Jones had kindly permitted us to stay on his farm at Tafarn-y-Gelyn, close to Loggerheads in North Wales.

But it was work before play, and Bill and I had been asked to take photographs at a large house in Caldy on the Saturday afternoon. Photographs taken, we returned home and Mum said, "There are a couple of official looking manilla envelopes addressed to you both". And they certainly were official. Inside we found our calling up papers. "You are to report to the RAF office in Peter Street, Manchester, bringing towel, soap, toothbrush etc, and if you require a rail warrant for your journey you can obtain this at your local police station." So, small bags packed, warrants collected, off we went to Manchester.

At the RAF recruiting office we were given vouchers to stay at a local hotel, The Black Swan, which was very nice and comfortable. The landlord, after showing us our rooms, said, "Gentlemen, dinner is at 7.00pm and breakfast is at 8.00am, and what paper would you like?" We debated on whether to have The Times or The Financial Times and then decided on the Daily Herald. We are fairly certain that the landlord realised that this would probably be the last day that we would be addressed as 'gentlemen', and the next day we would be lowly aircraftsmen, second class. In fact, it was the last time that we were to be civvies for six and a half years. Bill remarked, "This is the life isn't it, even better than camp?"

We reported the next day to the RAF office with 10 others, all in civilian clothes. They decided to send us to Debden, a fighter station. "Where's Debden?" our Bill asked, and he was told that it was in Essex. Bill seemed to be showing the quality of leadership, and he knew where Debden was, so the Corporal put him in charge of the squad, and he handled the travel documents.

Upon arrival, transport collected us and we were taken to the aerodrome where a real corporal took charge and Bill was demoted. We were formed in twos – left right, left right, and off we marched to the clothing store where we were each handed three biscuits, not to eat, they were little square mattresses, which, when placed end to end, made a normal mattress. Formed up once again we were marched to our bedroom, very different from last night at the hotel, this was a very big bedroom – a hangar, empty of aircraft, and we were allocated a space on the rough concrete floor. It was only a temporary measure of course, and we were used to roughing it as we went camping regularly.

The next morning Bill decided to rise early, and to go looking for the cookhouse. I stayed in bed. It had been cold during the night, and we had pushed our beds together. Well! A Warrant Officer came around to see how his charges were getting along. You should have seen his face, he wasn't at all pleased. He shouted, "Get those bloody beds apart". I told him it was my twin brother's, but that didn't make any difference, he was still very annoyed. I told him my brother had gone for a walk. Life seemed to be so different in the services and NCOs weren't always polite.

It was all quite exciting. We drew our uniform from the stores, and if the trousers were two inches too long they could be taken to the camp tailor to sort them out, and our irons (knife, fork and spoon to you), well, the stores supplied a set of ten steel punches, number 0 to 9, and we stamped our numbers on the handles – 750832 – yes, everything was numbered in the RAF except, we suppose, the CO. We didn't ever find out whether he had a number.

Well, here we were with our uniforms on, the trousers just the right length, not too long, in fact we looked quite smart. Bill said, "Wouldn't Mum like to see us now?". I said, "That's an idea, why don't we ask for a couple of days leave and let her see". The next day we went to see the Warrant Officer, the one who had told me to, "Get those bloody beds apart". We didn't both go, I asked Bill, he's the hard-faced one of the two of us. Bill told the Warrant Officer that we had a little business, and that we had been called up very suddenly, in fact we had come away the same day we had received our calling up papers, and would it be possible for us to have a couple of days leave to sort things out. The Warrant Officer said, "Leave things with me."

Later in the day he sent for us and asked which was our nearest aerodrome. We said either Hooton or Sealand. He then said, "Draw parachutes and be down on the airfield tomorrow morning at 0900 hours." and that they would fly us home. We were staggered, here we were in the service less than a week, and being flown home in a Fairey Battle. If anyone else had told this story we wouldn't believe them. It's true though. We learned that it was a training flight, so we weren't surprised when the pilot took a couple of small branches off the top of a tree with his undercarriage when we were coming in to land. However, we landed safely. There is no doubt that our bright star was shining.

Mum thought that we looked very nice in our uniforms, of course she would, wouldn't she; and even the neighbours who had called us a couple of little villains when we were young now decided that we were a couple of nice young men. It just shows what a difference a uniform makes.

Here we were settling into Debden which was a fighter 'drome and they decided that they would teach Bill and I to fight. So we were paraded onto the shooting range, told to lie on our stomachs and each given a rifle. We didn't do very well, and so we were shown how to fix a bayonet onto the end of the rifle. We were quite good with the bayonet, and in some cases, were able to penetrate the suspended sack of straw, right through with the bayonet coming out the other side. Bill was able to give his bayonet a little twist so that he could do the utmost damage to the enemy. The sergeant was very pleased with him.

I think that the officer I/C decided that we were unlikely to make any bayonet charges, and our next job was working in the underground control room fixing maps of Europe on one of the walls for the planning of raids. This was a far better job than fighting the enemy in hand to hand combat, which we weren't used to, and the wall covered in maps looked very good, even though we say so ourselves. We did not find much class distinction in the services, even when the Fl/t Lieutenant chatted away showing us the town in Switzerland where he had been educated.

We were fortunate to be in amongst the plans because we were able to borrow a couple to plan our route home, hitch-hiking. We loved going home especially if there was a dance on at Hulme Hall, in those days the girls always wore long dresses and at many of the

above, Debden was a fighter station in Essex

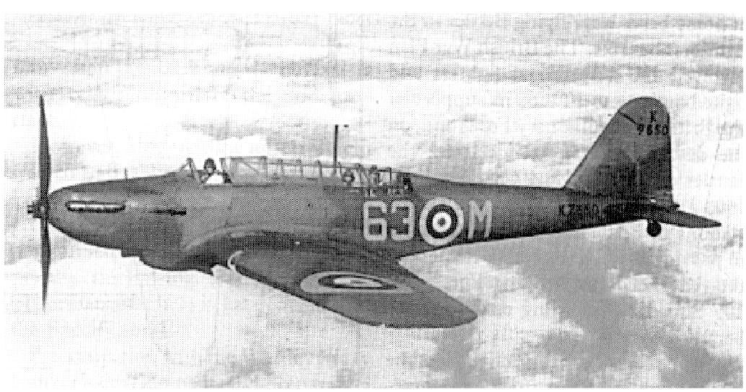

right, We were flown home in a Fairey Battle

dances we wore dress suits. It was far more of an occasion in those days.

Our next job was sitting at a large plotting table pushing little discs around representing enemy aircraft, officers telling us where to place them. That was exciting but it was early in the war and there was not much activity. There was lots of spare time and, having taken a Spanish course at evening classes, I took my Spanish book whilst on duty. I was learning Spanish. I cannot recall just why I should have chosen Spanish, Bill said it was because there was quite an attractive girl in the class. Anyway, here I was studying, or trying to, because I kept dropping off to sleep. Bill had to keep knocking me with his pusher lest I were punished for sleeping on duty.

One day we were told to report to the Orderly Room. We did so and one of the clerks asked us whether we would like to go to France – they required two clerks. We said, "No thanks, we are awaiting training as photographers." It was nice that they asked us whether we wished to go instead of just posting us. Seems our lucky star was shining!

The great moment arrived and we were both posted to RAF Dishforth, a heavy bomber station in Yorkshire as 'Photographers under training'. It was here that we learned about aircraft cameras, settings, loading and fixing them in Whitley Bombers. We enjoyed Dishforth except during the winter months when it snowed and we were freezing cold, especially on guard duty patrolling the huge perimeter of the airfield. How we hated that! It is rarely that we write about 'hating' anything, but I have just looked the word up in the dictionary. Yes, it was the correct word – it was all of those things mentioned.

Our free days were spent in Harrogate, where Bill met Hilda. She became Bill's girl friend. Her father was a Petty Officer but we did not ever meet him. We met her Mum, however, and were invited to tea on a number of occasions. Bill took me along and as Hilda didn't have any sisters, he let me take her out once or twice. That's one of the benefits of being twins – the girls usually don't mind which twin they go out with.

One day Bill became ill. I went with him to the hospital in Harrogate. The hospital was at the far end of the Valley Gardens. It turned out that Bill had appendicitis. I did not have mine until much later. After Bill's op' it was quite pleasant. We were invited by the nurses to their dance and Bill made friends with the sister who wrote to him when we were overseas. It was quite peaceful at Dishforth and although we loved going home, we certainly disliked the bombing that we experienced when in poor old Merseyside. It was horrendous.

All was going quite well in our photo section, with a good sergeant and a good corporal. So, there was bound to be a hiccup. And there was. Jack, that's me, was called to the Orderly Room and told, "You are posted overseas." "What about my brother?" "Sorry, just you." This called for immediate action and letters were sent to the CO asking if Bill could come too. That lucky star was shining up there – Bill was posted too.

That was our introduction to the Royal Air Force ...

6: Greece, Beauty and Horrors

So, after that short explanatory interlude, it's back to Egypt:

After almost twelve days leave in Cairo we left Beni Yusef, and our camp beneath the Pyramids, bound for Helwan Aerodrome. We encountered another severe dust storm on the way, so bad that it obscured our bright star, causing us to rise at 2am in the morning so we could board the train at 3.30am. This caused us much 'chagrin', or as they would say in the RAF, we were 'cheesed off' and even more so when we sat on board the train for four and a half hours without moving. Ah well, there was a war on! We thought at the time that this sort of occurrence was one of the reasons why servicemen swear so much.

We arrived at Alexandria and there she was, the 'Ulster Prince', our next 'cruise ship' waiting to transport us to Greece for further adventures, and, oh boy, what lay ahead!

Sitting, in the cruise ship restaurant, well, sitting on the deck, eating our lunch – bully beef and hard tack biscuits

The 'Ulster Prince' was an Irish Boat of about four thousand tons, more at home in the Mersey than the Mediterranean, but OK for our short two-day cruise. The weather was lovely, and although the sea was rough, we were by now seasoned sailors and actually enjoyed the plunging movement of the ship. There we were, first sitting, in the cruise ship restaurant, actually sitting on the deck, eating our lunch – bully beef, for the first time since arriving overseas. There were no plates, just our small round billy cans, not dissimilar to small frying pans, and our irons – the RAF name for knife, fork and spoon.

It seemed ideal, there we were sitting in the lovely sunshine, not knowing from one minute to the next whether we were going to be blown out of the water, or indeed the mess we were sailing into. However, as was our way, we looked on the sunny side of life, pushing anxious thoughts onto

above, We board a train, half as big again as an English train

left, Larissa, was north of the plain of Thessaly – very wet

below, We paddled our boots in drums to wash off the mud

one side and placing a good deal of faith in our bright star.

Sadly, the next time we saw the Ulster Prince was 91 days later – she had been bombed by the Germans, burning from stem to stern – a complete wreck, and we were in a desperate situation.

But, back to our cruise; the passengers were of different nationalities and we made friends with some Cypriot soldiers, thus taking the opportunity to learn some Greek words:-

Thank you very much	*aekaristo polee*
Yes please	*marleesta parakalo*
No	*ohkee*

During our short stay in Greece we learnt about three hundred Greek words, and obtained much amusement using them. The Greeks also seemed amused, and flattered, that we were learning their language.

Slowly Piraeus appeared on the horizon. There was a heat haze and as the Greek coast came into focus we marvelled at the beauty of the scenery – the deep blue carpet of the sea, and the white cottages gleaming in the early morning sunshine. It was no wonder that we waxed lyrical about the sight. However, coming back down to earth, we hoisted our kitbags onto our shoulders and boarded the coach for a delightful excursion to Athens to visit the Acropolis, Well, not really – we climbed onto a three-ton truck with wooden seats and passed the Acropolis in the distance. As we travelled along the street the Greeks were calling out 'Bravo English' which was a bit embarrassing – they must have meant the other chaps on the truck because neither myself nor Bill felt very brave!

We arrived at Elevsis Aerodrome and found it not to be an Aerodrome as we know it, but a grassy meadow with masses of wild flowers; blue, yellow and red in colour. There were about thirty tents and a few wooden huts, and to frame the scene, about two miles away, craggy mountains. Ah, this is the life we thought, and indeed it was very pleasant, just as long we didn't think about the future. We met up with some Greek Airforce Photographers with a super German-made Photo-Trailer and although none of the Greeks could speak a word of English we got along famously. We tried out our few Greek words – good morning, although it was afternoon – give me an egg – yes and no, and thank you.

The next day we boarded a train, it was huge, half as big again as an English train – of course they have to be massive, as three quarters of mainland Greece is mountainous. Travelling by train was not as uneventful as one might think. Ploughing its way through the gorges and tunnels the train stopped about twelve times during the day and night and each time it stopped the lads would climb down. At one place they tried to ride a donkey, not very successfully, and the Greek peasant who owned the donkey just stood shrieking with laughter at their efforts, whilst the donkey hee-hawed. It was not possible to travel through a Greek village without hearing the braying of donkeys.

At another stop our cooks tried to buy a sheep but the shepherd wanted 240 drachmas for it (about 10 shillings old money) which they considered to be too expensive. Bill and I walked to the front of the train and tried out our Greek on the driver. Kalimera (good morning) we said. Tee Kanatay (how are you). The driver smiled and invited us into his cab where we travelled for a few miles and as a special favour he allowed us to toot the whistle.

It was a lovely time of the year. Spring is a special time in Greece and as we passed through olive, vine and orange groves there were white and pink blossoms in profusion and it seemed as though there was a picture around every corner.

Reaching our destination, Larissa, a garrison town north of the plain of Thessaly, which we found to be a very wet plain, we learned two more Greek words – polee laspy (much mud). In fact, there was so much mud that the whole squadron of five hundred men were each given a pair of gum boots and every building had a round metal drum with water to paddle ones boots in and wash off the mud – well we tried.

We were billeted in brick barrack blocks which had just been built, but were half finished. The walls were without plaster and the floors were rough concrete, we didn't even have a cupboard, table or chair. We did have beds though, and these were composed of three bedboards which were placed on tiny wooden trestles about six inches off the ground. Upon these we placed three 'biscuits' which was the nomenclature given by the RAF to small mattresses, general issue in those days at English RAF stations too.

'Nomenclature' was used by the RAF instead of the simple word 'Name'– daft wasn't it?

They decided that it was about time we did some work and so we were remustered from photographers to armourers. For our first stint, which was a visit to the railway station, we had to load 250lb bombs onto our unit trucks. This was quite heavy work but we were young and strong and we quite enjoyed the change. We didn't face any danger as the bombs had not been primed, the only danger was dropping one on our toes. We made such a good job of loading the bombs that the next day we were specially chosen to visit the local town and collect logs for our cook-house stoves. Later on we used these stoves in the desert. Our mouths would water when our convoy stopped and we saw the cooks unloading the stoves from the truck. Meals were cooked and tea brewed – very useful cooking facilities.

We made a very good job of loading the 250lb bombs

Bill and I are non-smokers and we visited the local hospital – *Nosokomian* – another word for our vocabulary. As a present we took our cigarette rations*, we felt so very sorry for the Greek soldiers, they were fighting in the mountains of Albania under the most terrible conditions.

They were poorly shod and were suffering from both wounds and frostbite.

Whilst at the Hospital we took a group photograph of about fifty of the walking-wounded and made a copy for each of them to send to their families or sweethearts. After all, we were members of Toc-H and like the Lions and Rotary, Toc-H is a Christian organisation that does good works.

* *Every airman overseas was given a free ration of fifty cigarettes and 2 boxes of matches each week.*

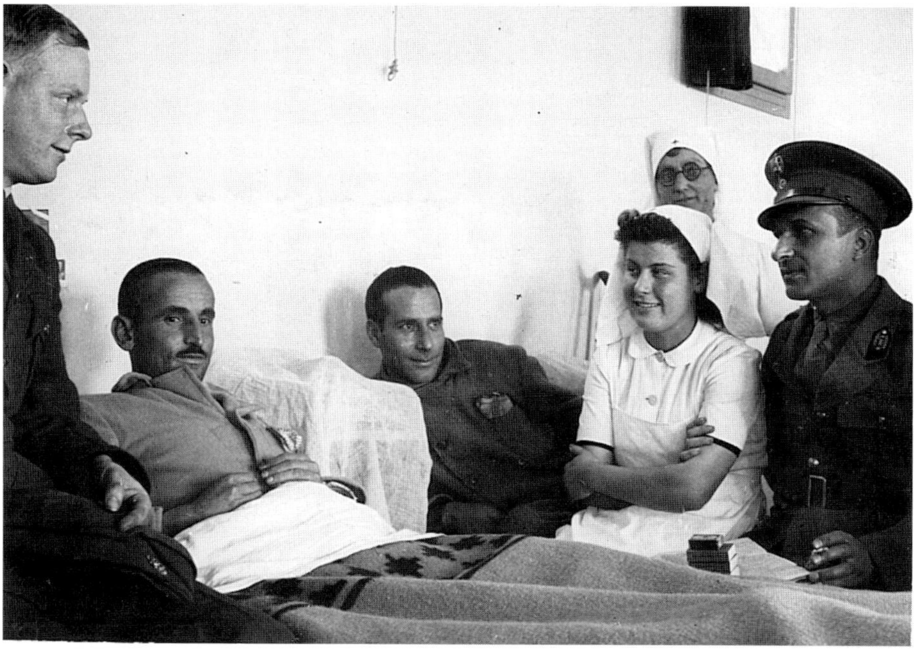

above, We gave our cigarette rations to the Greek soldiers in hospital as we did not smoke and we felt sorry for them

below, We took a group photograph of about fifty of the walking-wounded

above, Jack and his mate Dunmore are loading the camera into the aircraft

left, Just like our pilots, the old Greek shepherds wore sheepskin coats for warmth

below, Bill, and his friend Tommy, had sought the safety of an irrigation channel

7: Greece, Bombers and Brothels

Well, the brothers Fairs had a job to do. Our work was to produce photographs that had been taken over enemy territory, and it so happened that Air Commodore D'Albiac, who was the Commander of the RAF in Greece, and General Wilson, who was in charge of the army, were anxious to know what was happening on the war front in Albania,

So, a job for Jack and Bill. Air Commodore D'Albiac couldn't tell us directly, of course, as we were only LACs, and orders had to pass down the chain of command. So – to the CO – to the Adjutant – to the Photo Officer – to our Flight Sergeant, who said, "Get fell in you two and load the camera". The photo opposite shows Jack and his mate Dunmore, loading the camera into the aircraft. Bill could not be in the picture, he was on important business – in the tent, making a cup of tea.

Meanwhile, our first reconnaissance plane had returned from its sortie and revealed a grim picture of massed tanks, and of overwhelming German mechanised units in Rumania, with aerodromes bursting with aircraft, ready to invade Yugoslavia and then on to Greece. We knew just how important it was for the battle commanders to know the position, but at the time were not quite so sure whether it would have been better to be ignorant of the perilous plight we were likely to find ourselves in before long. We remember thinking, how nice it would be if we could take a short cruise across to Turkey, but then, unfortunately, Thomas Cook had cancelled their cruises!

No sooner had our next aircraft taken off when our attention was attracted by a number of airmen pointing to the sky. We heard the droning of aircraft, and saw, high above, four Italian bombers, making circles with their vapour trails, around the airfield. Oh dear, we thought, they must be targeting the 'drome, and we had best beat a hasty retreat.

Scared stiff, we fled. Although, scared stiff was hardly an apt expression. We were scared, yes, but not stiff. Every muscle in our bodies was flexing as we fled from the target area, panting for breath as we sought the safety of an irrigation channel. It wasn't nice, the thought of being blown up, especially as it was our day off. However, the bombing was soon over, and our breath was restored. We noticed a small village about half a mile away and thought we might as well go visiting to quieten our nerves. We do not think that the village had ever had foreign visitors before, certainly not RAF men, because the whole of the village turned out to follow us.

The head man, who spoke English with a strong American accent, bid us welcome. A table and chairs were produced, and we were entertained and given Turkish coffee in small cups, very strong and sweet. The cups were half full of coffee grains. We had this on a number of occasions, always supplied with a glass of water. We spent a pleasant hour learning about the Greek village way of life. We thanked our host and made our way to Larissa town.

The Germans had been spreading stories about, that whilst the Greek soldiers were fighting and dying in Albania, our servicemen were carrying on with their girlfriends. Because of this, fraternization with girls in Greece was forbidden. When we attempted to talk to the girls, they said 'Astinomia' (Police) and then, indicated with their hands that they would have their hair cut off.

On our way to town, Bill and I were walking behind two young Greek airmen and their girl friends. We thought that we would have some fun. We had been learning a Greek song, which was sung to the tune of 'The Woodpecker Song' a very catchy tune, very popular in those days. So off we started.

"Coroitho Mussolini, Canneenas, Thameeni Yseekay Italia. Eepra Thoosalia, Cremetoily Stoharkee." I suppose we were swanking a bit, but it was an overwhelming success. "Bravo, Bravo" they chorused. Then, chatting amongst themselves, one of the airmen turned and said, the girls, who were quite pretty, had suggested that we might kiss them if we wished. Our bright star was still shining. Quite unusual, but, realising we would be missing female company, they felt a little sorry for us. Well, we arrived at the town, having been sent on our way with a kiss.

The shops were quite a surprise, they were as different as chalk and cheese from those at home. Talking of chalk and cheese, they had open containers of goat's cheese which tasted a bit salty and sour. There were large square tins of fish eggs and sacks of lentils, rice, ripe figs and large white beans. The loaves were oval in shape, quite large, with hard crusts and tasting of wholemeal plus, with a slight edge of salt. The tea, called Chy, was served in glasses without milk. No sweets, so far as we could see, but flat cakes made with seeds and honey, which tasted quite nice. We returned to camp for tea and then back to town on duty, and here's why:

Earlier in the morning, Bill had called me over to the Orderly Room. It wasn't really an Orderly Room, but a tent with a wooden notice board outside. "Get an eyeful of this", he said, "just look at DROs." (Daily Routine Orders)

'750832 J. Fairs, 750791 W. Fairs – will report to the Guard-room at 1900 hrs and proceed on Brothel Patrol'.

The only patrol we had been on so far was Guard Patrol. This was a surprise and we wondered whether we had been chosen because of our knowledge of the Greek language, but on second thoughts, our twenty Greek words, partially comprising:- Good Evening – Kalee spera. Yes please – Marleesta parakaio. Give me an egg – Thostemoo avgar, would perhaps not have been quite appropriate, and so we were given the services of an interpreter. We went armed with rifles, but we were not quite sure whether it was intended that we should shoot the erring airmen or the girls!

It was all quite a new experience and our first time in a brothel. We normally spent our evenings in the cinema. What we do remember is, that they had little charcoal fires, like those we use for barbecues, in the rooms, and one of the girls was blowing through a bamboo tube to fan the embers. It was all very strange!

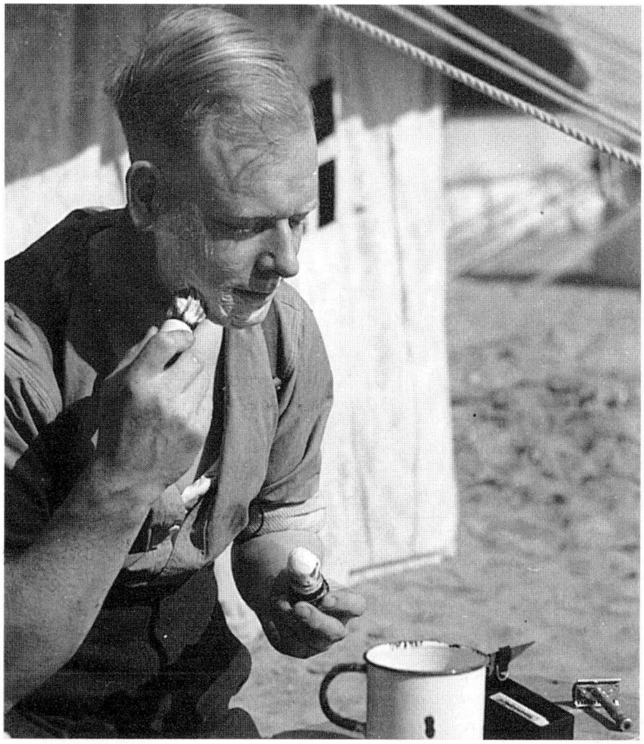

right Bill is shaving in cold water, but the sun was shining and since Mum had sent some English shaving soap – all was well!

below, Bill is writing home. His desk 'A' is a packing case in which they stored their clothes and the box 'B' is where they kept their very precious negatives

above, The whole of the village turned out to follow us

left, We sat at a table and were given Turkish coffee in small cups

below, A group of ladies were making scarves for the menfolk

8: A Village Visit

There was not a great deal to do on the unit and our flight sergeant had suggested we could have the day off.

We had made friends with a Greek sergeant and he and I were learning a few words of each other's language. We were looking at the adverts in a Greek newspaper and I was asking him to pronounce clearly some of the words for me, which I was them writing in a book, just how they sounded.

What a strange language it was! Observing an advert for chocolate I read OKOLATA... which was pronounced as 'socolarta'. Another advertising a film with Clark Gable in the lead was KLARK IKEIMIIA, I could somehow understand the 'Clark', but 'Gable' in no way! The sun was shining during our Greek lesson. We had a few good laughs and this was one of those pleasant interludes that made our time in Greece just a bit like a holiday.

Lessons over for the day, we decided to visit a village and learn a little of the countryside. Popping into Larissa first, we visited a lovely little church beautifully designed with a dome and two towers – one with a clock, the other with a bell. We entered and sat for a while saying a prayer of thanks for our good fortune, that our parents and friends, exposed to awful bombing on Merseyside be protected, and that God would be with us whilst we were overseas.

We passed a basket-maker on our way. He seemed so poor in his dress, although he was extremely skilled and we saw the same type of baskets that we had been filling with wood the previous day. Almost certainly they would have been made by him – but we did not have enough Greek to tell him. We also saw the village postman, a very important man at this time when the husbands and boyfriends were fighting the Italians in Albania.

Our very important cookhouse had requested volunteers for the collection of logs to feed the camp stoves, and Bill and I had come in a three ton truck to do their bidding; after all it was much better than heaving 250lb bombs about as we had done a few days earlier.

Walking back towards our aerodrome we noticed what looked like a family having a picnic. They signalled us and we walked over wondering just what they wanted! There were about one dozen peasants. It seemed to us that the whole family were there including the grandma and grandad. They had a little baby lying contentedly in a basket among the wild flowers. The women had spread thick woollen cloaks on the ground and they invited us to be seated. As we had approached they had said 'Kalos aristate' which we learnt meant welcome.

They had been working in the fields planting onions and had lit a fire and were cooking lunch in a huge blackened pot. It smelt good and when it was ready we were invited to help ourselves. The main dish was a stew of beans, onions and garlic. It was quaint really; they had not one word of English and so we racked our brains to make a little conversation in Greek. We told them we were airforce photographers (eeposmeneeus photographus) and pointing to ourselves, we told them that we had been in Larissa for three months (Larissa sto tres menas) and that Bill was my brother (adelfosmu) yes, we were twins (theethema) and just to swank, I said 'psomi parakalo'. Please pass me the bread.

We passed a very pleasant lunch hour, so unexpected, and although our Greek was very limited, about 100 or so words, we had used them so often, yes, over and over again, we had become reasonably proficient and confident. If we made some mistakes we did not care, life in this respect was not to be taken too seriously.

We had decided to spend an evening in Larissa and called in at one of the tavernas. How very different from home where the bread was usually white, here it was made of whole grain flour, a sort of rough wholemeal, big oval loaves and quite heavy, though we found it quite nice to eat. We were offered a drink of Turkish coffee in small cups which were half full of coffee grains and it was usual for a glass of water to be supplied. Then we were given Retsina, a most popular drink in Greece.

We visited a lovely little church beautifully designed with a dome and two towers – one with a clock, the other with a bell

above, We passed a basket-maker on our way. He seemed so poor in his dress, although he was extremely skilled

below, To make Retsina, a little resin tapped from the pine-trees is added as a preservative

below right, We also saw the village postman, an important man at this time when the husbands and boyfriends were fighting the Italians in Albania

Bill and I do not drink in the accepted sense of the word inasmuch as we don't care for beer. I did however try the Retsina. I shuddered at the taste and thought that it tasted of turpentine. We asked what the taste was and found that when the wine is young, a little resin tapped from the pine-trees is added as a preservative. Retsina, together with ouzo, a drink tasting of aniseed, are the drinks that almost everyone tries when they visit Greece and, despite my non-drinking habit, I was no exception.

A scratchy record was playing on an old hand-cranked gramophone and a number of Greek men were dancing to what I think was called bouzouki music. They were dancing in slow motion in a circle with their hands on each others shoulders, stopping now and then to snap their fingers in rhythm We were invited to join in, which we did, and we managed very well. We were always keen on dancing at home, but always danced with girls rather than men ...

We found it interesting to observe some of the men who were sitting watching, twiddling what looked like rosaries. They were black 'worry beads' (Komboloy). It seemed to be an activity that kept the men occupied.

above, A Greek sergeant and Jack were learning a few words of each other's language. They were looking at the adverts in a Greek newspaper

Others were eating what seemed like flat seeds and when we made enquiries we were told that they were roast pumpkin seeds and we asked for a few and had difficulty in opening the husk.

None of the men spoke English, and so we spoke our party-piece of Greek phrases. They asked us in Greek, 'Do you speak Greek?' We were able to say 'Ohi, polee lyeega' which means, 'No – very little'.

There did not seem to be any bacon, eggs and chips so we tried octopus with fresh salad – no comment. We eventually settled for what was called 'Meze' which was little pieces of cheese, tomato and cucumber impaled on tooth-picks, and this was followed by small squares of Turkish Delight, also on tooth-picks.

It was a very pleasant, unusual evening, very Greek – filed away in our memories to be recalled again and again with pleasure.

9: Greece – Tremors and Teeth

At Larissa in Northern Greece we were accustomed to being awoken each day at Reveille by the sweet strains of 'Over The Rainbow' played by a very talented Greek airman, who told us that his trumpet had been captured from the Italians. That was indeed a lovely way to be awakened, but then came 1st March 1941 and a very different awakening. At eight minutes to six we awoke to deafening explosions with the ground trembling. Our Bill said, "It's those bloody Italians bombing us!" We had learned to swear since joining the RAF but we only swore when stressed – like now.

We were covered in bricks and rubble. Fearing that there was more to come, and as the ground was still trembling, we heaved our blankets and mattresses over our heads. After a minute or so of silence we uncovered our heads to discover that our 'oppos', Erb and Dunmore, were covered in bricks and needed digging out. Fortunately, they were not seriously hurt and we all scrambled out through the wall. There was no need for the door, the wall had collapsed – outwards, luckily.

Well it wasn't the Italians after all, it was an earthquake, or 'Seismos' in Greek – yet another word for our vocabulary – not that we felt in the mood for learning. It was becoming light and we were thankful to see that the barrack building was built of reinforced concrete pillars, infilled with light bricks. Thank you bright star. However, the nearby town of Larissa was not so lucky suffering badly with much damage and many killed. Our CO sent an ambulance, transport and airmen to give them what aid we could.

A very talented Greek airman awoke them each day with 'Over the Rainbow'

The weather was very cold and because we were still experiencing earth tremors the squadron went under canvas. This gave us some degree of comfort, but our nerves were still on the edge, not having

above, At eight minutes to six the earthquake struck!

left, Remains of the cookhouse!

opposite, Because of the earth tremors the squadron went under canvas. Mount Olympus can be seen in the background

below, Some Italian prisoners of war helped out in Larissa town

experienced an earthquake before. It was a funny feeling to see the suspended paraffin lamp swinging to and fro when there was no wind. When we had booked our 'cruise', the travel agent failed to mention that earthquakes were a regular part of life in Greece!

Matters were not helped the next day, when the Italians really did come over and bomb the camp. So we set about cutting the tops off four-gallon petrol tins. These were about fourteen inches high and eight inches square and we filled them with soil. We didn't have any sand bags and, indeed, we hadn't any sand, so they seemed a good alternative. We placed the tins around the tent, hoping that they would stop shrapnel and, also, they gave us a certain amount of security making us feel more protected.

The next day it was business as usual. We went into the cellar we were using as a darkroom to develop our reconnaissance films. It was a weird feeling, with the building giving a little tremble every now and again. We wished we were outside, but duty called – the war effort and all that.

We had large rolls of film with one hundred and twenty five exposures each five inches square. Our developing tank contained two rollers and, when filled with developing fluid, we wound the film from one roller to the other, then poured in fixer and water for washing. We had been warned not to wind the film too quickly as this could cause 'stress marks'. But, whoever gave those orders hadn't considered working in a cellar during earth tremors and, as we ourselves were 'stressed', we ignored the order but, fortunately, all was well.

Diary Entry;

Six of our Blenheims took off for our advanced 'drome at Paramathea. One, sadly, crashed into the mountainside. Three were killed and three injured.

I am now separated from Bill. I broke my tooth, and when I reported sick the MO said that I would have to be flown to Athens as we did not have a dentist on the unit....

Amongst the few nice things you could buy in Larissa were oranges, figs and almonds. Now almonds are even nicer when they are sugared but they are very hard and, if you are foolish, like I was, they can break your teeth. And they did!

above, When Jack was in Athens he had time for some sightseeing – the view from the Acropolis

left, With Palace Guard Evzone

below, The pretty little Greek girl

10: Retreat from Larissa

Brother Bill is writing this chapter.

Jack had been away for almost a week with his broken tooth, having been flown to Athens and I was on the Larissa airfield. It was 15th April 1941 and the Germans had bombed Larissa during the day with a force of 40 planes – an unwelcome experience. After the raid an uneasy calm pervaded the camp, and it was with some relief that I tumbled into bed. Sleep is a wonderful thing when all worries are usually forgotten.

I had been sleeping peacefully for a couple of hours when I was awoken by someone gently squeezing the lobe of my ear and saying, "Wakey, wakey, do you want to buy a battleship?" I wasn't surprised because on the squadron it was not unusual to wake a person who was required for a duty at some unearthly hour in this manner. "Whadye want?", I mumbled, and then the orderly room runner told me that the squadron was moving out in half an hour, and that we were to parade on the airfield.

The move came as no surprise, we had been told earlier to make a light pack of those things needed for a prompt withdrawal, and to file the rest of our clobber on one side of the tent, together with films and paper and other photographic equipment, ready for burning. Each tent had been provided with a four gallon tin of petrol, but on no account were we to open the can. We were told that the demolition party would be setting everything alight at dawn.

Making our way to the parade we met a couple of our pals who told us that they had been helping to empty the canteen. They had a bottle of whisky, a bottle of brandy and two bottles of peppermint. They said it would have been a pity to have left it for the Germans. We boarded a three-ton truck. It was a very tight squeeze, and as there was standing room only it was most uncomfortable – but there was a war on! It was an eerie feeling travelling along the mountain roads of Northern Greece standing in the back of the truck, especially having been awakened from a deep sleep. We didn't feel like singing "It's a Long Way to Tipperary" or "We'll Hang Out the Washing on the Siegfried Line". In fact, we didn't have any washing to hang out, it was waiting in our tent to be burned by the Incendiary Squad, before the Germans arrived.

Upon reflection, and we had plenty of time to reflect, things didn't look too good; photo reconnaissance had shown that the German and Italian airforces had over 1,000 aircraft

above, We had a very welcome wash and shave at the well
below, Jack was covering his new home in fir branches for camouflage

between them, and we had less than 80 and, as one of our fitters said, most of those were "clapped out" – an airforce expression meaning in poor condition. Looking back, I can recall thinking, although life at that moment was a little difficult, how lucky we were compared with those back home on Merseyside who were experiencing the Blitz, or our air crews and the troops at the front line in Northern Greece in the heat of battle.

Yes, truly we had much to be thankful for. It was our bright star shining up there. However, one little blip, our convoy had ground to a halt! We waited about ten minutes, during which time we said a little prayer that the Germans would not have any night fighters up to strafe our convoy, we were travelling with dimmed headlights. Everyone alighted and went to see what the problem was. Well, it was pretty obvious, with the bonnet of the leading truck raised and a couple of bods fiddling about inside. It was a breakdown and the whole convoy was held up for about 15 minutes on the narrow mountain road.

It was decided to push the vehicle off the road in order that the rest of the convoy could proceed. We were lucky – just about 100 yards further along the road was a steep ravine. There was no problem finding willing volunteers and away she went, crashing down breaking trees, tumbling over and over, with pieces flying off. Very exciting, just like in the cinema! We managed to photograph most things, but this was one subject we were unable to capture – we did not have a strong enough flash. Ironically, our photo unit had used a flash with the intensity of many millions of candle power. This could illuminate an area of about half a mile square enabling a photograph of a target to be taken.

Off we went again. By this time we had managed to get into what could be described as a reclining position on the truck, far better than standing, but we were stiff and every joint ached. The truck rolled on hour after hour, with 10 minute stops, but no real break for 10 hours. In fact, we did not stop until 11am the next morning.

Yes! Then we had a lovely breakfast, two whole hours. We ate bully and biscuits. The biscuits were what we called hard tack – they were about three inches square and about half an inch thick, hard and crisp. They were like dog biscuits, in fact the dog biscuit manufacturers had turned over to making them. They were the same biscuits that were stored on lifeboats, and were quite palatable and pleasant to eat. We received a very nice surprise whilst we were stopped at the camp. There were some Aussie soldiers who were handing out tins of peaches. Just the thing with hard tack biscuits!

A further four hours and our truck stopped at a small village by the side of a well, where we were able to have a very welcome wash and shave. There were some Greek soldiers there who, although they could speak no English, indicated that the war was over for them. A Greek lady was watching us together with her pretty little daughter. She smiled and I said in my best Greek, "Kalee Mayra" (Good morning), and I was surprised when she replied in very good English, "Hello, I'm sorry that things have turned out so badly for you". We chatted for a while, and I suggested that I take a photograph of her little girl, after all how could I resist, when it was my intention, God willing, after the war to open a studio specialising in photographing children.

Little did we think that the day would come when, not only did we send her a nice picture, but actually received a letter of thanks. That was to be two years later when we sent the picture from Cairo.

On the road again for about five hours, we arrived at Elevsis Aerodrome. There was a large shed about the size of an aircraft hangar, and there we slept until next morning. Our truck driver told us that Menidi Aerodrome was not too far distant, and that was where brother Jack was stationed, which was good news. We hated to be separated and could not be reunited quickly enough. We were so fortunate being identical twins – thinking alike and never tiring of each other's company.

It was four months since leaving England and so far we had not received any letters, although Mum and Dad had sent four telegrams saying that they were OK, and we, too, had sent telegrams. But I digress. At last we arrived at Menidi Aerodrome, which was 20 miles outside Athens, and then to find our Jack. After a few enquiries I was told that he was in the dispersal area, a rather beautiful wood located on the King's estate. I was just in time – another few minutes and I wouldn't have been able to find the tent. Jack was covering it in fir branches for camouflage to conceal his new home from the enemy who had already strafed the airfield that day setting one of our Blenheims on fire.

right, The result of the attack was the setting on fire of one of our Blenheims – in the confusion this was the best photograph I could get!

below, The view from our camp at Tatoi at Menidi aerodrome on the King's estate was so peaceful and really beautiful ... at least until we were attacked by dive bombers!

11: To Corinth

It's 22nd April at Menidi Aerodrome, twenty miles from Athens. Bill and I have been reunited. It's a lovely day, the sun is shining, and if there wasn't a war on everything in the garden would be lovely.

Who would have thought that a simple visit to buy a tablet of soap would have caused so much apprehension. It did though. We had just popped in to Dapper Dan's Cabin, which was our NAAFI, a tin shed in a wood adjoining the Aerodrome, and said "Tablet of Lifebuoy Soap please". Whilst making our purchase, there was some rather pleasant dance music playing on the radio, and then, "Here is a special announcement. The German forces are within forty miles of the Greek capital, Athens."

We were surprised – there was the BBC so far away, telling us what was happening on our own doorstep. "Don't bother with the soap", we said as we hurried out full of apprehension, "We can't spare time to wash." In fact, members of the squadron had been lying out all day in between German air raids, but we had not considered that the enemy was quite so close. Having already left one aerodrome in a hurry, we more or less had just what we stood up in, as the saying goes, apart from a toothbrush, toothpaste, towel and face-cloth – you know the things one takes when you go into hospital, Ah! and one very special something, a box of very precious negatives, which is how we are able to supply these photographs.

Suddenly the air was full of explosions and machine gun fire. WOW! Here they come! We flung ourselves into the air-raid trench. Just fancy being pleased to lie with your face in the soil – we were. Being bombed and strafed was most uncomfortable, I remember thinking that our heads were OK being covered with our steel helmets, but the rest of our bodies seemed terribly vulnerable, and each time the planes swooped down we pressed ourselves further into the floor of the trench.

But not so Paddy Duff, an Irish fitter, who earlier in the day had removed a machine gun from one of the damaged Blenheims and put it in a metal tube fixed on the edge of an air raid trench, and as they say in the RAF he was belting away, thoroughly enjoying himself, Oh, that we were brave like him! Paddy gave a great deal of assistance to the Adjutant – he was an organising genius with a filing cabinet brain. One would perhaps wonder what a fitter was doing working alongside the Adjutant, but we found that our mobile squadron was like that – everyone 'shoulders to the wheel' no matter what their job.

above, Paddy Duff removed a machine gun from one of the Blenheims and put it in a metal tube fixed on the edge of an air raid trench

below, Jack & Bill tuck into syrup butties outside Dapper Dan's Cabin

We were not surprised to hear after the war that Paddy had quite an important position in Kenya.

However, when quietness returned and we were able to climb out of the trench, we knew that we were neither hurt, nor dead.

Many of the most important members of the squadron had already been flown out. Unfortunately, we were just lowly LACs and our true worth had not yet been recognised. We were instructed to go to the airfield and wait. It was somewhat unnerving sitting on the perimeter of the airfield, aircraft were burning, and we just sat waiting with nothing happening. Our patience was rewarded, our prayers too, three trucks pulled up and we clambered aboard, and off we went.

Travelling through Athens we were surprised at the sympathetic attitude of the Greeks, it was an extraordinary experience when they shouted out greetings, and gave us the 'thumbs up'. They were still most friendly, even though we considered that we had let them down, and were leaving them to German Occupation. We were sad to leave, but did not fancy a stay in a German Stalag prisoner of war camp, having been used to the better things in life like corned beef and hard tack biscuits.

Later we learned just how lucky we had been. Those lads who had been captured were imprisoned in a bug-ridden holding camp at Corinth. Without food for three days, they had to swap rings and watches through the wire to obtain something to eat. The camp was filthy, the guards were beasts – that star was certainly shining brightly for us.

Crammed like sardines, we drove mile after mile into the country. We guess the driver must have known where he was going because we had neither an officer nor an NCO in charge, not on our wagon anyway. Phew! it was most uncomfortable, we were so packed that if you lifted a foot off the floor, there wasn't room to put it down again, without standing on someone's ankle and you were left standing on one leg.

We were tired and fed up and, if we were honest with ourselves, hot and weary. Passing burning lorries and with the day drawing to a close, we decided that we should show some leadership.

Bill crouches in the slit trench holding the small Kodak Duo camera with which most of the photos were taken

above, On the airfield at Menidi we just sat around waiting for ages

right, In Athens we were surprised at the sympathetic attitude of the Greeks

below, Hypo, our pet 'pooch', left behind, became a prisoner in a POW camp

12: To Nauplian

We are still in Greece, journeying along the road to Nauplian, where we hope to make our escape. I suggested to Bill that we leave our truck in case we are strafed and meet an ultimately end and so off we go to sleep in the hills. We invited a couple of our pals to join us, and off we went, just two fields away from the road, where it would be more peaceful. We found a nice little area for sleeping beneath a hedge. With a couple of blankets and our small kitbags for pillows, we slept fitfully for a few hours. We were heartened when we gazed into the night sky to see that our lucky star was still shining brightly.

When morning came we found that we had visitors, girls from the nearby village. *"Kallee Mayra"* (good morning) we said, and then in our best Greek, *"Thaylomen psomi avgar"* (give me bread and eggs), and if this all sounds a bit Greek to the reader, well we had not been in the country for very long. One of the girls went away, and shortly returned with – guess what? Yes, bread and eggs, but a snag – the eggs were raw, so we said, "Zesti paragallo" which means hot please. The young lady motioned to Bill to hand over his enamel mug, and filling it with water gathered a few twigs, made a small fire, and hey presto! Hard boiled eggs – no butter, but there was a war on.

We chatted with them for a few minutes. We were able to tell them that we had been in Larissa for two months, that we were photographers, and they told Bill and I that we were twins (theethamer) and brothers (adelfia) and bravo. I'm not quite sure where the bravo came in, maybe they were saying we were lucky to be together. We thanked them again, and they spoke quite a lot of Greek to us, which we did not understand. We seem to recall that part of their farewell meant 'God be with you'.

The sleep had done us good, and we felt refreshed. We were on our own now, and heading south towards the Corinth Canal. After a few miles we met up with some New Zealanders who had experienced a real pasting, losing their equipment to far superior numbers of Germans. They had been dive-bombed and suffered dreadfully. They, too, were heading south, and we were glad to have their company. Enemy aircraft were continually passing overhead, and we rushed to hide ourselves under the olive trees, our hearts pounding, and we were offering a few prayers. Fortunately, there were many olive groves and we were able to conceal ourselves. We at last reached and crossed the bridge over the Corinth Canal, so easily – just like that. We were quite oblivious of the tremendous battle that was to take place within a short time of our crossing.

above, Jack and his pal, Paddy Boreland, awoke under the hedge to find they had visitors – fortunately just girls and children from the local village

left, One of them went away and returned with bread and eggs. She took Bill's enamel jug and made a small fire and cooked his eggs for him

right, We were on our own now, and heading south towards the Corinth Canal

When we think of a canal in England, we usually visualise a narrow channel running through the countryside. The Corinth was not a bit like that, the canal was in a rock cutting 150 feet deep, with precipitous sides and a bridge over. This bridge was of such importance to the Germans that three days after we had crossed they launched a tremendous raid, 20 to 30 dive-bombers and about 100 German fighters swooped down on our troops who were defending the bridge. When they had silenced our guns they dropped hundreds of paratroopers. We had lost, or almost, but – and it seems like a film scenario – there were two young British officers, one of whom took a rifle and fired into an explosive charge which they had previously fixed to the bridge, causing a violent explosion and demolishing the bridge. To finish the story, which is true, the two young men reached Nauplian and escaped.

However, we digress. Although it was not very apparent, there was some organisation, because we were ordered to board a train, which we hated. This was about the worst part of the journey, travelling along in a noisy train, unable to see or hear aircraft, and visualising the train being strafed. It really was unnerving and quite a relief to enter tunnels. The train eventually came to a halt, and we clambered thankfully down. By this time, the number of troops had multiplied, and there were thousands, mainly Australians and New Zealanders, with the odd sprinkling of RAF and British troops. It was growing dark, and we passed a churchyard where hundreds of men were sitting around on gravestones. It was eerie, and we were feeling a bit low in spirits. We made our way to the jetty, this was the Port of Nauplian, and with a bit of luck it was where we would embark. Smoke was still rising from an ammunition ship which had been bombed and blown up earlier in the day.

There was tremendous activity in the dock area, with boats ploughing backwards and forwards. A large vessel had grounded near the jetty, and a couple of naval vessels were trying to pull her clear. We heard later that the vessel was 'The Ulster Prince', the ship that had taken us to Greece. The next day she was bombed and strafed, and, blazing from stem to stem, she was left a total wreck. Landing barges were ferrying soldiers and airmen to the ships, which were a short distance from the jetty. Fortunately, the sea was calm, and it was with a great sense of relief that we found ourselves clambering up nets that were suspended over the side of the troop transport 'The Glenearn'.

We were assisted on board by one of the sailors, and within minutes the finest cup of cocoa that we have ever tasted was handed to us by a seaman. Yes, here we were with sailors giving us comfort when they themselves, on that very day, had been dive-bombed and their ship's paint store set on fire. The ship had also lost both her anchor winches. We owe a great debt of gratitude to the Merchant Navy and the Royal Navy for rescuing us. The congestion on board was extreme, over 5,000 men crammed on board, including 30 cot cases of wounded. The ship was just less than 10,000 tons.

We hadn't any idea of our destination until one of the crew told us that we were making for Suda Bay in Crete. It was now after midnight, packed like sardines was a very apt expression. Although those who wanted to could find a space to lie on the deck, it was both hard and cold. Surprisingly, we were able to sleep for a couple of hours. We were awakened by the throbbing of the engines, and found ourselves underway. Looking at the time we saw that it was 4am. We were so thankful to be on our way, but very apprehensive with regard to being bombed. However, at 8.00 a.m. we had company, being joined by two transports, also crammed with troops, and a destroyer.

above, The 'Glenern' – we couldn't get onto this ship quickly enough, and now we are desperate to get off it!

left, We hurried into the hills, and finding a gully we broke small branches off some trees, and formed a canopy to try to make ourselves invisible from the air

13: Crete

Land ahoy! Strange how we couldn't get on this ship quickly enough, and now we are desperate to get off it. It's our worst cruise so far, no wonder that the travel agent hadn't included it in his brochure. In fact, it was to take another 50 years before Crete became a popular holiday destination!

We arrived in Suda Bay. Although it only had one jetty and a large shed, it was one of the finest anchorages in the Mediterranean. As soon as The Glenearn tied up we dashed ashore, where a couple of airmen were standing by a large stack of sandbags, not for filling though. They gave us eight each and said, "Sorry lads, no blankets or sheets left, you will have to use these to keep warm and protect yourselves from the mosquitoes". Oh, that we had some string and a needle, we could have made a sandbag quilt. However, they were better than nothing.

We hurried into the hills, and finding a gully we broke small branches off some trees, and formed a canopy to try to make ourselves invisible from the air, then gathering some clumps of a type of heather and long grasses, we fashioned a bed of sorts, almost like a huge nest for two, Bill and I. The bed wasn't a great success. I guess that we were not used to sleeping in a nest, with twigs sticking into our backs. Sleep did not come easily, so we talked about our life in civvy street, before the RAF.

We had both worked for a marvellous company called Commercial Solvents Limited in Bromborough, where there was a very relaxed, friendly atmosphere, and in between making out invoices such as:-

May and Baker Limited

3000 gallons of industrial methylated spirit

500 gallons of acetone

I would take a walk around the factory with a handful of papers, hoping to meet a rather pretty secretary. Bill had decided that photography was to be his life, and he asked me if I would like to take over his job, and that was how I, too, worked for the company. Bill left on the Friday and I started on the Monday. We were so alike that very few in the factory knew that a swap had been made. Thus Bill started in photography and I left photography, I had worked for Kodak before the swap. It was strange really, how throughout our lives we have shared so many similar experiences, sometimes it is almost uncanny.

And what about the pretty secretary? Well, I was home on embarkation leave, and had

left, We swapped places and Bill stayed with the pretty secretary, who didn't mind at all, she probably preferred Bill anyway

below, The great big bird down in the bay was a Sunderland flying boat, like a huge seagull with wings outstretched

dated her. We were in the cinema, when who should appear but our Bill, all smiles, to say that he was coming with me overseas. In error the RAF had just posted me, but he had worked the oracle and was coming too. We swapped places and Bill stayed with the pretty secretary, who didn't mind at all, she probably preferred Bill anyway. We usually spent the whole evening with our girlfriends, but this was a short embarkation leave, and we had to cram a lot in a very few days.

With these pleasant thoughts of home, sleep eventually took over. We slept fitfully, and awoke cold and hungry. We welcomed the dawn, but no cookhouse, no tea and no breakfast. Our sister had given each of us a tin of Horlicks tablets for an emergency, and we used them now. They were issued to aircrew and used on lifeboats, so our sister was a wise one. Bill suddenly called out, "Just look at that great big bird down there in the bay", and sure enough there was a Sunderland flying boat, like a huge seagull with wings outstretched.

"Let's go and investigate." I said, and stacking our sandbags in a neat pile, off we went. We made our way down to the jetty, and found a sergeant in charge. He was embarking personnel on to an air-sea rescue launch to be ferried out to the Sunderland. "Good Morning Sergeant" we said. It is always important to be polite to sergeants, particularly when you want something from them. "Could we go on the Sunderland?" The sergeant looked at us and said, "No, only important people are being flown out on this kite, the King of Greece flew out on this the other day".

We both looked a bit downcast, and he must have softened up a bit, because he asked us what trade we were. Bill spoke up and said, "We are reconnaissance photographers". He could have just said photographers, but reconnaissance photographers sounded more important. It worked, and the sergeant said, "Okay, go on", but wanting to have the last word he said, "There are already 65 on board and she usually only takes 30 apart from the crew".

We got on board, but were separated, It was so crowded that Jack had to share the toilet with four others. It couldn't be used anyway, because no-one on board could move, but Alexandria wasn't so far away, and although it was inconvenient, everyone had to contain themselves. The take off, where we appeared to be taxi-ing all the way to Alexandra, was nail-biting. We were hungry anyway, apart from the noise of the engines there was complete silence on board, just like a prayer meeting, and I'm sure that it was the combined prayers of those on board that allowed the kite to eventually take off.

This calls to mind that a Salvation Army Major who was a friend of ours, had printed on blotting paper the following simple sentence: – "More things are wrought by prayers than this world dreams of." That was in the days of fountain pens, before biros. The blotters were distributed to the troops in Cairo and in the desert.

We were not aware at the time that this was an epoch making flight, which would be reported almost every time that the Sunderland was reviewed. It was also reported in 'The History of the Royal Air Force'. We did not realise just how fortunate we were. During four days 20,000 troops were landed at Suda Bay, and here we were being flown out. We had been in the air for about 10 minutes when there was an awful racket, a tremendous resounding of machine-gun fire. Oh dear, we thought, we've had it, and to die so young. We needn't have worried; they were just testing the Sunderland's own guns, and as there were nine of them, hence the terrific noise.

We could feel the aircraft dropping lower and lower, and all of a sudden, whoosh and plonk, bump, bump, we had landed in Alexandria harbour. Other passengers were occupying the observation lounge, and so we couldn't see just what was happening.

However, we were down, and we offered a little prayer for our safe deliverance.

We clambered into an air-sea rescue launch to be ferried to the jetty. We little thought that Jack was to work on this very same launch in the future, but that is a story for a later chapter.

It was with a great sense of relief that we landed in Egypt. We were met with transport, and travelling through the city we experienced a strong feeling of normality. We saw lots of different uniforms and smartly dressed servicemen, and girls to whom one could speak without fear of them having their head shaved.

Very shortly we arrived at the RAF camp Abu Kir, and we luxuriated in using wash-basins with taps, hot and cold, and then to the cookhouse for corned beef stew, apple pie and custard. Certainly no complaints for the orderly officer.

Bill and I were soon tucked up in bed, the familiar RAF standard iron bed which had the appearance of having been made in Cammell Lairds. They were so heavy, and yet we thought that they were opulent, and slept like logs, better than having twigs sticking into one's back.

So ended our Greek adventure, just over three months, it seemed much longer. Knowing Eleven Squadron there was without doubt an interesting future ahead.

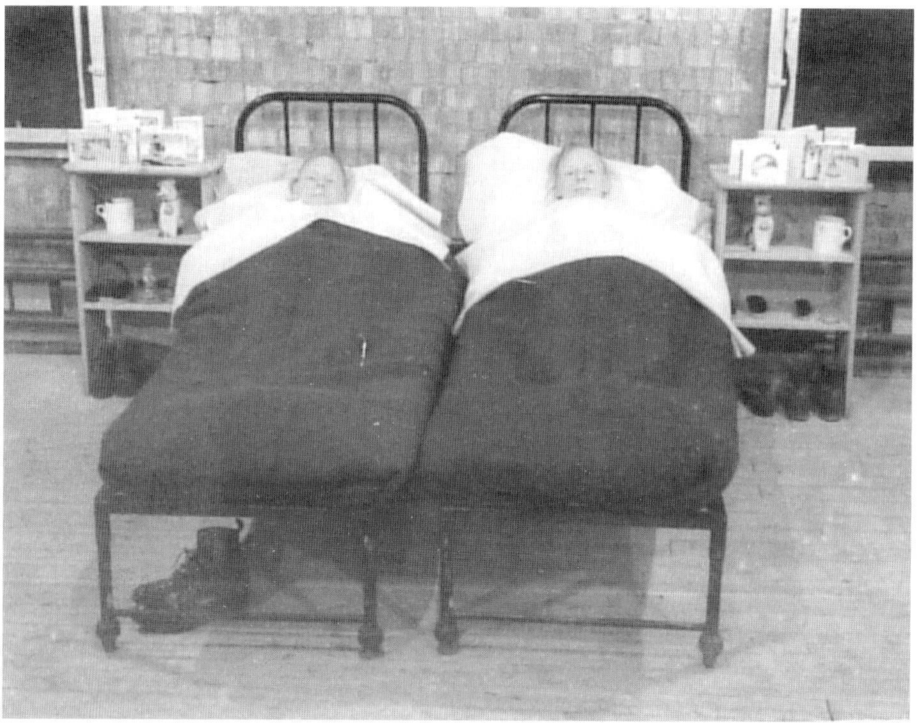

Bill and I were soon tucked up in the familiar RAF standard iron beds which had the appearance of having been made in Cammell Lairds

14: Letter from Israel

750832 LAC Fairs J
XI Squadron RAF
Middle East

Dear Mum and Dad,

This letter is to confirm our telegram "Both safe and well Egypt". It was indeed wonderful to reach safety, and to sleep comfortably at night. Having lost everything, the Squadron had to be re-equipped, and we, too, needed to be issued with new uniforms, khaki shirts and shorts, now that we are in the land of continual sunshine. It is the first desert that we have crossed, with thousands of square miles of nothingness except for scrub, sand and boulders. Sleeping at night was quite different, so quiet and pitch black. We had been warned not to wander away from the vehicles. To lose one's sense of direction could be very dangerous, and without water, perilous.

We were unaware of our destination which was most secret, and so we had to ask one of the cooks, who told us that we were heading for Palestine. The best time was when we stopped for meals, and the chuck wagon disgorged its stoves. Our cooks made very good stew under difficult circumstances, and one stove was used for brewing the all important tea. We have a waterbowser (tanker), and although the water tastes of chlorine, we aren't worried. Our convoy is very well equipped. It was at times when we stopped for meals that we considered that it was all quite exciting, and a bit of an adventure.

Our convoy consisted of about 40 wagons, and, oh boy, did they kick up the dust. See the photo enclosed – nose, ears, hair, full. We just looked as though we had been dipped in flour. Not too bad though, if that's all we have to worry about. A good brush down and we are smiling again. Smiling because we had arrived in Palestine (Israel) at Aquir Aerodrome, not too far from the lovely seaside town of Tel Aviv, with a very nice beach, but it gets a bit crowded at times. We have been lucky enough to manage a few visits.

We are now back with our shoulders to the wheel, and extremely busy at work, we cannot divulge any details because of very strict censorship. The camp is super, we sleep in fine wooden buildings, and have spring beds with huge fans whirring away on the ceilings, and we have mosquito nets. Each billet has a native whose job it is to clean our shoes and

above, Our convoy consisted of about 40 wagons, and, oh boy, did they kick up the dust

below, Mornings began with a yawn and a stretch and thoughts of food

polish our buttons, keep the hut tidy and to make our beds. All we have to do is wash ourselves and work. Truly that bright star is shining.

A couple of days ago we met with a Scottish lady in the St. Andrews Club in Tel Aviv, and she said, "Why don't you pay a visit to the Seiff Research Institute, I'm sure that you would find it interesting". Well we did. The Seiff Research Institute is in the village of Rehovot, a village about 14 miles from Tel Aviv. We travelled there by bus, and there was queue of about 40 waiting to board the bus.

We had taken our place in the queue when a young Israeli soldier told us that we could go to the head of the queue. We were entitled to do so because we were in uniform, so we did. The bus drivers are always most courteous, they own their own buses.

Arriving at the Institute we were met by two lady scientists, Dr. Hellinger and Dr. Weizmann. We were made most welcome, and taken on a little tour of the Institute. We learned that the Institute had been the dream of Dr. Chaim Weizmann, the brother of the lady doctor who was our guide. Her brother by the way is the President of Palestine, a brilliant scientist, his idea of setting up the Institute being the intensification of agriculture in Palestine. The Institute would study organic fertilizers, giving attention to such things as the milk industry, citrus, silk and tobacco, and especially chemical substances used in medicine. We were able to tell Dr. Hellinger and Dr. Weizmann that Commercial Solvents, the company where we had worked in England, used her brother's process for making acetone.

Dr. Anoushka Weizmann was born into a family of 15 children, and had lived in the tiny village of Motol in Russia, and so we were introduced to what we called Russian tea, no milk, but made with a slice of lemon, and being in the laboratory we drank from glass beakers. It was quite an honour being entertained by the President's sister. After a very interesting afternoon, we were asked if we would like to pay a visit with our hosts to listen to the Palestine Orchestra on the following evening, a very nice finish to the day.

Back at the camp we were quite surprised to see a gang of erks appearing around the corner of one of the huts with kitbags on their shoulders. Bill asked them whether they had all been posted. They said, "No, get your kit bag, there are masses of oranges around the comer, just waiting to be collected".

We went around the corner, and sure enough there was a lorry with thousands of oranges, sent by one of the orange grove owners. What a nice thought. We were reminded that this country is the home of oranges when we saw a signpost pointing to the town of 'Jaffa'.

This is a great country for growing fruit. Sitting cross-legged by the side of a road on our camp was an Arab with a large basin of pinky pawnee (this was water containing pot permang), and in this pinky pawnee were bunches of grapes. Our medical officer had forbidden the airmen to buy fruit unless it is so treated.

We are sending a photo taken at the Research Institute, and one or two others, and hope that the censor will let them through.

All for now.

God bless you.

Your loving sons,

Jack and Bill

above, The lovely seaside town of Tel Aviv has a very nice beach, but it gets a bit crowded at times!

left, Jack and Tommy on the steps of the Daniel Sieff Research Institute with the two lady scientists, Dr. Hellinger (next to Jack left) and Dr. Weizmann together with Professor Taub. (extreme right)

15: A Day in the life of Jack and Bill

Still in Israel, we'll tell you in a little more detail how we spent our day;

The day was 12th June 1941;

We were at Aqir Aerodrome, a few miles from Tel Aviv. The sun was shining and the sky was blue, but then the sun always seemed to be shining and the sky was always blue. It didn't ever seem to rain except in the months of November to April. We had an early breakfast and then off we went to the photo section to check the cameras and to load the film magazines which clipped to the camera body. The magazine held a roll of film of 125 exposures, 5 inches square, contained on a heavy spool, and so you will see that they differed very much from amateur films. It was our job to check the camera, and to adjust the controls, including lens settings, and film interval timing, so that the pilot who was so actively occupied had only to press a button when he reached the target area, and the camera, which was electrically operated, proceeded automatically to take line overlap photographs. The camera itself was mounted in the aircraft on rubber buffers to absorb shock, with the lens pointing earthward through a round aperture in the belly of the aircraft. The camera had a lens hood five inches in depth, and on one occasion one of the lads in the section inadvertently left a lens cleaning cloth in the lens hood, with the result – 'no pictures'. He was given 14 days in the glasshouse (military prison) for carelessness and endangering the pilot's life. We remember this incident because the young fellow came back to the unit with his head shaved, which in those days was very unusual.

Our next move was to the airfield, where we fitted the magazine to the camera in a Blenheim Bomber. We gave the pilot the thumbs up to indicate 'checked and ready'. The pilot was given clearance and, chocks away, he took off for Saida, a town on the west coast of Lebanon, where our enemies, the Vichy French, were giving us some trouble. The pilot told us on his return that he had experienced a marvellous spectacle of four British cruisers and four British destroyers in action pounding the Vichy shore batteries. Whilst the planes were away we prepared the chemicals, developer, fixer etc. to process the film. We used a large oval tank which contained two ebonite reels, the film being wound by hand from one side to the other. First it was soaked in water, then developer and finally fixer, the film then being dried, just as easy as all that ... or was it? We had to be careful to keep our developer etc. the correct temperature, not always easy in such a hot climate, although we were lucky,

left, The film magazine held a roll of 125 exposures, each 5 inches square. Here Jack and Bill are checking the film with the pilot

below, Jack with Miriam and Etti – a couple of smashers!

in the photo section we had an ice box which helped to keep the solutions cool, and was rather useful for melons too! When on duty we needed to take our job quite seriously, we were well aware the pilot was risking his life when he was on reconnaissance. Sadly the next day Pilot Officer Lea failed to return from a mission, but there was a hope that he may have been taken as a prisoner of war.

Film processed and dried, we worked a shift system on the unit and so we were able to pass the printing side over to the new shift to be made ready for the interpreters. We heard later that during the afternoon whilst we were processing the morning films, a formation of six of our Blenheims took off and bombed the enemy troops and transport at Kiswe which was occupied by the Vichy French. Anti aircraft guns opened up on our planes, and Sergeant Hudson's plane was hit in the rear gun turret, the gunner being wounded. Sergeant Hudson returned the fire hitting shells in one of the gun pits which exploded. Sergeant Hudson was the pilot of the aircraft in which six months earlier I had flown to Athens to see a dentist and we had made a forced landing, getting away with it. He was known as 'Lucky' Hudson.

Duty over, we were off to the guardroom to book out of camp. The M.P.s ask our name and number and that's it. They like to keep tabs on you and to make sure that you book in again. Even a bus journey was an adventure and, on the journey into Tel Aviv, we saw camels carrying loads of stone in a small quarry, orange groves with trees loaded with fruit, and a field of melons looking just like footballs in a field of desert sand. No greenery, and where did the water come from? These were scenes that we saw as we passed in the bus, there was probably a simple explanation for the melons but we didn't find out what it was. Ben Yehuda is the name of a principal street in Tel Aviv, but more especially the name of a very special cafe where two charming waitresses worked named Ruth and Ilsa. It made a pleasant change to chat with the fair sex. The Ben Yehuda was a cafe where, during the day, we sat on the sidewalk and watched the world go by, and during the evening we could sit inside and listen to an old Jewish gentleman playing a grand piano, Chopin and light classics creating quite a romantic atmosphere.

There were four of us RAF lads sitting enjoying coffee and ices. On the next table there were two pretty Israeli girls and their boyfriends. I remembered seeing films where the hero looked across the cafe and caught the eye of the pretty girl, and although not a hero I tried to catch the eye of one of the girls, she was a real smasher, and it worked. The girls and their boyfriends spoke excellent English. They seemed to enjoy their conversation with us. I am not quite sure how it happened, but happen it did, and I dated one of the girls. Her name was Etti Newman, I thought that she was wonderful. Bill wasn't left out, Etti had a friend called Miriam. We had a super evening, and were reminded of those pre-war evenings at home.

above, The Ben Yehuda was a cafe where, during the day, we watched the world go by

We had arranged to meet the two attractive girls, Etti and Miriam, at the beach, and to our delight they were there

16: The Enchanted Garden

June 13th 1941 still at Aqir in Palestine, and here we were on duty at the untimely hour of 0500 hours. We were very early risers on this particular morning, and had just fitted a camera into F/Lt. Rowbottom's aircraft. He was leading a flight of three aircraft to bomb some Vichy French motor transport, which was conveniently concentrated in a ravine. Our aircraft scored direct hits, damaging about 29 vehicles. The Vichy French were in Syria and the Lebanon, and were extremely anti-British and pro-German. Therefore our bombing was vital to help prevent the Germans from getting a hold and marching down into Egypt.

Mentioning F/Lt. Rowbottom's name reminds us of an amusing incident that happened at a big concert which was held in an aircraft hangar in Greece. The whole squadron was in attendance, and members of the audience were called upon to take the stage. Suddenly, F/Lt. Rowbottom found himself in the middle of a circle with hundreds of voices singing, "We call upon old Paddlebum to give us a song – sing – sing – sing", and to his credit he obliged.

However, we digress. Off to the airfield where we collect the film magazine, develop the film and hand it over to the other members of the section for them to print, ready for interpretation. Lunch over, we are off duty for the day, and making our way by bus on our favourite journey to Tel Aviv. Earlier in the week we had asked Ilsa, a waitress at the Cafe Ben Yehuda, if she knew of a Kibbutz we could visit. She told us of Ramat Gann, on the border of Tel Aviv, just a bus ride away. The camp was just a series of large wooden huts, but to many of the refugees who had escaped from the anti-Semitism that had swept through Europe, it was the Promised Land of Palestine. They had arrived with nothing, and were made so welcome that for them it was like joining a large family. If the refugees were Polish they joined the Polish group, Russians with Russian members; there were at least a dozen languages spoken, so conversation was not a problem. Where possible they worked at the job for which they had been trained, all jobs being of equal

Ilsa, waitress at Cafe Ben Yehuda

The Kibbutz of Ramat Gann was just a bus ride away

importance. Health care, education and housing were provided, even some pocket money! While we were on our tour we met a young couple with suitcases and a young child. On asking them if they were going on holiday, they smilingly informed us that, having spent some time on the camp, they had now decided to start a business in Tel Aviv. A measure of the importance of the Kibbutz can be judged from the fact that many important high ranking army appointments have been filled by Kibbutzniks, as they were called.

We were lucky enough to meet up with the two attractive young ladies, Etti and Miriam, when visiting the Cafe Ben Yehuda, and had arranged to meet them at the beach, and to our delight they were there. Sitting on deck chairs was very pleasant, and we chatted away, touching on many subjects. They wanted to know about our homes and families, and we learned a little about their way of life. After the chat it was time for tea, and we returned to the Cafe Ben Yehuda – we could not be blamed for feeling in a holiday mood, despite the war!

Tea over, we left the cafe, by which time it was getting dark. Etti realised that we were being followed – by Etti's boyfriend, Israel. Normally in the movies, when someone is being followed they are usually in a subway station and they wait until a train is just leaving and jump aboard. Alas, Tel Aviv did not boast a subway, so we jumped into the nearest taxi. Etti gave the driver his instructions, because with our limited knowledge of Hebrew, i.e. Shalom, hello and ice cream – Gleedah, we would not have got very far! Etti had asked the driver to take us to the Enchanted Garden – beautiful in the dim lighting, and certainly worthy of its name. We had a marvellous evening, because we had not enjoyed the company of girls for many months. We were young, and agreed with Richard Tauber when he said that girls were made to love and kiss. In his song he forgot to mention that they were also very useful when it came to cooking, washing and ironing!

Now back to Israel. No, not the country, but Etti's boyfriend, nursing his broken heart and threatening to throw himself into the sea because he thought he was being two-timed by his girlfriend. Despite telling him about the ships that pass in the night etc, he was still not very happy. Perhaps he is still wondering how ships came into a discussion about his girlfriend. Was she going to sail away with her new boyfriend? We were thoroughly enjoying life here, and happily this feeling lasted for the next few weeks. However, we did regret that so many of our companions overseas did not have the opportunity to meet the fair sex. Later, when we were more established in the Middle East, we were able to take some of the lads visiting with us and introduce them to families with whom we were friendly. In fact, one of our pals met his future wife at one home, and has been happily married for over 56 years.

17: The Zelcers

It was 22nd June 1941 at 1200 hours. There was great excitement on the airfield today.

We were watching a flight of six aircraft taking off to bomb the harbour at Beirut, led by Fl/lt Lawrence, when one of the engines of the leading Blenheim failed and the plane crashed on the field. It was a bad crash, and the ambulance and crash tender rushed over to the plane. Fortunately, there was no fire and we were relieved to see the crew climbing out. The air gunner had a leg injury and went off to hospital, the plane itself was a write-off but, fortunately, the rest of the crew were okay.

We mention these raids just to show that our squadron did some hard work, lest readers think that we were ALWAYS gallivanting around! (Which of course we were doing when off duty!)

We had a letter the previous day from Mum, she said that they had received quite a surprise when answering the door a few days earlier, to see two ship's officers who introduced themselves as Frank, the radio officer from the troop ship Empress of Canada, and his colleague, Bob, who had picnicked with us in Durban, South Africa. Frank had

Frank, the radio officer from the troop ship Empress of Canada, and his colleague, Bob, who had picnicked with us, left, in Durban, South Africa, had dropped in on Mum back home in Rock Ferry

above, Jack and Tommy on the Zelcer's balcony with the family and, rear right, Dr Esther Hellenger

below, The Mograbi Cinema in Tel Aviv

promised that if they docked in Liverpool they would call on Mum and Dad and tell them a little about our trip to Egypt, and here they were. Frank was as good as his word, and became a firm friend of the family. After the war Frank and his wife visited us and we went to stay at his home in Vancouver. We had a great friendship which lasted over 50 years.

But back to the war. Once again we are off by bus to Tel Aviv. We can still remember the feeling of being 'young and fancy free' with no commitments at home so far as girls were concerned. We were indeed lucky that, even during wartime, life should be so full of interest, and pleasant too, with just one or two unpleasant experiences, when we wondered whether we would still be alive on the morrow.

Who should we meet when we were alighting from the bus in Tel Aviv but Dr Hellinger, the President's secretary. She said, "I was hoping to meet you both because some friends of mine have suggested that you would be welcome to visit their home to meet a Jewish family. Their name is Zelcer. They are a very nice family and have two small girls, can you manage tomorrow afternoon?" We said that we would try, and in any case we would give her a phone call. We were certain that we would be able to work our duties so that we could be available. Our Flight Sergeant Jock Halliday was a real leader of men, and a joy to work for. If ever we erred in our work we felt we had let him down. The lads in the section held him in very high esteem, we were indeed lucky.

We managed to switch duties, and our visit was a great success, sitting completely at ease on the balcony, learning about orange groves, and chatting with the children. Such a complete change, that is a thing that one misses overseas, contact with families and children. We took Tommy Bromilow, an air gunner pal of ours. When convenient and possible we tried to include one or two of the chaps from the squadron, especially when visiting people's homes, they enjoyed sharing our good fortune.

The meal was so different. Camp grub was quite good, but when you are invited out, well, it's a bit special, and the fruit salad contained fruits that we hadn't tasted before. This was yet another event to file in our Memories Scrap Book, and we have just turned the pages to tell you about it.

The Mograbi Cinema:

We met our girlfriends, Etti and Miriam, later in the day, and went to the Mograbi Cinema with them. It was our first introduction to ticket touts who were at the door. It was sometimes difficult to obtain seats, and whereas the normal price of the seats was the equivalent of one shilling, they wanted one shilling and three pence – the scallywags!

Part way through the film we were quite startled. There was a very loud noise and a clanking and banging. We wondered what was happening, especially after our earthquake experience. We needn't have worried, it was just a large section of the roof rolling back to allow the hot air to escape. We certainly had some new experiences overseas. Jack Oakie was in the film with lots of dancing girls, but as we had our own girls we were quite satisfied! It was about eight months since we had been to a cinema with girls. The last time was when Bill and I shared the pretty secretary from Commercial Solvents, and here we were with a girl each – our bright star was still shining.

After the show Etti said, "Would you like to come home and meet my Mum?" I guess her mother wondered who her daughter was walking out with. I remember thinking what a good job I was wearing my Van Heusen shirt, quite smart really. We went home and were introduced with a nice cup of tea (lemon not milk).

Etti told me later that I had passed the test, and the picture I took shows a contented mother and daughter.

left, Jack strolls on the promenade at Tel Aviv with his friend George

centre, The Brocks had three little girls, and as one can see from the photograph, we were very busily engaged!

below, With Mr Dixon and Tommy at Ben Yehuda Cafe

more'. We chatted about what a wonderful job the Jewish people had done reclaiming the desert, and how they were irrigating huge tracts and planting trees. We learned that our new friend was a Mr Dixon, and he was the Chief Censor for Tel Aviv. He asked us if we would like to visit his home for a meal. Of course we said we would be very pleased to do so. He told us that he was not married but that he had a good housekeeper who would look after us. Two days later we had a lovely meal, and for those readers who have not heard the expression before, this visit was called by servicemen 'getting your knees under the table'. We were of the opinion that many civilians overseas felt that they would like to play their part in entertaining the boys, knowing how much they missed their families and homes. Indeed, many were homesick at times, although we ourselves cannot recall feeling homesick. We had a longing for home but that was a different feeling.

One night we went to a camp open air cinema, quite different from back home. No deciding whether to sit on the balcony or in the stalls, there were just rows of wooden forms, no carpet on the floor, just sandy gravel. In Palestine the evenings were pleasantly warm, and darkness always came more or less at the same time, about seven o'clock, and it took just about two and a half minutes for the sun to go down. Meanwhile the natives had been scurrying around selling peanuts and fried eggs on bread rolls, which were hot, and we enjoyed them. Seems odd doesn't it? Hot eggs in the cinema! We guess it was different in the Middle East. There was the usual chatter before the show started, and one of the lads stood and shouted across to one of his mates "What's the time Whack?" He was obviously a Liverpudlian, and at this various lads stood up and shouted "How's Scottie Road these days?". "What about a plate of scouse?" There was quite a bond between the Merseysiders. Darkness had descended, and once again we were in the land of make believe. Films played a tremendous part amongst the lads overseas, filling a real need.

Life wasn't always a bed of roses, and we had trouble with bugs, bed bugs to be precise, and wearing shorts was a disadvantage! They had made their homes in the joints in the wooden forms, and they had decided to have their evening meal just after 7pm. We could just imagine the little devils saying, "There's a nice bit of leg over there, fresh too, and it's white." In the billets, too, they were a nuisance, but we declared war on them. We would paint the joints of the metal beds with methylated spirits, set it alight and cremate them. We would also stand the legs of the beds in small tins of paraffin to make swimming difficult for them. Sorry about this rather unpleasant subject, but it was part of life in the Middle East, and we think everyone experienced this problem.

We met Dr Block, one of the scientists from the Sieff Research Institute, during the next day, and he kindly invited us to his home, asking us whether we could manage the following afternoon. We took our friend Tommy Bromilow along and we had a great time. They had three little girls and it was all so different from being in a camp full of men, and one can see from the photograph that we were busily engaged. Surprise, surprise. Dr Block said that if we wished we could borrow his flat for the weekend as the family were going away. We obtained weekend passes. Hey presto! We were residents of Tel Aviv, living in a flat doing our own cooking, so unusual during wartime that we were, as they say in the RAF, 'proper chuffed'. Tel Aviv was a beautiful place, so peaceful, no dirt and no beggars sleeping on the pavements. So different from Cairo, and it was with a touch of sadness that we were leaving. We think it true to say that the last three months were amongst the happiest of our six and a half years service, due in no small measure to the kindness of the Palestinian people, in such a small space of time for us to make so many friends was unusual.

When Mum received this photo she wrote telling Bill, "not to climb trees"

19: Crossing the Desert

Time marches on – it is now 2nd August 1941, 1400 hours – and we are leaving Palestine today.

Having said goodbye to Aquir, we were off on further adventures, making our way to our first port of call, which was the port of Haifa, just one and a half miles away. Our convoy of 50 vehicles was to park for the night in an olive grove, four miles out of town.

It was afternoon when we arrived, and Bill and I decided to walk around the block, or should I say, the district. We didn't even like olives, but we did like dates. We were passing some date palms, and our Bill (who is the adventurous one) decided that he would climb up and collect some of the mouth-watering fruits. I shouted up to him, "Hold it and I'll take a picture of you for Mum." Bill was climbing down with his booty when a man in European dress stopped and spoke to us. At first we thought, "Ah, here comes trouble," but not so. He had stopped for a chat and he was quite interesting. He told us some facts about the date palms, we learned that the fruits were not only eaten by people, but also by many animals. We were amazed to learn that on some date palms a single bunch could hold as many as 1,000 dates; also that the trunks supply timber, and that the ribs of the leaves were used for making furniture and crates – a very useful tree!

Mum eventually received the date palm photo and wrote (just like a mum) telling Bill, "not to climb trees".

We wended our way back to our truck, and found that the cooks had prepared a nice cup of char, and some corned beef sandwiches, which were improved with some HP sauce bought from our NAAFI. We were often able to add to our diet with little extras from our unit canteen, which consisted of a wagon and a tent, much of the food coming from Australia and South Africa, especially tins of fruit, so we were not a drain on Britain's supplies.

It was time for sleep, as we were making an early start next day at 0600 hours. We scooped a small hollow for our hips and slept well, reflecting upon the last time we had passed a night in an olive grove, when we were in the southern part of Greece retreating, but unlike then, here we could sleep peacefully without fear of bombing. We had the luxury of blankets and pillows, although the latter were not RAF issue. However, they were a great improvement on the webbing sidepack which was often used for resting one's head.

We slept well, and in fact did not leave for Mafraq until 0800 hours, which was quite a change, giving us that extra hour of sleep. We passed through some quite interesting country as we made our way to the border, where we crossed into Jordan. It was different from our usual travel, it was hilly so that we were able to look down into the valley and see the convoy on the road far below.

A short stop for lunch and we reached Mafraq at 1300 hours. Here we were surprised to see that we were to be escorted by four Bren Carriers of the TransJordan Frontier Force. We assumed that this was because our convoy was not armed, and there was always a chance that we may be attacked by marauding bands of Arabs. This was a most turbulent country. The Bren Carriers took us as far as the Iraqi border, where two Rolls Royce armoured cars from No1 RAF Armoured Car Squadron took over the escort duties.

We received many surprises whilst overseas. Stationed at an aerodrome in Britain one would not be aware that the RAF had so many unusual careers; Have you considered driving a Rolls Royce armoured car, or being a military policeman riding an Arab stallion, not to mention managing a lemonade factory or piloting an air sea rescue launch! Truly there was no end to the career possibilities in the RAF!

We cannot remember just how it happened – 58 years is a long time – but we do remember crossing the desert and approaching one of the pumping stations on the pipeline which transported the oil from the oilfields of Iraq to Haifa; There was an army unit located at this station, and they kindly invited us to lunch. Just why we shall never know, because they were totally unprepared for visitors. Hard to believe, they had partly filled a bin with broken hard tack biscuits (like very big dog biscuits), added tinned pilchards and water to mix, and stirred the lot up. Bit difficult to describe the taste – ugh, or perhaps 'horrible' might be better!

Undaunted, we thought that there was always corned beef and so we opened a tin. We had not taken into account that it was a boiling hot day, and when one boils corned beef the fat turns to oil, so if you open the tin over your knees, you can imagine the state of your shorts! Well, there was a war on, we had a good laugh, but from then on we took great care.

We cannot say that we were taking to the road once more, because there wasn't one – it was just desert, where sometimes the way was indicated just with old oil drums. Things were looking ominous, the temperature had soared, it was about 120 degrees Fahrenheit, and the vehicles in front were merely clouds of dust. On the horizon was a dark smudge which developed into a dust storm. The sun was obscured and it began to get dark.

For nearly an hour the dust storm continued, but the wind slackened and the sun reappeared, and we were able to relax and shake some of the dust off ourselves. It was everywhere, in our hair, our eyes and our ears. It might sound awful, but with the dust thrown up by the convoy ahead of us we were well used to dust and sand and took it very much in our stride.

above, Hard tack biscuits were added to tinned pilchards & water and stirred – Ugh!

right, Corned beef fat turns to oil

below, Rolls Royce armoured cars took over the escort duties

above, The camp was one of the most luxurious bases ever built

below, The tented village we later referred to as 'Hell Villas'

20: Habbaniya, Iraq

After the long journey from Palestine we arrived in Habbaniya in Iraq:

Following the five day crossing of a vast sun-drenched desert, we were surprised to find a town with street names such as Bond Street, Regent Street and Tottenham Court Road – but there the similarity ended – this was Habbaniya. With the sun beating down relentlessly, we hurriedly sought the shade of the eucalyptus trees which lined the streets. Our oppo' Tommy Row, a transport driver, wrote in his diary, "Arrived Habbaniya 7 Aug 1941, 5pm. No food ready – cheesed off – slept in tents pestered by ants", which suggests that he was not exactly impressed by Habbaniya. The camp, however, was one of the most luxurious bases ever built. It nestled between a long high escarpment and the River Euphrates, which supplied water for the gardens and eucalyptus trees. Amenities were plentiful; there were two cinemas, a church, tennis courts, soccer and hockey pitches, riding stables, a polo ground and the finest swimming pool in the RAF, to say nothing of 28 miles of roads lined with exotic trees, which were sure needed for shade! How we recall moving over to the shady side of the road. Life would not have been bearable without those trees.

That is enough of our holiday brochure description of the camp. There was no room at the inn for 500 desert weary airmen, so they had created a tented camp. The whole area was two inches deep in fine dust, which was just like talcum powder. We photographed the tented village and sent a photo home to Mum, avoiding telling her how unpleasant it was. It was not until we arrived home and were making up our photo album that we entitled the photo of the tented camp, "Hell Villas".

Our siesta during the afternoon was one of the least pleasant times, "charping it off" it was called by the squadron, because we lay on charpoys, light Indian beds made of cane, so light they could be lifted with one hand. They were so unlike those heavy Blighty beds which had the appearance of having been made in a shipyard. There we lay sweating away with just a sheet and a mosquito net. There weren't any side walls to the tent to allow the breeze to blow through; kidding – what breeze? I said to Bill, "Now I know just how a turkey feels in the oven." Oh, for those lovely cool spring mornings in Blighty. No doubt many servicemen reading this think that we 'did not know we were born' as they say, and they arc correct. We have been told a number of times, so we must point out these latest experiences are more of a report than a grouse.

We well knew that compared with many other servicemen we were extremely fortunate, and being so we were content, our bright star was shining, although it flickered a little. There was little work at the moment, just a leaflet raid on Iran, and no photography, and so I suggested to Bill that he pop into the travel agent and see whether there were any coach trips on offer (it wasn't really a travel agent – it was our Motor Transport Section). Bill was told that due to hostilities, coach trips had been cancelled, which was a great pity, because the RAF had one of the biggest coaches we had ever seen. It was a Mercedes Benz, it held 40 passengers, 1,000 gallons of water, had an ice box and was air-conditioned. We sure would have liked to take a trip in it. They were, however, able to offer a trip to Lake Habbaniya and a sail on the lake, or a trip to Baghdad. The trip to Baghdad was to buy books for our squadron library. During our retreat from Greece when we had destroyed all the squadron equipment, we had set fire to our library books, and these were to be replaced. Who knows, we may find a copy of 'The Forty Thieves'! Bill and I being the squadron librarians were chosen to go on the trip. Bill phoned Tommy Row, our pal in Motor Transport, and asked "Is the magic carpet ready to take us to Baghdad?" Tommy's reply, "I don't know about a magic carpet, there is a three-tonner over at the armoury having a machine gun mounted on the front. I will come and collect you when I'm ready, I'm just writing a letter to Freda." She was Tommy's girlfriend, 17 years of age, whom he had met while square-bashing in Blackpool. We mention this because in 1999, 58 years later Freda, came to stay with Bill and his wife.

Once again we digress: We were equipped with .303 rifles, and Paddy Duff, the squadron's volunteer gunner, was to handle the machine gun. Paddy was an LAC fitter, not a machine gunner. We have been reading a book called "Operation Mercury" written by Marcel Comeau, which gives an account of XI Squadron's adventures in Greece and Crete. The book was sent to us by the author Marcel, who was kind enough to write on the front leaf "To Jack and Bill who took part in many of the adventures recorded in this book – Marcel Comeau MM" – fame at last!

Extract from "Operation Mercury" ...

"A horde of German Me110s came shooting over the woodland and hit the Menidi Airfield, their bellies almost scraping the grass. A Greek Junkers burst into flame and a Blenheim collapsed suddenly on a broken oleo. The noise was terrific. A dozen columns of smoke arose amongst the Blenheims, and Paddy Duff, enraged at seeing XI Squadron's aircraft destroyed, wrenched an 84 Squadron Lewis machine gun from its mounting and ran down the centre of the airfield like a man berserk, firing from the waist at the oncoming fighter bombers. By a miracle he was not hit."

Back to the story. Well, there we were 'armed to the teeth' (not exactly). There were six of us with .303 rifles, and of course, Paddy sitting with the driver for easy access to his gun. We were travelling in a 3 ton Chev and some wit had painted on the door "Lifts for Servicemen".

There was a real possibility of trouble, and we were warned against taking any chances. However, we reached Baghdad without any problems. It was quite an interesting city with its natives, its minarets and mosques. We saw a native sitting on the sidewalk. He must have been a barber, he was shaving another with a piece of broken glass. Further along the road a person was asleep on a cart loaded with large round melons, and he was actually lying on the melons. A young Arab girl was leading four goats, she was no more than six years old and one of the goats was eating a piece of dirty crumpled paper. Observing scenes like this was far better than lying on our beds in an oven on the camp, and at times it was just like an overseas holiday. We reached the shop where our purchasing agent was to haggle over the price of the books. You've guessed it – our purchasing agent was the redoubtable Paddy Duff, who was described by Marcel in his book, as the Adjutant's right hand man and an organising genius with a filing cabinet mind.

above, Our big 'coach' was a Mercedes Benz, it held 40 passengers, 1,000 gallons of water and had an ice box and was air-conditioned

below, The finest swimming pool in the RAF!

above, The camp at Habbaniya was patrolled by mounted policemen
below, The lovely church was after the style of those in England

21: Habbaniya Memories

I was in Ward One of Habbaniya Hospital and a male nurse was standing at the foot of my bed, saying "I don't believe it", "You don't believe what?" I said. "I've just taken your temperature in the next ward." was his reply. He was nonplussed, and so I explained that it must be my twin brother, he, too, must have sandfly fever. He went on his way, still shaking his head. Half of our squadron of 500 men was in hospital during our five week stay in Habbaniya. Nothing too serious though, and usually suffering from sandfly fever or desert sores. About five days in hospital would cure either.

Desert sores were caused by a scratch or cut festering, and unlike home, where they just heal naturally, here they refused to mend without a short stay in the clinical conditions of a hospital, where they applied crushed tablets of M & B and, hey ho, one was cured. It was just as well that we were in hospital together, because we only had one razor between us, having lost one of them in our Greek adventure.

Habbaniya was Born; It was strange how we learnt about the origins of Habbaniya. Bill was chatting to the corporal in the next bed to him in the hospitaL, who was surprisingly well-informed regarding the history of the camp. He told Bill that in 1919 Air Marshal Trenchard had prepared a paper for Mr Churchill regarding the future of the RAF in the Middle East, as they were both very keen to establish bases there. The whole area was far from tranquil, and it was important that when trouble threatened they could act within a few hours, whereas a military expedition from Britain would take time and, of course, cost very much more money.

The barber was shaving another with a piece of broken glass

Subsequently, in 1921 at a conference Mr Churchill, who was then Colonial Secretary, decided that the RAF should garrison Iraq. A site near the River Euphrates and close to Lake Habbaniya was chosen because of the all important availability of water. Lake Habbaniya was also important for the Empire Flying Boats to land on their way to India, and so RAF Habbaniya was born.

The corporal told Bill that he had developed his interest in research to pass the time away. His two years at Habbaniya had just six months to go. He was cheesed off, and was looking forward to seeing his girlfriend again on his return to Blighty.

Visit to Camp; There was great excitement on the camp. We were expecting the visit of a high ranking officer, and sure enough at 0900 hours Inspector General Sir Edgar R. Ludlow-Hewit K.C.B., C.M.S., D.S.0., M.C. arrived to inspect J. and W. Fairs L.A.C.S., R.A.F., V.R., XI SQDN, and the rest of the unit. Ah, that the true importance of the more lowly members of the unit was recognised. Perhaps we should have mentioned that this visit took place on 19 August 1941, just six days before our 23rd birthdays, so it was all rather fitting.

Habbaniya's War; There is no doubt that 1941 was Habbaniya's most eventful year ever, not just for the fact that XI Squadron with Jack and Bill had paid them a visit, but Habbaniya had its own little war and, had we arrived 13 days earlier, we would have been in time for Habbaniya's four-day war:

A rebel leader called Rashid Ali organised a coup, deposing the Iraqi Regent, and with German encouragement decided to take over Habbaniya Aerodrome. He had an army of over 45,000 men, equipped with guns, tanks, armoured cars and 80 aircraft. Habbaniya had about 3,500 men, including 1,000 Iraq Levies, who were believed to be loyal, and indeed they proved to be. On May 1st Rashid Ali's troops were seen to be massing on a plateau overlooking the camp, and they were digging trenches and installing machine guns. They even set up guns as close as 500 yards from the camp.

The Iraqi Commander intimated that all flying should cease or the aircraft would be fired upon, to which the Air Vice Marshal replied that if this was to happen, a state of war would exist! The camp commander received a telegram from Winston Churchill saying, if you must strike, strike hard, and together with his officers he decided to launch a devastating strike on the Iraqis at 0500 hours the next morning.

Some Wellingtons arrived to help with the bombing, but the few days that followed were described as a nightmare. Most of our bombing was done by training aircraft (Audaxes and Oxfords), but the firing from the Iraqis was fierce, and after the third day only four out of 37 of our aircraft remained serviceable. It must be remembered that the pilots were instructors and were certainly not used to bombing. The whole camp set to, helping to load as many as 5,000 20lb bombs and a quarter of a million rounds of ammunition, as each of the 27 Oxford training planes could carry eight of the 20lb bombs.

But, fortunately, we missed all that!

Habbaniya Cinema; The open air cinema was our favourite venue, and as the temperature dropped about 30 degrees in the evening, it was quite a pleasant place to be. Once again, watching the films we were transported to a land of make believe, sitting with a couple of pints of lemonade, and for many of the lads some Chinese or Australian beer. It was most enjoyable. The lemonade was manufactured here on the camp, where the RAF had their own lemonade factory, and they certainly needed it with Bill and I each consuming a gallon each day, in addition to our usual tea ration. In this climate we needed an intake of at least eight pints of liquid to offset dehydration. At times it was hot beyond belief, with perspiration trickling down our shirts.

There was a lovely church too, built very much after the style of those in England,

above, The open air cinema was our favourite venue – the mountains of empty lemonade bottles being collected for re-filling give an indication of the amount of fluid consumed by the enthusiastic evening audience!

below, From outside the high screen of the cinema was clearly visible

appeared in today's issue of Cairo's principal newspaper. The photograph shows Bill and I developing a film in a portable darkroom in the desert, with the fighter pilot standing by his plane in the background. You cannot see much of Bill – only his boots are showing.

We had our hair cut today, very different from the barber at home. Here the cool breezes waft the hair away as it is snipped although in some respects it is the same, inasmuch as the barber prattles away with the news as he snips! The camp barber is an electrician and he cuts hair as a sideline. As one can imagine, amongst 500 men there are many talents. In most of the aerodromes in Blighty they have their own orchestras, but not in a mobile unit as ours – a cello would not travel too well because of its bulk. Our postman received two sacks of mail today and there was quite a queue outside his tent. We were lucky. We received four letters – one from you, one from Ken Speakman in India, one from South Africa and one from Etti in Palestine with a photograph, which I am sending on for safe keeping.

Tommy Row who, as you know, is a transport driver, is teaching Bill to drive in his three-ton truck. He made us all smile the other day. He was showing Bill how to do a three point turn and he said, "You shouldn't have a problem, with twenty miles on one side and two thousand on the other!" We sleep on the floor, or rather, the deck, as it is called here, which consists of 'mutty', a sandy clay-like substance which, when walked upon, grinds itself into a fine dust. You may have received the photograph showing the truck with the dust whirling up behind it. Today we have something approaching a dust storm. It may sound unpleasant but so far they have not been too bad. They are similar to sand devils, which we can see coming, about every ten minutes. We just close our eyes and stand with our backs towards them and wait a few seconds until the air clears and becomes once again beautifully fresh.

Life here has its lighter moments, we are sending a snap for the album showing Jack and a couple of lads dressed as Arabs. Everyone in the tent has gone to bed and I'm yawning my head off so I will join them.

God bless you all. Your loving sons,

Jack and Bill.

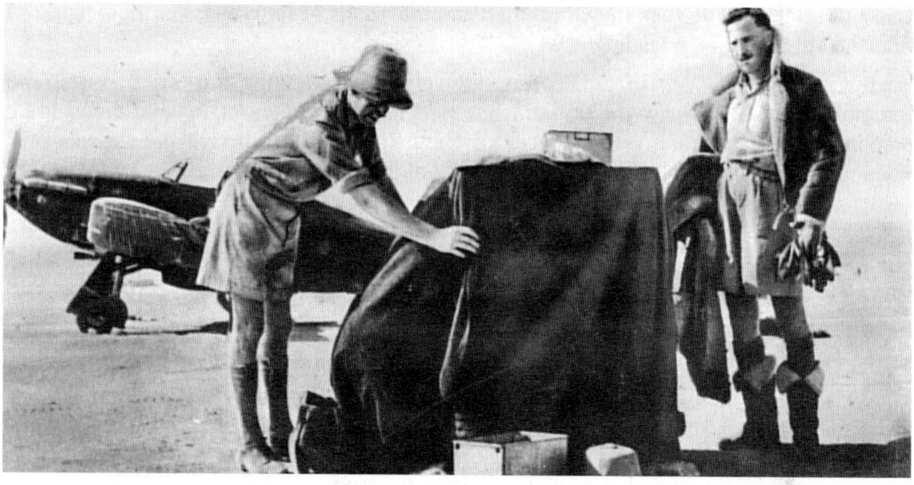

Bill and I developing a film in a portable darkroom, with the fighter pilot standing by. Not much of Bill – only his boots are showing!

above, Jack keeps up to date!

right, photo of Etti that Jack sent home for 'safe keeping'

below, We had our hair cut today, very different from the barbers at home!

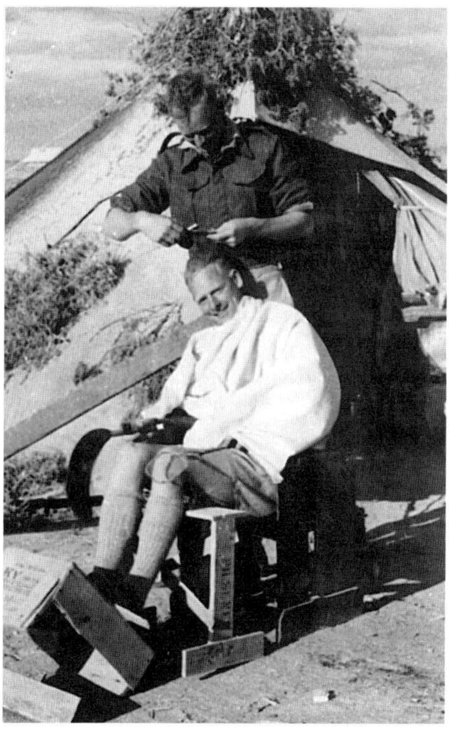

above, The pleased look of our group shows the relief at having completed their air-raid trench

left, The teapot and kettle were a four-gallon petrol tins; the tea wasn't Earl Grey, it was Shell Grey, a special chlorinated blend – but it was tea!

below left , Our medical section had a rather macabre sense of humour!

below, Desert Lilies, most unusual specimens found in many desert camps!

24: A Momentous Decision

Jack and Bill had arrived at a landing ground in the Western Desert in September 1941:

Given a few days in one location we were able to make quite a comfortable home and, as with most servicemen in the field, our first priority was to construct an air-raid trench. It was very hard and tiring work digging in the stony ground and the pleased look on the faces of our group shows the relief at having completed the job.

With hindsight we wonder whether the Germans used it; they captured this landing ground when we retreated – to be honest we hoped that they did. Our Long Range Desert Group, who operated behind the German lines, had mounted four machine guns on each of six Jeeps, and these appeared out of the darkness sweeping through the enemy landing grounds spraying the tents and aircraft with devastating results, destroying the aircraft and causing many casualties.

We can recall during one night hearing a tremendous banging and clattering of trucks coming towards camp. Fortunately, we heard next morning that it was our own lads with a convoy of empty trucks that caused such a rumpus – they had been delivering petrol to a forward airfield.

Our medical section had a rather macabre sense of humour which can be seen by the skull and cross-bones displayed in the front of their tent. Either they wished to indicate just what their business was, or else they wished to discourage the lads going on the sick parade.

Because of the scarcity of water there were very few flowers in the desert. There were, however, Desert Lilies, (Lillium Urinii), a most unusual specimen which was to be found in all camps in the desert. Those readers who served in the Western Desert will be familiar with them. They are not an easy thing to describe and so I have had a drawing made. I was going to add that they were well watered, but my wife, who looks over these articles, crossed it out.

Poor drainage is the greatest enemy of this species, but a sandy stony ground is ideal; they should be planted six inches deep. Strangely enough, it was not a plant hunter who discovered Lillium Urinii and introduced it to Egypt, but a Dr Shell of Ellesmere Port.

Looking through the album I see that we had a tea making ceremony like the Japanese or was it? You can judge. Our stove was a four-gallon petrol tin with three inches of sand in the base and into this we poured petrol. The teapot was also a four-gallon petrol tin; the tea wasn't Earl Grey, it was Shell Grey, a special chlorinated blend. The stove, sand and petrol were not our idea, it was common practice by the desert warriors.

During these days we were feeling a bit unsettled. Our work was spasmodic and, taking things easy had never been our way of life. In civvy street we had worked till ten most nights starting our photographic business. One day I saw Bill with a big smile on his face and I asked him what he had in mind, to which he replied, "I have made a momentous decision that we will go to Heliopolis". I wasn't too surprised, but suggested that as he was only an LAC he should rephrase that remark to, "We will apply to go to Heliopolis."

Heliopolis, the city in the sun. What a city. Superbly laid out and a place where the rich had their palaces, and it was there, too, that the powers that be had very wisely decided was a good place to build a very big pre-war RAF station – the home of No2 Photographic Reconnaissance Unit. Bill then said, "OK, point taken, you're the writer, you put in an application." And so I did.

I had called into the Orderly Room (tent) to ask about a letter of application to the CO and the corporal said that I must sign my letter, "I have the honour to be your obedient servant". When I suggested that seemed as if I was crawling he said, "Well, isn't it worth a bit of crawling to move to Heliopolis?" And so I had the honour to be the CO's 'obedient servant'! I was writing the application to the CO and during the evening asked Bill to go outside the tent to see if our 'bright star' was shining; he returned to say that it was and so we said a little prayer that we would be successful.

The next morning we delivered the letter to the Orderly Room after having spoken to our Flt Sergeant, Jock Holliday. He said that he hadn't any objection and that if we managed the transfer he would be sorry to lose us, which was rather nice.

Bill and I now anxiously wait to see if our application is successful.

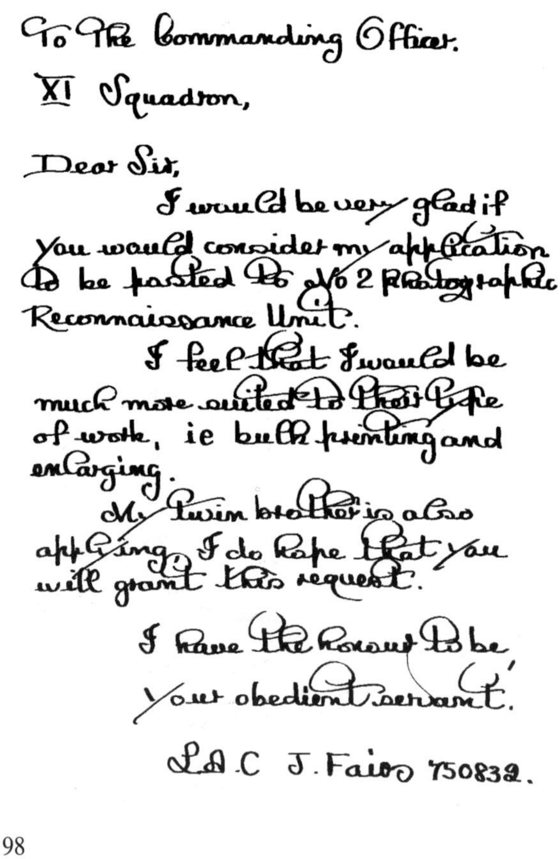

To The Commanding Officer.
XI Squadron,

Dear Sir,
I would be very glad if you would consider my application to be posted to No 2 Photographic Reconnaissance Unit.
I feel that I would be much more suited to that type of work, ie bulk printing and enlarging.
My twin brother is also applying. I do hope that you will grant this request.
I have the honour to be your obedient servant.
LAC J. Fairs 750832.

left, Jack's application

25: Posted to Helio

Another day in the Western Desert, but a day with a difference;

We had been summoned to the Orderly Room, a call which is usually received with fear and trepidation. But this time we went with anticipation, and it was justified as we learned that we both had been posted to No. 2 Photographic Reconnaissance Unit in Heliopolis. Although we were anxious to go, it was not without a little regret, as the desert was a very special place with its extreme quietness, especially at night.

It was so different, it even had its own newspaper. As there were thousands of troops in the Western Desert, Middle East Air Force had decided to publish a special newspaper for them, aptly titled the 'Dust Sheet', and it contained much of interest to the lads in the desert, as it was light-hearted and humorous. Typical of its contents is the drawing, below, of a lady as seen by men who liked their drink. Many newspaper men had been called to the forces, and it was with their expertise that the paper was produced.

Another humorous cartoon strip showed a NAAFI tent in front of which were two Sherman tanks, a jeep and some NAAFI groceries and a plate of NAAFI rock cakes. The first picture shows an army of ants approaching, the next where the ants had eaten the tanks, and in the last the ants were departing and only the rock cakes were left.

Back to the story – Someone at Middle East HQ had certainly got a move on. It was only 14 days since we had put in an application for transfer to Heliopolis, and now we were walking around the camp with a form to obtain signatures for each section to certify that as far as they were concerned we had nothing on loan from them – the armoury to certify that we had handed in our Smith & Wesson revolvers, the medical tent to say that we had handed in our crutches, and transport to confirm that we hadn't any cycles on loan.

above, The Pyramids of Giza suddenly appeared on the skyline, there was water, lots of water transported by irrigation canal

Little did we know that it would be three long years before we sampled the joy of riding an RAF cycle, or that it would be through the country lanes of Oxfordshire, holding hands with Betty, the girl who worked on the farm belonging to Christy's the famous hat-makers, very pleasant memories.

Having finally received permission to go, we said cheerio to our pals in the Photo Section. Our Bright Star was shining, and as the unit did not boast a staff car, a truck had been organised for an early morning start. The first part of our journey was across the desert upon what was called a 'barrel trail', marked out with empty oil drums. Eventually we reached the road leading to Alexandria and Cairo – and what a road! We were amazed at the stream of tanks and guns making their way towards El Alamein. They stretched for miles, and we recall commenting that with such tremendous weight of armour surely victory must be ours.

We had travelled about 180 miles from Fuka to Alexandria before branching off to Cairo. Our driver decided not to continue on the road, but to take to a desert track. We were rather pleased that he did because, as if by magic, the pyramids of Giza suddenly appeared on the skyline, and we were reminded of something that we had once read in a book where the Arab guide had said, "There are the Pyramids Effendi we shall be in Cairo this time tomorrow", and here we were, and we would be in Cairo within the hour. We decided that it would be very nice if we could visit the Beni Yusuf camp, which was only about half a mile off our route. This was where we had been stationed when we disembarked from the troopship. The driver said that this was okay with him as long as we did not hang about.

When we arrived at Beni Yusuf we found a complete contrast to the desert. There was water, lots of water. We were not far from the Nile and the river water was transported by irrigation canal, then raised to the fields by a variety of methods. This was the work for the fellahin, and we saw one fellah standing knee deep in muddy water by a steep bank. He was bending down, scooping up a bucketful of water, hoisting it shoulder high and pouring it down a narrow channel where it flowed into fields which were divided into squares by mud walls. What a job, hour after hour! We guessed it was that or go hungry.

Mindful of our promise to the driver not to delay, we continued our journey. As we passed through the small village we saw three dusky maidens with huge water containers on their heads. This was a picture we simply had to have, and happily they were willing to be photographed. Just how they managed to carry and balance those heavy containers on their heads was hard to imagine. The picture duly taken to send home to mother, we resumed our journey.

Our driver had not been to Heliopolis before and, by mistake, he took a wrong turning which led us into the Egyptian army barracks. That would not have mattered, but as we were proceeding apace we were confronted by an approaching Egyptian army truck the door of which swung open in our path. Our driver did not believe in doing things by halves, and we hit the swinging door and took it off completely. Both trucks pulled up to 'exchange details', but to our surprise, and our driver's relief, the Egyptian corporal who was driving the other vehicle came up to us with a big smile, saying 'marleesh, marleesh' (never mind). We all shook hands and away we went.

We arrived in Heliopolis in mid afternoon with the sun beating down. It was quiet, and there were just one or two mad dogs and Englishmen about. The main street had an arched parade, where the Englishmen could obtain some shade from the sun.

We knew we would be happy here.

above, The main street of Heliopolis had an arched parade, where we Englishmen could obtain some shade from the sun

left, In a small village we saw three dusky maidens with huge water containers on their heads

26: Another World

Jack and Bill had left the desert and were now approaching their new home in Heliopolis;

Little did we realise how lucky we were to be posted to Heliopolis, what a wonderful place, where wealthy people lived, no slums, and so clean. It had a swimming pool, a cinema and, best of all, two super clubs for servicemen. As we approached the camp, we noticed how smart the airmen looked. They were wearing blue, and their buttons and shoes glistened. What a contrast to our appearance in the desert. We were reminded that we had better make a quick call to the NAAFI to buy polish for our shoes and buttons, without doubt the old spit and polish days had returned, we did not possess any polish, not having use for this whilst in the wilderness.

We stopped at the guardroom to sign in (guardroom? – we had almost forgotten what they were!) We saluted an officer who looked as though he had just walked out of Gieves the Tailors. Oh yes, we were indeed in another world. We found our way to our billet which was at the top of the camp, it was one of a number of wooden barrack blocks, in such close proximity to one other, and a hundred yards from the hangars, that with our experiences in Greece and the desert we considered that dispersal should have been a real priority – thought we must do something about this. Settling in, we regarded this camp as heaven – hot showers, and water-water-water, lashings of it, and tea without taste of chlorine, and the tea was on tap in an urn, and if that wasn't all, we had liver and bacon for tea and fruit cake.

The next morning, after a good night's sleep, we reported to the photo section, and chatting with the lads they told us that the warrant officer I/C was a swine. We thought that rather unkind because the pig is quite a noble animal. Later on we were to find out that their assessment was quite correct. We should add, however, that other warrant officers whom we met in the service were both helpful and pleasant. We were to work a shift system, twelve hours on and twenty four off, we liked the

left, One of the super clubs for servicemen

below, Heliopolis had an open air cinema

sound of twenty four hours off. One of our first jobs was quite interesting. The public had been asked to send holiday photographs that had been taken around any foreign port or installation, and the snaps that we were given were of the Mediterranean ports and our job was to make copies of them.

Our next job was to make a mosaic of an airfield from twenty five photographs, that had been taken from the air. They were five inches square and were taken in line and overlapping, we carefully cut the prints and chamfered the edges, pasting them on a card, until we had a large photograph of the whole airfield. This we photographed and it was then returned to our interpreters to annotate showing the position of enemy gun emplacements and other features. This was again copied and enlargements made which would be used by our pilots when they were raiding the airfields in Greece, Crete, and the Aegean. Making mosaics was a large part of our work as they were used by all three services especially the Navy if they wished to shell a port.

The next day we were off to Cairo, about seven miles away, and we were waiting at the Metro tram stop when a black American Air Force man pulled up in a small truck. He literally screeched to a stop and said "Cairo, you wanna lift?" We climbed aboard, it had seats and an open back and there was no doubt that he was Air Force because we literally 'took off' and were almost airborne. We were so relieved when we arrived safely in Cairo because during the journey we had been clinging to the metal seats lest we be bounced out of the truck. We learned that we had been travelling in a wonderful new invention by the Yanks – a 'Jeep' – and resolved that we would not travel in one again driven by the American Airforce.

Well, here we were once again in Cairo, what a place! After the silence and isolation of the desert, the bustle and smells of Egyptian towns were both bewildering and irritating with its masses of people cramming the pavements, and noise which was, at first, shattering. We

We were waiting at the Metro tram stop to go to Cairo

made our way to the Toc-H hostel in Soliman Pasha, where we had a lovely dinner, and we renewed acquaintance with Gordon Turvey, the warden. It was peaceful and pleasant. They had a Scottish housekeeper, and apart from the Nubian servant dressed in a pure white galabier and a red fez it might almost have been England.

It was quite a while since we had been to a dance, and we did manage to find one, but so different from the dances at home – there were thirty girls and about three hundred service men! That was just the way in the Middle East with the hundreds of thousands of servicemen there. We managed a couple of dances, one was with a Greek girl named Olga. She may well have been Olga the beautiful spy and she was quite pleasant to look upon. Olga knew very little English so I tried my Greek, but the words I knew hardly added to the conversation, although spoken very fluently. They were thank you – good morning – its very hot – I want an egg – where is the aerodrome? We both had a good laugh, and she said, bravo, I'm not quite sure what for, but it did earn me an extra dance.

Today we had the great fortune to be introduced to the Steffell family. Colonel Steffell OBE was the chief of the Cairo Fire Brigade, and they lived in a pleasant apartment over the Cairo Fire Station, just at the back of the Cairo Opera House. We were invited to tea, and learned that the family came from Liverpool after the 1918 war. We were made to feel very much at home and were invited to dinner later in the week.

We little realised this was the start of a lasting friendship and that Colonel and Mrs Steffell would visit us in England after the war, and that fifty eight years later, in 1999 that I would be speaking to Colonel Steffell's daughter, June, in South Africa, on the phone of course.

Day over, back to camp, and a good night's sleep ready for our next day's work, remembering that there was a war on.

27: The Cotton Story

Jack and Bill have now settled in the big photographic reconnaissance unit in Heliopolis. It is 12th February 1942, and in this chapter recount a most interesting story;

Our heavenly star was still shining, and we could hardly believe our good fortune that we should become members of this very important section, No 2 Photographic Unit, which was to play a significant part in photographic intelligence gathering, and we feel certain the following story will be of interest to our reader:

Just before the war, a member of the RAF Air Staff Intelligence Branch, a chap called Fred Winterbottom, who, in the course of his duties, often travelled to Germany, recalling in his mind his experiences when he was a pilot in the First World War. Realising the importance and the valuable information that could be gained from aerial photographs, he decided that he would do something about it. He had gained the idea from some French colleagues who had secretly taken photographs from a civilian aircraft over Germany with excellent results.

Winterbottom had the good fortune to be introduced to a remarkable Australian, a man called Sidney Cotton who was probably the man most responsible for the remarkable progress of photographic reconnaissance in its early years. Between the wars he was with various flying ventures and he developed an air-mail service in Newfoundland, where he also tried his hand at aerial surveys. Later Cotton became interested in colour photography, and was now concerned with the manufacture of colour film, and in the summer of 1938 was busy establishing contacts in Germany. Cotton was a very clever man and somewhat unorthodox in his methods, he had invented a widely-used windproof flying suit named after him, 'The Sidcot' which was the forerunner of the siren suit.

Ready for adventure and being a civilian he was not bound up with the red tape of the services, and he put forward a plan to fly over Germany in a civilian aircraft secretly taking photographs. He put the proposal to The Chief of Air Staff, Sir Cyril Newall who was enthusiastic about the project, and although the idea was strictly civilian he gave it his blessing and authorised the purchase of an opulent twin engined Lockheed 12A plane.

They decided to fit three cameras, secretly hidden in the bottom of the passenger cabin, the central camera to photograph downwards, and the other two, one on each side to take oblique photographs. The three when operating together would take a long strip of the

Sidney Cotton's opulent twin engined Lockheed 12A plane, pictured here in 1991 after extensive renovation

countryside. Cotton based the plane at Heston Airport, where he engaged a young Canadian who had just finished his short term commission with the RAF.

Time and time again they flew to the industrial capitals of Europe, but most especially to Berlin, and each time operating their secret cameras, with great success, the reason of course that Cotton was able to make these trips was because of the company that he had established 'Aeronautical Research' which sold colour films.

During the months before the war began, the Nazis put on a special air display at Frankfurt, it was on the 28th July, just a few weeks before the war began, and Cotton was fortunate enough to be invited. The Germans were undoubtably quite interested to see his elegant duck-egg green Lockheed, and so he arrived to join the motley crowd of aircraft of all sizes. The agent for his company in Berlin was a Herr Schone who had been in the same squadron as Goering in the First World War, and he introduced Cotton to many of the senior officers including a number of Luftwaffe Generals who all wanted to have a flight in the Lockheed.

One of the generals who was chief of the Templehof Airport in Berlin said that he would very much like to have a flight in the Lockheed and, of course, Cotton was delighted to oblige. Cotton told the general that one of his aunts had raved about the beauty of the Rhine at Mannheim, and he would love to fly the General over, the General agreed, and indeed there were many more flights permitted.

There was quite a bit of competition to fly in the Lockheed, and Cotton flew hither and thither over airfields, ammunition dumps, factories, and fortifications, meanwhile he unobtrusively flicked a little switch and down below the cameras went into action.

This is a brief description of Cotton's early days in the RAF. He was typical of the many clever men who shaped the future of photographic reconnaissance. These included a teacher of psychology, a research botanist and many others, people chosen for their intelligence, with trained minds and with the dogged patience photo interpretation demanded. These were both men and women who would pour over photographs hour after hour checking for the smallest detail.

We are sure that you will have found that little story of interest.....

Wing Commander F Sidney Cotton OBE at his desk in 1941 – a man who shaped the future of photographic reconnaissance

As it was our day off, we went to Cairo and called in at Toc-H were Mrs Gould, the Scottish house-keeper, sold us tickets for a dance at the Y.W.C.A., they cost us five ackers each which was the equivalent of about one shilling in those days.

On reaching the door of the YWCA we found that the entrance was barred by one of the lady helpers, who was saying, "Not one of you shall come in here until this person has gone". This person as you might guess was a soldier who was seven sheets to the wind, he was very happy, thinking that he was on the threshold of another bar. Finding that it wasn't he took himself off.

We entered a beautifully furnished old house which had been the home of a wealthy Egyptian; upstairs was a huge room highly decorated. There were two balconies, one higher than the other, a magnificent ceiling, the floor was of wood block and smooth, it was ideal for dancing, we never ceased to be surprised at the quality of the club premises that had been chosen for service people in the Middle East.

An officer of the New Zealand Nurses asked us if we had danced, yes madam! The girls were quite nice, mostly Waafs and Wrens we hadn't seen so many service girls since we left home; they had not been in the country very long, and said that they were pleasantly surprised, because they had been led to believe that Egypt was a dreadful posting.

We passed a very pleasant afternoon, and when it was over, then came the tea and that was worth writing home about, delicious cream cakes, chocolate, and merangues, and only 1¼d each, I ate six.

Dance over, we wended our way back to Toc-H where we had an excellent dinner finishing with coffee. It was all so pleasant that we asked Gordon Turvey the warden whether we could bring a couple of the girls along one evening, he said, "Yes providing you bring one for me".

Our lucky star was certainly shining, and, reading through this epistle, I think perhaps our next chapter should show that we did some work!

left, Gordon Turvey and the Matron at Toc-H where an excellent service was offered

below, Many of Cairo's modern buildings were in stark contrast to the living conditions of the town's poor folk

28: Is Jack Guilty?

It was 26th February 1942 at 0930 hours and I was asleep in the billet after a hard 12 hour duty, when one of my colleagues from the section woke me by tweaking my ear saying, "The old battleaxe wants to see you over at the section." The battleaxe was the Warrant Officer. I dressed myself quickly and went to see him, and was told that I was on a charge.

Guilty – and of what you may ask?

The answer is of 'a dereliction of duty' and a total disregard of the need for accuracy in the production of important photographs. That's typical of the high falutin' language used in a court of law, and simply means that I had produced enlargements of the wrong size. Next morning there I was on a charge, standing outside the Station Commander's office flanked by two burly policemen and the Warrant Officer standing with the charge sheet in his paw.

C.O. "Enter"

W.O. Grunts, "Attention – Left turn – Left turn – Left, right, left, right – Halt – Remove hat."

C.O. "Read out the charge Warrant Officer."

W.O. "On 25th February 1942 at 0245 hours L.A.C. Fairs. J. with a grave dereliction of duty and total disregard for accuracy did produce enlargements of the incorrect dimensions."

C.O. "What do you say L.A.C. Fairs?"

L.A.C.Fairs "Sir, I have always put forward my best endeavours in executing my duty in the effort to beat the Hun. The reason for the error was that the apparatus that I was using was faulty. It had been modified and was not standard issue, it had been tampered with to enable larger size photographs to be obtained."

C.O. "Warrant Officer, was this the case?"

W.O. "Yes sir, the enlarger had been modified."

C.O. "Case dismissed."

Strange really, here was I who had to face three charges during my service career, and Bill not one. Perhaps it was because I was the elder (by one hour). The only good thing about the charge, apart from the fact of getting off, was that I was able to gain experience in preparing my defence for the further two charges that were subsequently to come my way. I guess that I had better tell you just what they were!

You will probably remember that I had a girlfriend in Tel Aviv, Etti. Well, we were still in touch and I thought it would be nice to send her some sugar; it was in very short supply. A Jewish friend of mine, Ikey Rosenberg, was travelling to Palestine, and said that he would take it for me. Unfortunately, the military police on the train checked his baggage, found the sugar, which was okay, but the secret message contained in the envelope? Now, that was suspicious!

The C.O. read the message, which he understood. It was the usual thing that young fellows write to their girlfriends, and he himself wasn't so old. But it was the code at the end of the letter, a series of crosses, apparently was the query, but I had the feeling that he himself had evidently used the same code, because he was actually smiling and said, "Case dismissed." My bright star was still shining.

Oh, the insolence charge! Well I told the C.O. that the Corporal had provoked me, and that I had suggested that his parents had not been married. I told the C.O. that I didn't really mean it, and that it had been said in the heat of the moment, and that I was sorry. The C.O. said, "Just watch your step L.A.C. Fairs. Charge dismissed."

It was our day off, and so we were off to Cairo which was only seven miles away by Metro; a very good service every few minutes, and all for a handful of peanuts. I must explain: When the conductor came to collect our fares we found that we had only a fifty piastre note and no change. I said sorry and indicated an empty pocket, whereupon the conductor opened his bag, which was virtually empty, and said, "Mafeesh, no change – nothing – nothing." We were in quite a quandary when we hit upon the splendid idea of barter, so we offered him a handful of roasted peanuts, shook his hand and smiled. He shrugged his shoulders and all was well. We should mention that the Metro carried many non-fare-paying passengers. We are sure that of all the world's tram systems, the Cairo Metro carried the most non-payers. They consisted of the natives and young children who would run alongside and cling precariously to the footboard, most dangerous of course, and we saw many who had lost limbs as a result. We thought we ought to mention this tram ride to Mum and Dad, and consequently took a picture. The afternoon was spent pleasantly, taking a few photographs of one or two local scenes including the two little girls. Despite their tender age, here they were tending a herd of goats.

Home to bed after an eventful day. We had been in bed for about ten minutes, the lights had been switched off by the hut corporal who occupied a small room at the end of the hut. Suddenly, there was quite a racket. Two of our airmen had arrived in a happy state. It wasn't unusual for the two of them to come in the worse for drink, nor were we surprised to see one of them sporting a black eye.

Both of these airmen carried knuckle-dusters made of brass, and they frequented the bars and some of the less desirable parts of Cairo. Big Mac, he was about 33, and, perhaps, just a wee bit rough. I recall asking him what he did in civvy street and his answer, "I was a burglar." I said, "No, you are pulling my leg." He just looked at me and smiled. Now what sort of person would carry a knuckle-duster? By sheer coincidence the following morning Bill and I called on a small native plumbing shop and asked the plumber if he would obtain two seven inch lengths of hosepipe and insert three inches of lead in the end for us. They were called coshes.

We should perhaps add that we had to travel along about three quarters of a mile of desert road, and on one occasion some Egyptian soldiers had run their truck towards us missing us by inches, and so we had a feeling that a little bit of protection would not go astray.

I'm sure that no-one could imagine Bill and Jack carrying coshes – well, just once in a while, and they were for security. – We slept well.

above, Despite their tender age, two little girls were tending a herd of goats

right, The conductor who came to collect our fares posed happily with us after accepting the handful of peanuts!

above, The El Gindi home, what a place, it's like a palace, and so comfortably cool, with high ceilings, all very ornate

below, One of our lads on the unit married a very attractive Greek girl

29: Letter from Heliopolis

Dear Mum and Dad,

Phew, it certainly is hot, although cooler than yesterday. It is 90 degrees, and we are consuming large quantites of lemonade. At times like these we feel that it would be wonderful to have a good old English fog, or better still a downpour of rain. A cold shower makes things more tolerable.

Our friend Farid el Gindi, the film producer, was in touch with us, saying that he had not seen us for some time, and he invited us to his home for coffee this morning. His home! What a place, it's like a palace. Comfortably cool, with high ceilings, and all very ornate – you will have a better idea because we are sending a photograph taken in the lounge. In the garden is a shooting lodge built in the style of a Greek temple, with columns, showing all the trappings of wealth, but Farid and family are very friendly, and although it's all very posh we feel quite at home. Farid and Bill are off on location, where Farid is producing a film. This afternoon's filming is in a courtroom, and Farid has promised to get a still picture for Bill to send to you for our album. Whilst your son Jack has decided that he will take a young lady out and opt out of the trip with Farid. Our bright star was still shining and recently we have been fortunate enough to be introduced to a charming English family called Mather, and guess what? They have four very nice daughters! My choice is Alice. She is a red head with sparkling eyes, and she is very good company. We were invited to their home so that old Mather, that's the dad, could give us the once over, and he did, evidently deciding that he could trust his daughters in our care. Bill is friendly with Mary, the elder daughter, who is two years older than Alice. Alice and I spent a very pleasant afternoon in a lovely garden, with grass and trees.

Egypt has virtually no rain, and grass does not grow unless it is irrigated, but this garden was just near to Gezira Island, and as the River Nile is just yards away, it has lots of water and splendid lawns. Just a little background. Although the girls are English, and they were educated at the English School in Heliopolis, their mother is Greek and their father stayed out here after the First World War.

They live in a nice little apartment in Heliopolis, which is very convenient for us. We will send you a photo, but this will have to be under separate cover because we cannot include anything in this Airmail Letter Card.

There are a lot of Greeks living here in the Middle East, and earlier this week we went to a wedding. One of our lads on the unit married a very attractive Greek girl. We did take pictures at the wedding, although the one we are sending was taken previously. John and his bride will be able to live out of camp which will be very nice for them. The reception was held in the bride's home, which was quite unlike our homes. Because of the hot weather the floors are usually tiled, or in some instances, marble. I would describe the furniture as very heavy, with carved chairs that to me resembled miniature thrones, quite different from our armchairs and settees at home. Unlike English weddings, where the cake is carefully cut and divided, here it was cut into whacking great slices, although I must say that it was much lighter than ours, almost akin to a sponge cake. Bill and I toasted the bride and groom, and champagne flowed like water.

We had dinner later on at Toc-H and told Padre Jackson of the wedding. He was not too optimistic about the success of mixed marriages. The bride might not be very happy living so far from her family, and after enjoying continous sunshine the English weather might come as a shock! Bill and I have no intention of becoming too involved with our girlfriends during the war. Naturally, though, because of our age we enjoy their company – it's great being young! Lest you think that it is all play, had we taken you into our workroom yesterday, you would have heard us humming whilst we watched the image appearing on a glass plate as we gently rocked the dish of developer backwards and forwards. Our next job was to print hundreds of aerial photographs, develop, fix, wash and dry them – very tiring but most satisfying this photo game. We are so much happier on this unit, there is never an idle moment, and in many cases we are able to see the job through from beginning to end, which is most rewarding.

My choice is Alice, a red head with sparkling eyes, and very good company

We are glad that all is well at home. Mail is coming through in good style, we received 16 letters in four days, but that is unusual. Thank you for sending cash out and your suggestion, that as we were walking out with the girls and may need some extra, made us smile, we called in to Barclays Bank in Sharia Kasr el Nil and opened an account.

We mentioned to our photo officer, Fl/lt Langdon about opening the account, and he said "Good, you can cash a cheque for me". I told him that we had not yet received a cheque book, to which he replied "A piece of paper will do, just as long as it has a two penny stamp upon it". He wrote the cheque out, Jack signed it, and sure enough it was accepted. Quite a surprise wasn't it?

Once again as I am writing this letter, my eyes are almost closing, so I will sign off now.

God bless you,

Your loving sons,

Jack & Bill.

30: One of our planes is Missing

Today is the 7th March 1942. We have heard from our sister unit No 1 Photographic Reconnaissance, that one of our pilots, F/Lt Alastair Gunn, stationed at Leuchars in Scotland, had not returned from a sortie over Norway on the 5th March 1942. He was presumed shot down by an enemy fighter and had lost his life. This was one of the difficulties – verifying what had happened to reconnaissance pilots: Because they flew alone on a sortie, if they did not return, they were missing, presumed to have been killed, unless they were able to write home from a German prisoner of war camp, having parachuted to safety.

German pilot Heinze Knoke

To continue this little story, we must jump forward a good number of years: in fact to April 1999. Yes, fifty seven years. Strange how things happen. Bill was on holiday staying with friends in Sydney, Australia, when he learnt that the pilot, F/ Lt Alastair Gunn had been shot down by a German pilot called Heinze Knoke.

Apparently, No 1 PRU had been making a habit of flying over this particular part of Norway, which was covered by Heinze Knoke's squadron, who were determined if possible to shoot them down. A bottle of Hennessey brandy had been offered by the commanding officer Captain Losiekeit as a prize to the pilot successful in doing so.

We are indebted to Mike Hatch of the RAF Air Historical Branch at New

It is a Spitfire, leaving a short vapour trail

Scotland Yard for his help in unfolding this unusual story, which was told by the German pilot Heinze Knoke.

The story:

A German Airfield in Norway – 5th March 1942.

A shout from the operations room "There he is again" out through the window. Into the snow twenty or thirty long strides and I am in my aircraft, seconds later I am off.

Climbing steeply into the cloudless sky.

12.10 hours: altitude 15,000 feet. I adjust my oxygen mask.

It is bitterly cold. "Bandit in Hanni-seven-zero."

"Victor, Victor; message understood," I reply.

Altitude 22,000 feet: I'll climb to 25,000. I must get him today. He appears to be sweeping round the northern tip of the sound, heading towards the anchorage of our warships. I am now at 25,000 feet, scanning the skies around and below, and ahead, when I discern a tiny speck in the sky against the unbroken white landscape below. It is the Spitfire, leaving a short vapour trail behind him, I maintain my altitude and study my prey, now over his objective the Tommy flies round in two circles, he is taking photographs.

He is so intent on his task that he does not notice me. I am now about 3,000 feet above him. I open my throttle wide, and check my guns as I swoop down upon him. In a few seconds I am right on his tail. Fire! My tracers vanish into his fuselage and now he begins to twist and turn like a mad thing. Must not let him escape. Keep firing with everything that I have. He begins trailing smoke which gradually becomes denser. I fire yet again. I veer to the right in order to be able to observe the Tommy through the side window. He is gradually losing speed, but is still flying. Suddenly another Messerschmitt comes into view climbing from my left. It is my old comrade Dieter Gerhard, and I radio him to say I can no longer continue to fire.

"Then let me finish him Heinz!"

He opens fire. The Spitfire's right wing sheers away.

Like a dead autumn leaf, the plane flutters earthward.

The pilot? Is he alive? If he is why does he not bale out?

The Spitfire goes down like a flaming torch now hurtling towards the snowfield and with it the pilot. I find myself shouting, "Bale out, bale out!" After all he is a pilot like me, with the same love of the sky and clouds that I feel and perhaps he too has a wife? "Bale out, bale out!"

Then a body becomes detached from the flames and falls clear. A white parachute spreads open and drifts slowly down onto the mountain. A feeling of pure joy is in my heart now. This is my first combat victory in the air. I have got my man and he is alive.

Later, Dieter brings him to the mess after landing in the mountains, in a Fiesler Storch fitted with skis, and rescuing him. He is a tall, slim F/Lt in the RAF. A stiff drink of brandy does him a lot of good. We toast one another and have a good laugh when I tell him that the brandy that he is drinking is my prize for shooting him down.

F/Lt Gunn was sent to a POW camp for Officers.

We must now leave Germany and, return to Heliopolis, where we were walking down the main boulevard when Bill said to me, "Just look at those green roses in that florist's shop," and sure enough, they were Green Roses, the first that we had ever seen. We examined them, carefully thinking that they had been dipped in dye, but strangely they looked perfectly natural. We haven't ever seen Green Roses since, nor have we discovered the mystery of them.

Bill said, "And what do roses bring to mind – Loggerheads?", and so they did. It was in the nineteen thirties, and we were staying at our camp, 'No Work Villas.' I was walking up the road from The Loggerheads to Llanferres with a young lady called Irene Blodwin Jones, (I think she was Welsh!), a young man was walking towards us and Irene said, "Oh goodness here is my boyfriend, I must go." And off she went.

I wasn't too perturbed. All is fair in love and war, but here's where the roses come into the story. The next morning, there was a knocking on the door of our bell tent, and who should be there but Irene Blodwin with a lovely bunch of roses... just to say that she was sorry for having left me the previous evening. Wasn't that a nice gesture! It must be a Welsh custom to give the men roses. She was a lovely girl – our lucky star shone in Wales too!

We were chatting to a friend in our unit, John Gawsworth, telling him of our lucky star, when he said, "You are twins and you each have a star in the Constellation of Gemini, one is called Castor and the other Pollux."

I sometimes wonder whether you think that one or two of these tales are true! They are! John Gawsworth just appeared on the unit, out of the blue; a superior type, and a marvellous artist, he wasn't a photographer, just someone from Intelligence Dept, and after two weeks he disappeared, but not before he had drawn a picture of himself in our autograph book and signed it.

Irene Blodwin Jones, lady with the roses

Two faces of Egypt, above, A beautiful modern villa in the centre of Cairo, and, below, In a village only a couple of miles away, separating the grain from the husks, as they have done for thousands of years

31: Letter to the CO

Whenever Bill and I had a day off or were on a day shift we would go for our morning stroll, that is, we would walk around the boulevards in Heliopolis.

It was very pleasant first thing in the morning before the heat warmed up the 'oven'. We would chat, putting the world right, and on this particular morning, we set about putting the camp right. Bill suggested that he was unhappy about our being billeted in one of four huts which were in such close proximity to one another, and just about one hundred yards from the hangars. He said that a bomb could write off very many valuable well trained airmen, (well, naturally, we thought that we were). He said: "You know what a super place Heliopolis Town is, and these huts leave a bit to be desired during the heat of the day, so hot in summer ... why don't you suggest to the CO that the men are moved into town." I said: "I cannot do that. Remember we are only LACs ... OK. I'll try. Nothing ventured nothing gained."

The next day I made an application for an interview with the Commanding Officer to put my suggestion to him: firstly the application has to be placed before the Officer in charge of the unit. I had spruced myself up, wearing my Van Heusen shirt, and my buttons glistened so brightly, they would have done credit to a guardsman. He read my application. At first he looked surprised, and then he frowned and said: "I cannot pass this to the CO, LAC Fairs, you know we officers are running this unit." I said: "Well I would be glad if it could go before him." His answer: "Just leave it with me", and he placed it in the drawer of his desk.

I have an idea that he thought I was too big for my boots, although, here in the Middle East, unlike in England, we wore shoes, and by coincidence it was just a week earlier that I had been to see him, complaining that the new shoes that I had just drawn from the stores had cardboard soles, or so they seemed to me. Just where he got the idea that I was too big for my boots I shall never know, with the knowledge that we had gained in the Western Desert and Greece regarding dispersal, we regarded it as a must where possible. I mentioned this but his answer was: "Just leave it with me."

This interview was on our day off, and to hide our deep disappointment at the outcome. we took ourselves off to Cairo.

Ah! Before we continue with our trip, I will tell you a little anecdote recounted by one of the lads in the billet when I told him about the shoes with the cardboard soles: He had served with XI Squadron when they were stationed in India, where he went to order a pair of shoes from the village cobbler, who told him to put his feet in a basin of water. He was told to walk across the concrete floor, the cobbler then measured his wet footsteps, and three days later when he picked up the shoes, they were the most comfortable he had ever worn.

We took the Metro tram to Cairo, and walking across the city hitched a lift in an army truck which was taking supplies to one of the outlying camps on the Mena Road. Seeing a beautiful villa, we asked the driver if he would kindly stop. Thanking him, we then took a photograph of the glamorous residence. We had decided that we would spend the afternoon seeing how the other half lived, or perhaps I should say how the other 95% lived. I do not think that I am too far out in my estimate.

We were going to visit one of the villages in the desert, and we thought that the posh villa would contrast well with the mud huts of the Fellahin. Our path lay alongside an irrigation canal, fed by water from the Nile, and the village was about two miles into the desert. We stopped to watch a man threshing corn. He was sitting on what looked like a sledge which was being driven in a circle by two water buffalo, round and round over the outspread sheaves. The heavy sledge was breaking up the corn, and detaching the grain from the husks and stalks and we had no doubt that this was the same method they had been using for the last five thousand years. We left the canal path, and also the lush green fields, and made our way to the village: Oh dear! what a mess it all seemed. The hovels, which is what they were, constructed of mud bricks, with heaps of soil in the passage ways. There was no litter, because the goats ate any paper that there was, and no old tin cans, because tin cans were useful, especially in the towns; should they happen to be boot polish tins, there the natives would fill them with goo (orange peel and a putty like substance) and sell them to unsuspecting and newly arrived servicemen.

Two shy maidens outside their home

One can get a general idea of the dwelling from our photograph. On one side of the doorway, (there was no door) can be seen a crude drawing of a cow, and on the roof, stacks of maize stalks and dried camel dung, which they use as fuel for cooking. No glass in the windows, and inside, the floor is of beaten earth, and a raised platform of hard dried mud, where the family lie down to sleep.

On the back of the photograph of the two girls, which was sent to our mum and dad, I have written ... these two shy maidens have four or five years before they get married, (generally at fourteen or fifteen).

Despite the extreme poverty, the natives almost seemed content and there was an air of tranquillity about the village, with greetings and smiles as we said 'Salaam aleikum' (hello).

A very interesting afternoon, thought provoking, and we must say: "Al hamdu lillah that we live in Heliopolis" (praise be to God).

32: The Stirling Story

Our section had received a 'first priority' job to make a photographic mosaic of a German airfield in the Western Desert and F/Lt Grinsell was standing, looking over our shoulders, telling us how urgent it was, and that he was waiting to annotate it.

We were pasting the line overlap photographs on a sheet of card and then F/Lt Grinsell would print in the position of the anti aircraft guns, and the petrol storage supplies etc. This done, we would re-photograph the mosaic, and hey ho! – it was ready for the SAS.

It may interest readers to learn a little about how the SAS and The Long Range Desert Group got together:

This was brought about by David Stirling, a Scots Guardsman, educated at Cambridge and a member of the First Army Commando Unit. He was six feet five inches tall, adventurous, keen on climbing and exploring, and, indeed, a natural-born commando. David was with a unit which had been sent to the Middle East with the object of capturing the island of Rhodes. Well, that was the idea but, unfortunately, the ships and equipment were not available. A brother officer, Jock Lewes of the Welsh Guards, was working alongside David, and they had to decide on another operation to hurt the Germans. Knowing the Germans had been greatly concerned about extended supply lines in the Western Desert, they discussed the possibility of causing havoc behind their lines to add to their problems. It so happened that they came into possession of fifty parachutes, that had 'fallen off the back of a wagon', and, although neither of them had any training as parachutists, together with two others they decided to have a go, thinking that this would be a good way to get behind enemy lines.

Soon afterwards they were able to obtain the use of an ancient Valentia aircraft and they rigged up their own static lines fastening them to the seat frames in the aircraft. The Valentia was not a good choice of aircraft for parachuting, because of the possibility of parachutes snagging the tail-plane and, unfortunately, this is just what happened to David Stirling. Holes were torn in his parachute and with his sixteen stone, he crashed heavily onto the rock-hard ground injuring his back so severely that both legs were paralysed for some time.

David spent two months in a Cairo hospital and used the time planning deep raids behind enemy lines. His preference was for a small number of men to be parachuted some

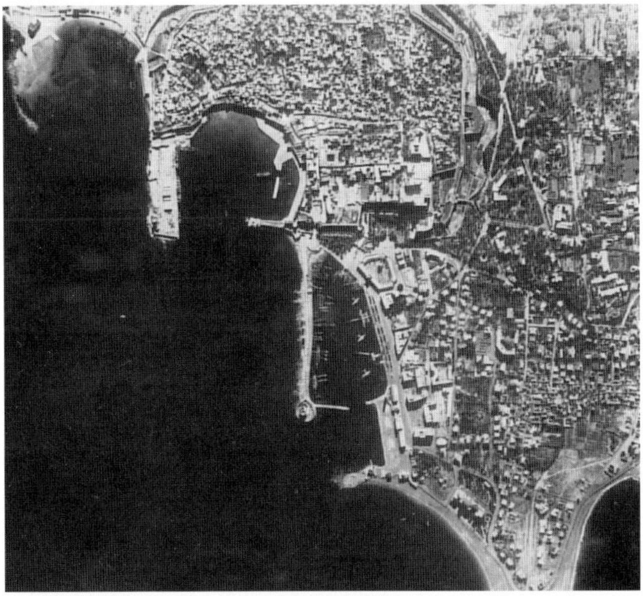

above, Making up a photographic mosaic map by pasting together lines of overlapping pictures

left, The town and port of Rhodes

below, The SAS in action behind enemy lines in the Western Desert

distance from an enemy airfield, hiding during the day and striking at night, believing that the enemy would not expect to be attacked by saboteurs from the ground. He was very enthusiastic, saying that, in his opinion, small teams could wreak havoc and possibly do more damage than a fully-supported air raid or a naval bombardment and with far fewer losses.

After his hospital treatment, David was able to walk about on crutches, and decided to deliver his plan in person to the Commander In Chief, General Sir Claude Auchinlech. He considered his chances of being granted an interview by such a high personage were, at the least, very limited being a mere subaltern. It was typical as a commando whose unit motto was 'HE WHO DARES WINS' that he would ignore the usual procedure for obtaining an interview and seek to go direct to the C In C. David made his way to GHQ Middle East, smiling to himself at the idea he was reconnoitring a commando raid.

The HQ was surrounded by a high wire fence and, waiting until the coast was clear, he climbed over although not without some difficulty and somewhat painfully. He then walked to the main administration block where he located the General's Office, but found to his dismay that he was out. By this time security staff had been alerted, and he was fortunate to discover the office of the Deputy C in C, Lieutenant General Neil Ritchie, before he was detained. He bowled into his office, saluting the surprised General and said quietly "I think that you had better look at this, Sir!"

Lieutenant General Ritchie not only looked at the paper, he questioned David closely for over half an hour and then requested him to return at 14.00 hours for further discussion. When David returned to the office, he was surprised to find that no less than the C in C, General Sir Claude Auchinlech was also present, and he was requested once again to present his plans.

It was quite evident that the plans had been discussed at some length by the Generals because, when David had completed outlining his plans, the Generals informed him that he had been promoted to the rank of Captain. David was told that he should call on The Long Range Desert Group who had an office in the headquarters building, and discuss his plans with them as they were very experienced at operating behind enemy lines. It seemed a splendid idea to be escorted by the Group, a body of men well versed in travelling behind enemy lines.

They had for some considerable time been carrying out reconnaissance for intelligence purposes and they conceded that they would learn much, in fact, both units did collaborate with a great degree of success.

All David's hopes were realised: with units of as few as twenty men they achieved remarkable results, destroying over one hundred enemy aircraft during the next few weeks.

The SAS is such a cloak and dagger unit that it may be interesting for you to have learned a little of their exploits. We have no doubt that our mosaic, annotated by F/Lt Grinsell, was used by them on one of their raids, and are proud that our unit played a small but important part.

Photographs for this chapter were kindly supplied by Roy Conyers Nesbit, author of 'Eyes of the RAF'.

instructions for use of this form in K.R. and A.C.I.,
. 2349, and War Manual, Pt. II., chapter XX., and
s in R.A.F. Pocket Book.

SECRET.

OPERATIONS RECORD BOOK

Page No.

of (Unit or Formation) 2. P.R.U

Place	Date	Time	Summary of Events	Reference to Appendice
EIRUT	1942 1/5	14.00		

/LT Pierce carried out a successful P.R. sortie of
uda Bay and the Crete aerodromes A/C Spitfire
P 904 Time 4.0 p.m.
HELIOPOLIS 9/5 0700
/LT Whelan carried out a successful P.R. Sortie
of Leros + Rhodes

above, The actual No2 P.R.U.s Secret Daily Operations record for 1st May 1942

below, The Gezira Sporting Club where Jack & Bill had a successful landing with Anna and Sabrina

33: Suda Bay

The month is May 1942, and we are now able to tell you a little of what we do at the No2 Photographic Reconnaissance Unit;

Today F/Lt Pierce took one of our kites to take a 'shufti' over Suda Bay, that was how we would have described it in unit parlance; in plain English we would say that he carried out a successful Photo Reconnaissance Sortie over Suda Bay and Crete Aerodromes. We were particularly interested in the Suda Bay photos, because it was just 12 months ago that we were hiding from the Germans in the hills overlooking Suda Bay, on the island of Crete, and we were able to pick out the place where we had slept overnight. Restrictions have been relaxed upon publication of classified material, and we are able to print part of the actual No2 P.R.U.s Secret Daily Operations record for 1st May 1942.

We met the aircraft, collected the magazines, developed and dried the films and printed two off each, 250 five by five prints. Our photograph shows some of the lads in the workroom, and one can see the enlargers in the background. It wasn't quite so simple as that, the prints had not only to be developed and fixed, and washed, but also dried. I should

above, At work in the darkroom with the enlargers in the background have mentioned that the films also had to be referenced and each exposure had to be numbered by hand with indian ink, the prints sorted into numerical order and then sent to the interpreters.

Duty over for the day, off we went to Cairo; we didn't ever stay in the camp, 'charping it off' on our beds ... (sleeping that is), there was far too much of interest in the world outside. There was the same cloudless sky that enabled F/Lt Pierce to carry out his successful sortie over Suda Bay, and Bill and I decided to set out on a sortie of our own. We were not flying, but in this instance we were fortunate enough to travel by a large American staff car. We generally tried to hitch-hike, but were not always successful and were often reduced to travelling on the Metro Trams where the natives expelled their foul breath laced with garlic into our faces. It was at times like these that we thought longingly of England where garlic did not seem to have been discovered.

On with the target, where we made a successful landing on the Gezira Island and found our targets for the day – Anna, and Sabrina who is Polish. We spent a pleasant afternoon chatting to them in the grounds of the Gezira Club. For a little more about Anna I will quote from a letter that Bill wrote to Mum next day:

"Yesterday I went out with a charming girl called Anna. She is Italian, I took her to dinner, at Toc-H. It is the first time I have been out with a girl since leaving Palestine, and it was quite a pleasant change, we find the different nationalities most interesting."

We have just been issued with a new set of 'Blue' (uniform) and have taken them to a civilian tailor, outside the camp, who we have heard is quite good. As I write this something comes to mind – that is just how the RAF came to wear blue uniforms; When the Royal Flying Corps and The Royal Naval Air Service amalgamated in 1918 there arose a problem; the Navy wanted blue to be chosen, and the Army thought it should be khaki. The War Office suggested a neutral colour, green, but neither the Navy nor the Army liked the idea of green.

It was here that a civil servant solved the problem. He told of hundreds of bales of blue material stored in a government warehouse, cloth that had been ordered by the late Tsar of Russia for his Imperial Guard. The Russian Revolution put paid to the Imperial Guard, and so today we have the pleasure of wearing blue. Isn't that a nice little story?

Bill's charning friend, Anna

Lest readers who served in the army feel left out I will recount why their colour was chosen;

A long time ago in India the British troops actually wore white tropical uniforms, but it was found that they were an easy target for the enemy, and so, it was decided that a colour would be chosen that would enable them to merge into the background.

What better than a very light brownish straw colour! They experimented by staining their white uniforms with dilute coffee which produced a colour not unlike the dusty earth. In Hindustani the word for 'dusty' is 'khaki'. So there we have it, and now the standard colour for British uniforms is khaki, and also for the RAF tropical uniform K.D (Khaki Drill).

34: Helio Bombed

There we were, comfortably settled in our wooden hut, when all of a sudden there was a huge explosion. Oh dear, I thought, one of our kites has gone into the deck, (meaning that one of our planes has plunged into the ground). We rushed outside to find that one of the hangars was on fire, the plane that we had heard overhead and thought was one of ours, was not, it was German.

Bill rushed back for his camera, and I, the coward of the two fled to the nearest slit trench, fearing that there was more to come, all was quiet for a couple of minutes, and then the CO's voice came over the Tannoy. 'Will all personnel go to the hangars and drag the planes out.' I did not hear very well and so I stayed where I was. It was all very upsetting, but taking into account that we had not been bombed since our adventures in Greece, it was

We rushed outside to find that one of the hangars was on fire

above, We looked the part going to the Opera by car and chauffeur
below, our unit was moving to Heliopolis Town, into palatial headquarters

evident that our lucky stars were still shining. In the comparative safety of Egypt we hardly knew there was a war on whilst our folks at home on Merseyside were having an awful time being bombed night after night, it didn't seem fair, we were supposed to be the warriors. Next morning we both went down to Sick Quarters to give a pint of blood – we would much rather give it that way than through a piece of shrapnel.

A few weeks ago I had put in an application to the CO with the suggestion that the personnel be moved to the nearby town of Heliopolis. Unfortunately, the application had finished up in the Photo Officer's drawer. It just goes to show; if that stick of bombs had been a few yards from the hangars a lot of valuable photographers could have lost their lives instead of an aircraft being destroyed, which could easily be replaced – that was my thinking.

We had a good lunch at the camp, and lots of tea to make up for our loss of blood, and decided that we would like to get away from the aerodrome for a while, and so we went off to Cairo. We called at Colonel Stefell's and told Mrs Stefell about the raid and our loss of sleep, she said, 'You boys can have a sleep here'. She was a great one for mothering us. Mrs Stefell invited us to tea and would we like an omelette? She then took us up on to the roof. The roof was flat and there was a native looking after a hen coup, so our eggs were really fresh. We had a very nice tea served by the Colonel's daughters, Lillian and June, we asked them whether they would like to come with us to the Opera House to see a play. They both said, 'Yes please', so off we went to book a show at the lovely Opera House which was just round the corner.

We decided to do things in style, so we booked a box, after all, we were going to arrive by car and chauffeur, and we should look the part. Lillian's fiancée arrived and stayed to tea, he was an army lieutenant, and he surprised us by producing a little white paper packet and spilling a small pile of diamonds onto the table. Today's value would have been over £7000. We learnt later that he was a jeweller in civvy street. No doubt there were some very strange goings on in those wartime days! Two days after the bombing of the aerodrome the Germans tried another attack, but this time we were ready for them with a barrage of night fighters. They did not stand a chance and failed to reach the aerodrome.

Fourteen days have now passed and someone at Middle East Headquarters has apparently woken up – our unit is moving to Heliopolis Town, into palatial headquarters. No 2 Photographic Reconnaissance Unit had originally been set up in June 1941 but it had grown so much that a decision was made to move the Interpretation Section Headquarters out of the RAF Station into the town and call it Middle East Interpretation Unit – MEIU for short. Plans had indeed been made as early as May to form the new unit but it was not until August 1942 that the move took place. Just what we had hoped for. It was most exciting, a new Targets Section began, and we started to receive the same ground information from secret agents, which, so far, had only been received by Middle East Headquarters. Consequently, this information became available to the interpretation section. The result was that it became possible for our unit to send specific questions, arising from photographs, to the organisations responsible for the interrogation of prisoners of war and escapees from occupied countries.

For instance, where, say, an escaped prisoner of war was able to confirm severe damage inflicted on a railway marshalling yard, this would save a further raid and no doubt the risk of further loss of aircrew. Our new unit was out of this world. We even had a 'chai wallah' whose job it was to sit in the entrance hall all day, just making tea, no milk but sugar. It was supplied in cut-down beer bottles.

Now if that wasn't heaven what was!

above, We assisted at the crippled children's party each month

left, Toc-H had taken over a lovely house in Soliman Pasha Street, Cairo

below, Nubian servants with red fez and spotless galabyas would not have looked out of place in the best hotels

35: Toc-H

Jack and Bill, once again deviating from their story, recall some earlier days in Birkenhead as memories of the past come flooding back:

It was 1933: Bill and I were 15 years old, and with a pal, Ken Speakman, had been down-town looking for a room to rent for a boy's club we had formed. We had ideas that we may see a hayloft over a stable or some such accommodation. We say a stable, because when we were young, in those early days, horse transport was much in evidence. Co-op bread was delivered by horse and cart. Milk, too, was carried in a type of horse and trap, the milkman going from street to street calling 'Milk, milk'. We would go out with a jug or basin to collect a pint, and he would dip a metal ladle into a 12 gallon urn, or if we wanted a gill, which was a half pint, he would use a smaller ladle. For funerals too, the hearses were drawn by horses. They were a very ornate affair, with the horses wearing plumes in their headdresses. The hearses had large glass sides, and were very elegant – a splendid send off. Because horses were a general mode of transport in those days, there were lots of stables, so it wasn't too unusual for rooms over stables to be available. We were unsuccessful in our quest, and were making our way home along Church Road, Tranmere, when a gentleman asked if we could direct him to Bedford Road in Rock Ferry. We said that it was a little distance away, but that we would be pleased to help him if he would like to walk with us.

We entered into conversation, and told him of our endeavour to find a room for our boys' club, whereupon he introduced himself, telling us that he was Padre Ambrose, and that he was on his way home after a meeting at Toc-H, which sounded very mysterious to us. Padre Ambrose then suggested that if we would like to call at Toc-H House on the following Tuesday, he was fairly sure they would be able to help us. He told us that Toc-H House was at No 47 Clifton Road, off Whetstone Lane. The meeting started at 7.30pm and we should just ask for him.

The next Tuesday we three called at the House, and were welcomed into a large room where there were about 20 men. We saw a notice hanging on one side which said 'ABANDON RANK ALL YE WHO ENTER HERE'. The meeting started with the Ceremony of Light. The room light was put out and the lamp, illustrated above, was lit with a taper by Padre Ambrose who then read a short prayer ...

They shall grow not old as we that are left grow old
Age shall not weary them nor the years condemn.
At the going down of the sun and in the morning
We will remember them ...

We found it all very interesting, and were amused when we heard one of the men addressed as 'Sparks' and another as 'Gas'. We learned that they were an electrician and a gas man respectively. Another, addressed as 'DC' was a District Commissioner of Scouts. We were also introduced to Mr W F Bushell, the headmaster of Birkenhead School. Toc-H Club was in one of those large houses which had been owned by a rich merchant, and contained a big basement and it was decided at the meeting that we could have the use of the basement for our boys' club. The Jobmaster gave one of the Toc-H members the job of helping us.

It would seem that even in those far off days our lucky star was shining, indeed it was a surprising outcome of our boyhood dreams that we were able to obtain premises for our boys club, and without having to pay any rent. We little realised that we should eventually progress from a boys' club to the Clifton Camping Club, and we have to smile when we see amongst our old papers, where one of the lads who had access to a printing press had supplied us with a printed letter heading for the club, with the secretary and treasurer's name. We had great ideas even then! The camping club was in being from 1932 until the outbreak of war, and each weekend we would cycle twenty five miles to Loggerheads. It was wonderful.

Our introduction to Toc-H was to have a profound effect upon our future lives. We were to join an organisation with Christian principles, whose main aim was service to others, much the same as Rotary and the Lions today. After a period of probation, we joined Toc-H, and amongst our jobs was hospital visiting. We visited Manor Hill Hospital, which was for the severely wounded from the First World War, and we made friends with the men and took them for walks in their wheelchairs. We were to continue hospital visiting during the war in Greece, Germany etc. Another job was to assist at the crippled children's party. This was held on the first Saturday of each month.

We will take you back: I am sitting alongside a lady, Leonora Crampton. She is a doctor's daughter and is one of those kind volunteers who provide transport, whilst Bill and I act as guides, and also we assist in lifting the children into the car when it is necessary. We play games and sing, and there are usually one or two extroverts amongst the children, and the parties are always a lovely happy event. The children looked forward to the drive in the car. Most of them had not ever travelled by car – in those days not many people owned a car.

Toc-H was started in the First World War, in Belgium. About ten miles behind the battlefield was a pretty little town called Poperinge, and in one of its streets was a house named Talbot House. And so it happens that the Army signaller's code for Talbot House is 'Toc-H', so there we have it – a code for a house. That's where the name came from.

This was no ordinary house, no 43 Gasthuistrasstraat. It was opened in 1915 as a sort of soldiers' club where men could get some peace and quiet, away from the battle front, but especially, visitors had to abide by the Toc-H motto 'Abandon rank all ye who enter here'. Tommies and officers alike, the atmosphere was relaxed and very special. It was Senior Chaplain Neville Talbot who decided to call the house Talbot House in memory of his brother Gilbert, who had been killed in action. Chosen to run the show was Padre Tubby Clayton, who was untidy, jovial and charismatic, with whom everyone felt at ease. Such a

For Tommies and officers alike, the atmosphere at Toc-H in Cairo was relaxed and very special

haven for officers and other ranks, it had an atmosphere so special that after the war it became the inspiration for a worldwide charitable organisation, known simply as Toc-H.

Toc-H grew so much after the First World War that by 1940 it had hundreds of branches all over the world, 30 in London alone including the House Of Commons. Readers may be interested to know the names of some of the members of Toc-H in the year 1940. They included:-

The Duke of Devonshire

General Sir Charles Harrington, GCB

The Archbishop of Canterbury, GCVO

Admiral Sir Richard Phillimore, GCB

LACs Jack and Bill Fairs

Air Chief Marshall Sir Robert Brooke-Popham, GCVO

Major General Sir Arnold Sillen, KCM

(We thought it permissible to include Jack and Bill – all rank abandon ye.)

Readers may wonder what this has to do with the Middle East. We'll explain:

Toc-H had taken over a lovely house in Soliman Pasha Street in Cairo, as a hostel, and it was here that servicemen could stay for bed and breakfast. Everything was done in such splendid style. Mrs Gould, the Scottish matron, was very particular, and the Nubian servants with their red fez and spotless white galabyas would not have looked out of place in the best hotels. We often called in for afternoon tea, which was always a delight, served at 4.00pm, toast, muffins and jam. The tables had white tablecloths and damask serviettes. Proper posh it was. The atmosphere was very genteel and so different from the canteen or unit cook-house. Dinner was served at 7.00pm and Bill asked the Warden, Gordon Turvey, whether he could bring a girlfriend, Anna Gwandanini, and Gordon agreed to his request. Anna was a charming Italian girl, whose family lived in Bolzano in Northern Italy. Bill and Anna enjoyed a very pleasant friendship, without getting too serious. We also had the pleasure of staying at Toc-H hostels in Palestine (Tel Aviv) and Alexandria, and counted ourselves very fortunate to belong to such a splendid organisation.

After the war we visited Leasowe Open Air Hospital for long stay patients, and adopted Loyalty Ward, where we chatted to any of the patients who did not have visitors, and here over 50 years later we are still in touch with one of the patients who hasn't ever walked.

and realising the importance of books for the troops when they were not occupied, we felt that something should be done to send more books to the troops in the forward areas of the desert. A couple of days previously, when we were at the Gezira Club canteen, we had been speaking to a young New Zealand soldier who was working for their post office, and he had suggested that there were many books and periodicals that were unclaimed, and he felt certain they would be available for such a good cause.

We had lunch with Gordon at Toc-H. and chatted about our idea. He was quite enthusiastic, and said that the books could be sent to Toc-H for forwarding, and no doubt some means of sending them up the desert could be worked out. Acting on the maxim of 'do it now' we made our way to the New Zealand Post Office, where we met the lieutenant in charge. We explained the purpose of our visit and found him most helpful. He promised to send eight sacks of books to Toc-H. He was as good as his word, and the books were delivered to Toc-H the following week. Captain Wilcox of the Salvation Army took the books in his van to the Eighth Army in the forward area. Sadly, he was captured by the Germans, and the last we heard was that he was in a prisoner of war camp in Italy.

Now, referring to our title 'We Join the Army', it was the Salvation Army, and we were just attaching ourselves for a couple of half days. Our purpose was to take a series of photographs of the Red Shield Hostel, to be published in the famous 'War Cry' sold throughout the pubs in England.

Mr Fadil, the man from Syria, was as good as his word, and here we were seated at the home of Mr and Mrs Fadil, where a lovely meal had been prepared. It was roast beef and Yorkshire pudding, just like mother used to make. The difference from a meal at home is that here a servant was waiting on us, and by each place was a finger bowl containing warm water. Most of the homes that we visited here used finger bowls, and Bill suggested to me that the reason must have originated in the tents of sheiks were they tore the lamb to pieces with their fingers. The fruit salad contained fruits that we did not recognise, and we ate figs that were shaped like small pears, not the dried type that we were used to at home.

Mr Fadil told us that he had just taken delivery of some very special green leather from England, which he had ordered for an album that he was making for King Farouk. I told him we wanted to buy an autograph album, and would it be possible for him to make one for us and bind it with the same leather that he was using for King Farouk. He said most certainly. Major Pearson made up the party, and we spent a most interesting evening, and although it was not Jerusalem, it was quite evident that we had two wise men in our company. Once again, our lucky stars were still shining.

Captain Wilcox of the Salvation Army welcomes one of the lads

I have just been looking at the album whilst I have been writing this chapter. It is a bit unusual, because in addition to autographs it has 154 photographs of people, many of which were taken in the Middle East.

Bill and I share the album. He keeps it for some months then it is my turn. My wife kindly lets me keep some photographs of past girl friends.

37: Tea Sar

That's a strange title, isn't it. All will be revealed a little later.

It is the 23rd of July 1942 and we are in our wooden hut at the top end of Heliopolis Royal Air Force Camp in Egypt. I was sitting in the hut polishing my shoes (the ones with the cardboard soles) when Bill dashed in with a big grin, saying 'I've got a surprise for you', he was holding an envelope with an Egyptian stamp on it, and I thought oh! It's a letter from our Egyptian friend Farid el Guindi, but, no, it was from the Gezira Sporting Club, and here is the letter:

The Gezira Sporting Club, Cairo

18th July 1942

Dear Brothers Fairs,

The members of The Gezira Sporting Club welcome you to spend a week's leave on the Puritan Houseboat, which they have hired to provide accommodation for servicemen on leave, and they hope that your leave will be a comfortable and happy one. Bed, hot bath, morning tea, breakfast, lunch, afternoon tea will be provided for you, and you can buy on board drinks and cigarettes at reasonable prices. You are close beside the club grounds, where arrangements have been made for you to play games, and if you ask at the Secretary's Office, you will be shown where you can play football, tennis or squash – rackets, shoes and balls are available.

You will also find bowling greens and croquet lawns, and if you are a golfer, some members of the club will be glad to lend you clubs and arrange a game for you. You may have a swim in the bath after 6.00pm. This letter will serve as a pass to the club grounds. Members of the Club will visit you from time to time to see if there is any way in which they can help you to have an enjoyable leave.

We hope that you will make yourself at home.

Yours sincerely,

Cecil Campbell, Chairman General Committee, Gezira Sporting Club

A week later, and we were on our way. We travelled light, each carrying a small brown paper parcel. Getting to our destination was easy, we just caught the Metro a little distance from the camp gates, and travelling about eight miles, with a little walk we were on board. It

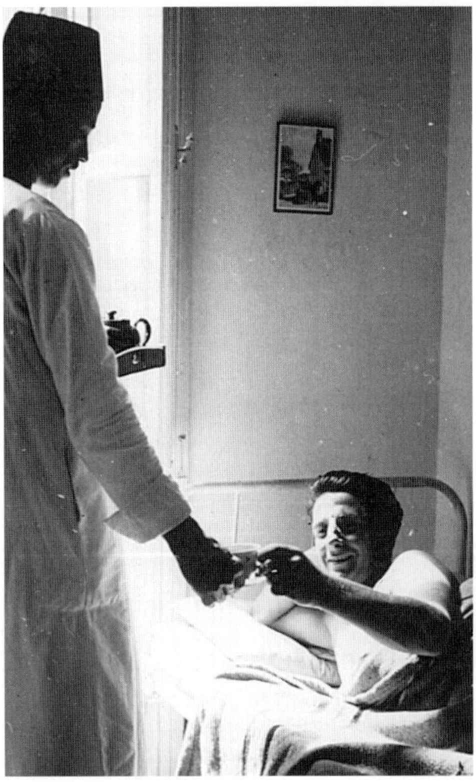

above, The Puritan Houseboat was moored in the Nile beside the club

left, Next morning a servant kept saying 'Tea Sar', until we awoke

below, The charming, Tatiana, WOW!

wasn't dark, and so our bright star was not yet shining, but we were allocated a cabin on the top deck. It had just been redecorated, and was lovely. It had two comfortable bunks, feather pillows, a wardrobe and thick white carpet. It must be remembered that we did not have wardrobes and carpets in our camp, they were just part of civvy street memories.

The ship had a number of lounges, and a radiogram which played eight records without any attention, just the sort of music that the lads liked, Deanna Durban and Strauss. We were waited upon hand and foot, and the next morning were awakened by a native servant who kept repeating 'Tea Sar', 'Tea Sar', gradually raising his voice until we were awake. The lads loved this tea in bed – all very posh. Breakfast over, we only had to cross the road and we were in the club grounds, where we played a game of croquet. We were quite good at that, having played quite often a Loggerheads before the war.

One day after a very good lunch we tried our hand at a new game, to play one must throw a horseshoe shaped piece of iron at a metal stake driven into the ground. Whilst we were playing, along came an Air Vice Marshall and a Wing Commander, who watched us for a few minutes. The seemed very interested, and challenged us to a game. After half an hour we succeeded in beating them 60 points to 38 – well done other ranks. The next evening there was a gala dinner and dance on board, and it addition to the 50 servicemen, who were divided approximately one third from each of the services Navy, Army and Air Force, some girls had been invited to partner the lads. We were lucky and sat on the Captain's Table. Well it wasn't really the Captain's Table, it was the Club Secretary's, and our bright star was really in evidence, because who was seated at the table but the Secretary's assistant, a charming Latvian girl, Tatiana, WOW! I've put the wow in here, it really comes later on when Bill and I dated her (one at a time of course, we did not play gooseberry).

These articles are, as the readers probably know, derived from letters home, and perhaps I should mention that I did not put the 'WOW' in the letter, because you know what mothers are, she would have been asking what the wow was all about, and I would not have wanted to tell her. Nor am I going to mention the reason here.

The dancing was most enjoyable, and although being wartime the boat did not move, we did – especially during the quick step. It was almost like the dances at home. It's 57 years on when I'm, writing this book, and I have just looked in our autograph book, and I see that Tatiana wrote the whole of Tennyson's poem 'IF' on her page. She also mentioned ships that pass in the night. It was our good fortune that this ship did not pass in the night. It was anchored in the Nile. This was the start of a very pleasant friendship, we both walked out with Tatiana. We met her friends, and attended a wedding with her. (As I write this it seems like only yesterday.)

The next morning found Bill and I sitting comfortably in the Gezira outdoor canteen. Bill was saying just how lucky we were to be enjoying such a splendid holiday, and he wondered what we would be doing if we were still with our old squadron, and where we would be stationed.

When we were in the Western Desert with XI Squadron, we had become somewhat fed up with long periods of inactivity, and that we had requested if possible we be relocated to a unit where we would be fully employed in photography. We were fortunate to be transferred to No 2 Photographic Unit in Heliopolis, a lovely town where conditions were just like peacetime. There is little doubt that were we to have stayed with XI Squadron, we would surely have been in a front line zone, and our lives would have been most uncomfortable, we would have been in India.

Our pal Tommy in XI Squadron was keeping a diary, and the following entries give some idea of what we would have been experiencing....

Extracts from Tommy Row's Diary:

Three of our Blenheims made a raid on Burma, unfortunately one was shot down and PO Williams and his crew were killed.

Twenty four Japs raided Feni Aerodrome, destroying three of our Blenheims, and killing a number of natives.

Thunderstorm. received vaccination for Cholera and TAB

Good news, sixteen Japs raided the Chittagong area and twelve were shot down by our fighters.

Cheesed off, there has been a continual downpour of rain and our tent is flooded. We killed a snake in the tent.

Paddy fields are under water. We went punting but the boat sank three times and I was bitten by leeches.

Mail has been very much delayed. I received 30 letters today, 25 from Freda.

Tommy had met 17 year old Freda whilst training in Blackpool. They had fallen in love, and eventually married. Freda is a widow now, and she spends her annual holiday with our Bill and his wife.

above, The impressive approach to the Gezira Sporting Club where Jack & Bill spent many happy days

38: Twenty Four Hours

It is five thirty on the morning of August 14th 1942, and we have been on duty since 8 o'clock last night. We are working a 12-hour shift, in the darkroom, and then we will have twenty four hours off. I will tell you how we spent our 24 hours.

We stopped for a break at 9.00pm and Bill asked for permission to go to Lady Lampson's RAF Club, which was just two or three minutes from our unit. We guess it was called that because Sir Miles Lampson was our Ambassador in Egypt, and his wife had been responsible for the club's inception. How very fortunate we were to be stationed in the town. Bill could get permission to go out and buy some cakes for the shift, and unknown to the sergeant pop around to see his girlfriend Mary, who lived just two minutes away. I am not too sure whether we asked for a cup of char and two wads, which was NAAFI language for a cup of tea and two cakes, because the club was kindly staffed by English lady volunteers. I think it was the latter. We just bought cakes and toast in the evening at the club.

The interpreters often worked 24 hours

Tea for the shift was made at the unit in a bucket, which was heated over another bucket which contained about an inch of cotton wool in its base, and this was soaked in methylated spirit, and so we had a spirit stove, a little bigger than most. We had lots of meths on the unit. It was used to accelerate the drying of the film, and the cotton wool was used to dry off the surplus. As the reader will see, we had

above, We look out from the balcony of our home in the plush new apartment block – I do not pride myself that my suggestion to move to town had been heeded, but rather that common sense had prevailed, and here we are and it is wizard

Fl/t Lieut Lamboit

other uses. Bill was saying the other day 'I would not be surprised if the methylated spirit which we used was refined by Commercial Solvents of Bromborough, the company for whom we both worked pre-war'. They used to refine thousands of gallons every week.

Things were certainly hotting up in the Western Desert, and from the reconnaissance photographs that we had been developing we could tell that the Germans were getting ready for their big push. We have produced some hundreds of prints during this shift, but it is difficult for us to gather any information from them. To do so we would require to look through a stereoscope, and would need to be interpreters, someone who could decipher and clarify the images. We had little problem, however in deciding what was happening on one of the pictures. It showed quite a large ship on fire, which was being towed by two tugs. We heard later that it was a seven thousand-ton merchant vessel which our people had bombed, and the Germans were towing her back to Greece.

6.15am. We had finished our jobs, and we asked the sergeant permission to do some buckshees. I think that we had better explain that these buckshees were personal photographs. They were mostly of people and places, and indeed the photographs illustrating these articles are copies of those sent home to mother, that is those not liable to censorship.

During the war, most photo sections had what was loosely termed a 'racket', where they sold photographs, but Bill and I produced many hundreds of photographs for the lads and the girls. We didn't ever charge, they were 'buckshee'. Work over for the night, our sergeant allowed us off a little earlier, and within a few minutes we were eating breakfast, and in no time at all we were in heaven. Well of course it was not heaven, but it was heavenly, and here's why:

Our unit personnel had moved into town, and our billet was delightful. It was on the second floor of an attractive Moorish apartment block. Our bedroom was lovely and cool, with shutters over the windows, and we could, if we wished, sleep out on the balcony. It was quiet, so off to sleep for a few hours. Readers may recall earlier that I had requested an interview with my commanding officer to suggest that the men be moved to the nearby town, because the four wooden huts in which we were located were extremely vulnerable should the station be bombed. My request had to go to my photo officer first, and when I handed it to him, he looked a bit puzzled, and then he frowned and said 'I cannot pass this to the CO, L A/C Fairs, you know we officers are running this unit', to which I replied 'Well I would like it to go to him'. He then said 'Just leave it with me', and placed the letter in his desk drawer. A few weeks later the aerodrome was bombed and the hangars set on fire just a few hundred yards from our huts.

Shortly after the bombing, I was called in by Fl/t Lieut Lamboit, our photo officer, and he said, 'Something is now being done about moving the men to town Fairs, and you can have your application back'.

I do not pride myself that my suggestion had been heeded, but rather that common sense had prevailed, and here we are and it is wizard. Climbing the stairs to our bedroom in

above, We told the guard, Hussein Sunheil, that we wished to learn a little about the house, and something of the history of Heliopolis

left, Baron's Folly was a house built by a Belgian Baron, and was modelled on an Indian Temple, and it was called a Folly because he did not ever live there the new apartment, we were intrigued with the light switches on the stairs, they were large push buttons that switched the lights off automatically when we had reached our landing. We little knew at the time that some 50 years later we would have the identical type switches in our own apartment block next to our shop, and we still have them today.

Back to the story. It is midday and 12 hours have passed. One of our oppos has called into the billet for his irons (knife, fork, spoon and mug). He is off to lunch, and by arrangement he wakes us for our lunch too. Four hours was enough sleep, and we had plans. Bill has suggested that now we are residents of Heliopolis we should learn a little of the history of the town, and probably a good start would be to visit 'Baron's Folly', which was only seven minutes walk from our billet. Now, what you may ask is 'Barons Folly', and the answer is that Baron's Folly was a house built by a Belgian Baron, and was modelled on an Indian Temple, and it was a Folly because he did not ever live there.

We walked to the large gates and called to a native, who was in a small gatehouse 'Talaheena mafadlak' (come here please). Imagine our surprise when he said in almost impeccable English 'What can I do for you?' Yes, I think we were bowled over with his reply, and we told him that we wished to learn a little about the house, and something of the history of Heliopolis. We were made welcome and invited into the grounds, and the following is his story:

Once upon a time there was a wealthy Belgian nobleman and entrepreneur, called Baron Edouard Empain, who had made a great deal of money in the Congo and in building the Paris Metro. He was so successful with the Metro that he was able to persude the Egyptian Government to grant him a huge tract of desert land on the outskirts of Cairo. There he decided he would like to build a small city. The Baron being a director of the Cairo Electric Tram Company thought it would be a good idea to make money from the rents of his properties, and also from his trams which would serve the city and transport the residents to Cairo, which was seven miles away. He chose an Englishman, Sir Reginald Oakes as his architect, and it was a coincidence that they had heard of Port Sunlight, and were inspired by its concept.

Heliopolis, however in no way resembles Port Sunlight. It was built in radial grid patterns; its wide avenues lined with apartment blocks with Moorish facades, and its green shrubberies giving it a feeling of a garden city. The Baron's guard Hussein Sunheil (for such was his name) told us that Heliopolis was a place where the rich lived. Although Bill and I were poor, we too lived here in an apartment. There is no doubt that our lucky stars Castor and Pollux had placed us in this very desirable location.

We thanked Hussein with some of our unused cigarette ration, and went back to the unit for our evening meal. Eight o'clock and the end of our 24-hour stint, not too untypical of our life at Helio. We wrote a letter to Mum and Dad, and so to bed.

One of Wirral Champion's readers, David Bloom, knowing of our interest in Heliopolis, has been kind enough to pay a visit on his recent trip to Cairo, and here is what he said. 'The present day Heliopolis is far removed from the vision you and Bill experienced almost 60 years ago. It is westernised, with many restaurants and nightclubs. The racecourse has been turned into a rather tatty amusement park, there are fast food outlets on almost every corner, with the inevitable Macdonald's and Kentucky Fried Chicken restaurants.'

We cannot help but reflect upon our good fortune that we lived in Heliopolis when it was an unspoilt and delightful place to be, even with a war going on.

above, The local church, called St Andrew's, was built in the style of an English village church

left, Our job was to photograph the harbour at Tobruk, so that our bombers could identify the shipping

39: First Priority

It is August 1942, and Bill and I are extremely busy at the Middle East Interpretation Unit where we are producing photographs by the thousand. A full moon is due, and Rommel, the German Commander in the Western Desert, is expected to make his big push to defeat our boys of the Eighth Army and capture Cairo and the Delta. On the unit our Production Department is working flat out. Jobs are normally classified in the department as ROUTINE – URGENT – FIRST PRIORITY, but now they are all FIRST PRIORITY.

Rommel has two main supply routes from Crete to the ports of Benghazi and Tobruk. It is these ports on the Mediterranean coast of North Africa where he must receive supplies for his army before he can begin his offensive in the Western Desert, and it is our job to photograph the harbour at Tobruk, so that our bombers can identify the shipping.

The sorties flown, we produce the photographs, and these go via despatch rider to RAF Middle East HQ, when our Beaufighters and the American heavy bombers are sent to make a precision attack. This is made on the main jetty, sinking a merchant ship and many barges. It does not sound a very important thing, sinking barges, but these barges can carry as much as 1,500 three-ton trucks. Whilst returning from the sortie, our pilots spot a huge concentration of motor transport and armoured units, seemingly just waiting to be bombed and strafed. We heard later that a combined effort by the South African and the US Air Force had succeeded in destroying many of the vehicles.

So much for those brief reports from the battle front. Now we will tell you a little of Jack and Bill's off duty hours: some snippets that have been culled from five letters sent to Mum and Dad during August 1942 to keep them acquainted with our life in the Middle East.

August 25th is our birthday, we are 24, and we have passed the day quietly. One of our girlfriends presented us with a birthday cake, and another insisted upon treating us to the cinema. We are very lucky, as we can choose from six different cinemas, all within 20 minutes distance of our camp. The cinemas show mainly English films with Arabic subtitles, which run at the side of the screen, and at the end of the performance the Egyptian National Anthem is played, and our troops quite often sing some rude words. Fortunately, I am sure the Egyptians do not understand. The weather is very hot, and when we are not on duty during the afternoon, we take a siesta, almost everyone does, and most folk, including the military, work what are called Middle East hours, working mornings and then off until 5pm resuming work until 8pm.

We tell mother that we have our laundry done twice a week, and we change for dinner each evening. We each have four pair of socks, so we are quite well off. We are quite clothes-conscious, and had our uniforms tailored. We really mean that our uniforms were altered to make them a better fit. It paid dividends too. Bill was adjudged the smartest man on parade, and was awarded a 48-hour leave pass.

Today is Sunday, and at 8am we are not on duty, but rose at this unearthly hour to have breakfast, and later we will be off to church. Not the usual church parade held by many squadrons, but we are able to wend our way to the local church, called St Andrew's, built in the style of an English village church. There are many English people living here in Heliopolis, and the church is well attended, everyone dressed in their Sunday best. The sun is streaming through the window, and some black Basuto soldiers are singing a hymn in their own language, which is most enjoyable. We notice that the three Mather girls are in church, and we hope to see them after the service. It's almost like home really, and rather nice for being so. We manage to have a short conversation with the girls and then back to duty, reminding ourselves that there is a war on.

The next day Bill has a date with his friend Mary, and not wanting to play gooseberry, I decide to have lunch in town, and then perhaps go dancing. On my way I spot a crowd, and being curious I push to the front, and am very surprised to see a couple of policemen who had detained two Arabs. They are standing beside a coffin, which was full of white loaves, most unusual! I make enquiries from a European gent standing nearby, and am told that he had observed a funeral procession of about 40 people, but unlike the usual procession there wasn't any wailing or tears, in fact they all seemed to be enjoying themselves. The police had arrived and the crowd had fled, and only two men had been detained. It seems that the bread was being smuggled, and was black market bread, very scarce at the moment.

Strange place the Middle East – it isn't unusual to see a number of natives just lying asleep on the sidewalks during the afternoon, having their siesta. The other day we saw a sword-swallower – he was in fact swallowing a piece of flat iron about two feet long by one and a half inches wide, it made us feel sick!

I am now sitting in a cafe by myself having tea and cake, debating whether to go to a French club, not being too sure whether to go because they all speak French. Here I am though at the door of the club and the attendant tells me I cannot go in because it is members only and so I sit and wait on the off chance that I may know one of the members still to arrive.

Well my lucky star is shining – the young lady whom I met at a previous dance invites me inside. Some of the girls are wearing Jasmine garlands around their necks, and I am sure the scent from them will travel for miles. I have been here before – the club is called The Circle Recreative, and I now recognise one or two members whom I have met previously. The floor is quite small, in fact it is a tiled plaque, and the dance is a short step shuffle because room is so limited. It is in the open air just in front of the clubhouse. Bill and I have learnt a few French words, "May I have this dance please? You dance very well." (We say this whether our partners do so or not, and quite often they burst out laughing).

Reading the letters home to Mum and Dad, whilst writing this book, it surprises me a little that we should feel so much at home in the Middle East. I think perhaps it was because we were young at the time, and a bit adventurous.

right: The whole unit were photographed out on parade in their Sunday best with us discreetly hidden at the far end

top, Two or three men can easily lift the 'tanks' into position

centre, The Sherman tanks, were disguised to make them appear as lorries

below, We were adopted by the Steffell family

40: 'The Magicians'

It was strange how we got to know about 'The Magicians'. I had just delivered a batch of photographs that Bill and I had been printing, which had been taken over the Western Desert, to Fl/Lt Richmond Brown. He selected two of the photographs and placing them side by side under the stereoscope he said, "Just look at these and tell me what you can see." I looked and said, "They appear to be lorries dispersed over an airfield". He said, "Yes, they are ours, and now I will surprise you. They are not lorries, they are Sherman tanks, and they are disguised to make them appear as lorries. These photographs have been taken as a check to see how good the disguise is."

Fl/Lt Richmond Brown said, "Pop in again in about an hour when I have done a little more sorting." I did so, and he again suggested that I look through the stereoscope and tell him what I could see. My reply was, "Masses of tanks." He said, "Yes, ours also, but once again they are fake. Some are made of light wood covered in hessian, and some are actually made of inflated rubber." He said, "It is quite amusing that two or three men can lift the tanks into position. In addition they are constructing realistic guns out of pipes and hollow frames with netting, as though they are partially camouflaged. We are hoping that when Gerry comes over with his reconnaissance planes that he will be deceived. We will even have men moving about when we hear the planes approaching."

We learned that this was just the tip of the iceberg, and that elaborate schemes were being perpetrated to try to fool Rome. It was on a colossal scale, with hundreds of men being engaged in the manufacture of these fake vehicles and guns under the codename "Bertram". In this attempt to deceive the enemy, hundreds of tanks disguised as lorries and squadrons of wooden and rubber tanks were located a long way from the front, to make the Germans think that a thrust was to take place in the wrong area.

If I recall correctly, we used fakery on a much larger scale than the tanks and lorries. When Gerry came over bombing our airfields, some distance away we would have a dummy airfield where we would light fires to attract his bombers. I can remember when we were in North Yorkshire at a heavy bomber station, how sorry I felt for those airmen who were detailed to man the dummy fields. On an even bigger scale, and much nearer to home, about 15 miles from Liverpool in the Formby area which had been commandeered by the military, many of the trees were cut down. When the enemy planes were overhead they were used to create fires with the idea that the enemy would think they were the Liverpool docks, and thus waste their bombs.

It must be said that using dummies was not new. The Germans also used them, causing our interpreter's job to be more difficult, and making necessary the use of long focus lenses, and in addition, low level flying which was of greater importance, to enlarge the ground detail and detect the dummies. We were seldom able to learn what our photographs were being used for, and it was refreshing in this instance to know of their importance.

It is said that, "All work and no play makes Jack a dull boy", and Bill too, so we will leave the war for a short while and tell you a little about our private lives.

We are 'Adopted'

We have had the good fortune to be adopted by Colonel Steffell and his family who originally came from Liverpool. Not officially with documents, of course, but then if we fail to appear at their apartment for a few days, Mrs Steffell asks, "Where are my twins?" We were so lucky to be welcomed into the family. There was a mum and dad, the two girls, and Harold their brother. He was an army officer. June was a school-girl, and Lillian was about two years older than we were, and was married to an Italian Captain. Colonel Steffell was in command of the Central Fire Brigade in Cairo, and the family lived in an apartment over the fire station. It was a pleasant apartment, with a balcony, where we used to sit and watch the world go by, and as it was in Egypt, the world was quite colourful. The family would entertain a good deal, mostly officers, and although Bill and I were of a lowly rank, I cannot ever recall that we felt other than at ease with the company.

Colonel Steffell used to ride and shoot and we enjoyed wild duck. We quite liked sweet potatoes, and enjoyed Mrs Steffell's cooking, it was like mother used to make. There was a good wine cellar, but Bill and I being tea-total had soft drinks. It seemed that right through life we were given the opportunity to drink which others would have welcomed. Strange really, Before the war we both worked for companies that had beer bottling plants on their premises; Bill for T B Hall & Company along the Dock Road in Liverpool, and I for the L M S Hotel Services in Exchange Station, where there was a bottling plant underneath the station, and yet we did not imbibe a drop.

Being family we were lucky to be able to borrow the Colonel's car when it was not being used, a big American Nash and chauffeur, Mahmoud, and we did so on many occasions, usually when we booked a box at the Opera House, and to arrive in such style was 'proper posh'. We had some lovely evenings out with our adopted sisters, Lillian and June, and they were not a bit jealous when we used the car for other girlfriends.

'Maid of the Mountains' at the Opera House

It is pure coincidence that as I write this very chapter, I have just received a letter from South Africa from June, which includes a photograph of her and her grandson – 58 years on and we are still very good friends. And yet another coincidence, I discovered after the war the girl that I married was a friend of Colonel Steffell's sister – what a small world we live in!

41: The Battle Begins

It is 9th October 1942 and our morning is most exciting, as we find ourselves developing photographs showing the landing grounds of El Daba and Fuka where we were stationed about 12 months earlier, and where we had put in so much effort in digging a very useful air raid trench. We were informed later by our interpreters that due to the Autumn rains, the grounds of the airfield were soft, and that it was such a morass that the Axis planes were unable to take off.

This was just what our lads had been waiting for, and our fighters and fighter-bombers gathered in strength, even to the extent of taking planes off training flights, and they gave Gerry a real pasting. We heard later that many of the enemy planes had been destroyed or damaged. Nevertheless we hoped that the Germans had been able to use the air raid trench that we had so carefully made and that they personally had escaped harm.

I was chatting to Harry Blackmore, one of the lads on the section, and he was telling me that he was stationed on the next landing ground to Fuka, and just how unpleasant it was. Apparently, the Germans would deliberately set out to keep the squadron without sleep. They would send over a single bomber and drop just one bomb, and keep repeating this during the night, so that the next day everyone would be far from alert. This went on for a few nights, and then we wised up to them and on three occasions surprised the Gerrys by shooting their planes down without warning. Yes, we were rescued from this predicament by one of our night fighter squadrons.

A very frightening time was experienced by Harry when the Germans would fly over the landing ground and drop a cluster of flares, which hung like great chandeliers in the sky, illuminating the camp as though it was a bright summer day. Harry said they had warning of these visits, because in the morning a Shufti Kite would come over at a great height (Shufti is Arabic for look, an expression very much in general use by the lads). Unfortunately, these German reconnaissance planes were a daily occurrence. Lying in their slit trenches illuminated by these huge chandeliers with bombs dropping was most disturbing, although thinking back that was not the way the lads described the events!

Later in the month, on 23rd October 1942, Montgomery started his offensive at El Alamein, and consequently we were exceptionally busy on the unit having received a brand new camera, the F52. It was huge and the negative size had increased from 5ins x 5ins to 8ins x 7ins and the film to 500 exposures, with the camera using a 36 inch lens.

Our shift excelled themselves one night, producing over 1,000 prints, of the German

The huge new F52 camera

gun batteries, which had to be left for the next shift to dry on a row of large chromium plated rotary drying drums. The Eighth Army had requested these. A big push was imminent and with this knowledge, together with their own sound-ranging and visual spotting, they could then decide which of the German batteries would be likely to cause them the most problems during the advance.

Our interpretation officers had become so skilled at checking the photographs that they were able to determine the location of the German guns to within fifty yards or less. Our artillery selected 25 of the enemy batteries and gave them a very heavy concentration of fire in order to shatter their morale and cause much damage. During the battle, only about half the enemy batteries concerned continued firing, and almost every prisoner of war brought in during the first few days told of the guns destroyed and heavy casualties amongst the crews. This we learned later. The knowledge of the effectiveness of our photographic contribution towards the success of the battle, which was undoubtedly responsible for saving so many lives, gave our unit great satisfaction. Jack and Bill, too, felt that their 12 hour shift, after which they had virtually collapsed on the bed, had been worthwhile. We thought perhaps we should add this last little bit, as most of these stories give the impression that we might be on holiday.

However, enough of the war – let us see what we were up to during this month of October 1942: I have looked out four letters that we sent home during this month and I think that if I select one or two little items of news from them you will see just how we kept Mum and Dad quite well acquainted with our goings on. Here goes:

We were off to Cairo and came across a native carrying a crate of live chickens on his head. This was not unusual but when he placed them on the ground, he selected one out of the crate, put some seeds in his mouth, opened the bird's beak and blew them in – well it was so different, so far as we were concerned, to think that someone would buy the bird later in the day – YUCK!

You will remember Captain Wilcox of the Salvation Army, who takes our books up the desert for the troops. Well, he is unfortunately now a prisoner of war in Italy, so there is no doubt that the hundreds of books that we were able to send went right up to the forward area.

We have recently received a pay rise. It works out at about a shilling a week after tax is deducted. Handsome isn't it? That's the bad news, and the good news is that Barclays have received the £50 that you sent us – thank you very much.

In a recent letter we mentioned the Mather sisters. A couple of days ago we spent a very pleasant evening in their home. The girls are good looking, with lots of personality, and they dance well.

Jack & Bill's Maltese friend Romeo

Back from breakfast we are getting ready for church. This morning we are going to an RC church to see whether we like the service, and also because we have been invited by two pals. One of our pals is Maltese, and his name is Romeo. We tell him his parents chose his name well because he has a moustache! He is dark, and looks a real Don Juan. He told us an interesting little story;

Romeo's parents had three daughters born to them. When the first was born she was called Juliet, but unfortunately, she died. Another was born and they again called her Juliet. She, too, died and yet a third, whom they also lost. Hard to believe, but I was assured it was true. So Romeo was alone, and I guess that one of these days Juliet will answer from her balcony, but she won't be Romeo's sister.

Dad, you mentioned reading H V Morton's 'Middle East'. I guess that you will be able to tell Bill and I something about Egypt. I must be honest and confess that we have been to the pyramids twice and wandered about the bazaars, but find far more interesting eating, dancing and visiting our friends. When we come home and are asked, 'And what did you see in Egypt?' we'll say 'Gone with the Wind at the Heliopolis Roxy'.

Jack and Bill with the four good looking Mather girls – lots of personality, and they also dance well!

above, On our way to the Mokattam Hills we passed by the Monastery of the Whirling Dervishes

left, Bill spoke to one of the priests who were calling the faithful to prayer, chanting out their calls from the top of the minarets

42: The Dead City

The battle in the Western Desert was going fast and furious and, I guess, our Commanding Officer was feeling that he would like a bit of the action. He had assembled his officers and addressed them as follows; "Gentlemen, we are unable to lead our troops into battle and so I require you to lead them on a series of guided tours." Thus it came to pass that each officer chose a tour of his special interest. We volunteered to go with our boss Fl/t Langdon, and his choice of places to visit wad, The Moquattam Hills, The City of the Dead and The Citadel. The following are extracts from a long letter we wrote to Mum and Dad:

Firstly, we were off to the Mokattam Hills, and on our way we passed by the Monastery of the Whirling Dervishes where Bill spoke to one of the priests. We had been wondering for some time just what the priests, who were calling the faithful to prayer, were saying when they chanted out their calls from the top of the minarets.

Here is what we learned: The priest was called a muezzin and he sang out, "Allahu Akbar, Allahu Akbar" (Allah is most great) and this he sang out four times. "Hayya 'ala I salah" (come to prayer) twice. There was more too. But we were satisfied that we had learned a little of what we had been hearing, five times a day when we were in our digs and at our work, both places being in very close proximity to mosques and minarets certainly within hearing distance.

To reach the Mokattam Hills, we had four miles of tramping the rocky barren landscape and it was hot! It was just like stepping into a furnace and not only stepping in but staying there. The only reason I can think of for the choice of the Mokattam Hills is so that we would appreciate the relative coolness of the mosques in the City of the Dead, which was our next visit.....

The City of the Dead was a gigantic mausoleum, so silent and comprising dozens of streets, some lined with roofless single storey houses, some with huts, mostly built with mud brick walls.

We suppose it will be hard for readers to realise that people then should continue to build houses, and in these houses to place the bodies of the dead.

We were told that the poorer people, such as the fellahin, would often just cover the body lightly with earth and then take the coffin back home for subsequent use, and if they could not afford a mud house, they would just hire a room.

The rich were there too, with magnificent mortuary palaces, and there were exquisite domes of the mosque tombs of the Pashas and royalty. Some of the tombs were made of marble and had taken years to carve. We visited the tombs of the present king's relatives. It is hard to convey the splendour and elaborate furnishings of these buildings; solid heavy brass doors, thick carpets covering the floors and superb stained glass windows.

The contrast; the deserted dusty streets as one emerges – no, we are wrong when we say deserted, because seemingly from nowhere, emerges a mob of young urchins yelling for "Backshees" (money) – what a country! There were no half measures about our leader. Here we were visiting the Castle of The Mamluks where we took a picture of our pal Roy standing in one of the windows looking out over the Dead City with the famous Citadel in the background.

When we reached the Citadel we had to remove our shoes before stepping across the threshold on to holy ground. In some of the mosques, canvas overshoes were provided and these were known as 'unbelievers shoes'.

What a scene! There were hundreds of worshippers all on their knees facing Mecca, just some of the thousands who come each week, bare-footed having removed their shoes before entering. The Citadel was one of the most spectacular places we had ever seen. Built in the seventeenth century it contained the most elaborate alabaster and marble workmanship, and our guide informed us that it was all worked by hand. We find it difficult to put into words just how beautiful it was. We were struck by the simplicity, the coolness and silence. No pews, no altars, no candles, no saints, just orderliness, space and so cool after the Mokattam Hills.

In a country where the sun always shines we could understand why the muslims found a satisfaction in visiting their mosques. As usual, Bill and I and a couple of the lads found ourselves on forbidden territory – one of the Halls of Bats, rarely visited by tourists, and of course we wanted to photograph the bats which lined the roof in their hundreds.

We had brought some Sashalite flash bulbs and, pointing the camera towards the ceiling, we let the flashes off. Wow! Just after the flash almost the entire company took to the wing. The din was quite frightening and just to show their displeasure the bats decided to shower us. Fortunately, we were wearing our khaki shirts and not our blue uniforms.

The tour was drawing to an end and our Photo Officer, who had organised the outing and had made such a good job of it, completed its excellence by arranging for us to have tea in Groppi's, one of Cairo's best cafes.

Tired out but very satisfied, we climbed into a three ton Chevvy, which our Motor Transport Section had arranged. It was the usual open-backed wagon with slatted seats, the type we had travelled in across the Western Desert, not our usual transport, but then we had a very successful day. We guess our lucky star had once again been shining.

The Dead City today:

Our tour took place in 1942 and it may be of interest to know how dramatically things have changed in Egypt since we visited the Dead City during the war. The Dead City is no longer dead – it is teeming with life – there has been a population explosion. Thousands of squatters have moved into Dead City and it is even crossed by an Express Highway. Whole families now live amongst the tombs, houses and huts, in a place which was once silent.

How fortunate we were to see the city when it was truly a Dead City. (Evidently our lucky star was shining.)

above, The City of the Dead was a huge mausoleum, so silent, comprising dozens of streets, some lined with roofless single storey houses, some with huts, mostly built with mud brick walls

right, Our pal Roy standing in one of the windows looking out over the Dead City and Citadel

above, One of the bats from the Hall

left, When we reached the Citadel we had to remove our shoes before stepping across the threshold onto holy ground

below, The Hall of Bats just before we disturbed them all!

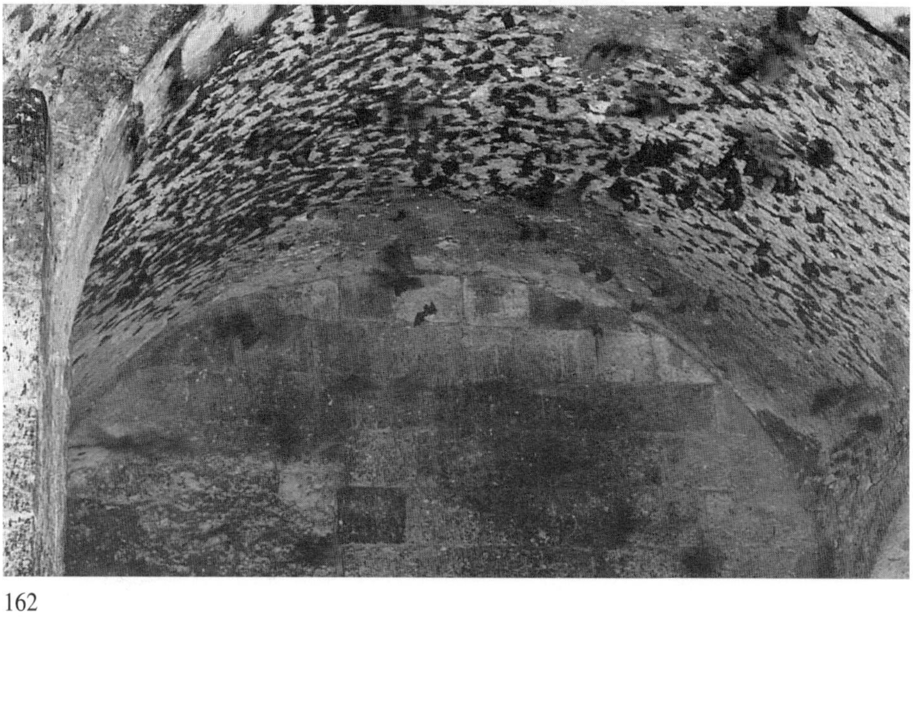

43: Jack Joins the Navy

21st August 1943
LAC Fairs 750832
Chief Naval Intelligence Centre
C/o FMO
ALEXANDRIA

Dear Mum and Dad,

We had a nice surprise the other day. The boss asked if one of us would like to be attached to the Navy for two or three weeks, and to go to Alexandria. We call him the boss, being RAF Volunteer Reservists, and just in for the duration, regular airmen would of course call him Fl/Lt Langdon. Bill suggested that I go on the trip to Alexandria: he is walking out with a young lady called Anna, and he is rather smitten.

Jack with the F24 Aircraft camera

There is little doubt that we must be 'blue eyes' that we should be given the opportunity as to whether or not one of us should go to Alexandria. It is probably because we are continually making suggestions for the improvement of the work practices of the unit, as well as both working extremely hard.

I am now at Alexandria and I travel each day along a magnificent road, which is about 13 miles in length, passing a series of delightful beaches and many lovely villas, of which our HQ is one. The sea is deep blue. On these calm summer days it seems like a holiday, and it's hard to believe that there is a war on.

I have quite a pleasant job photographing each ship of the Sicilian invasion fleet, for which we have adapted an F24 Aircraft camera, which is quite heavy, and not really ideal for the type of photographs that I am taking, but despite that the results are quite good. The camera takes 125 exposures on each roll, saving re-loading, which is not so easy whilst wallowing about on the air-sea rescue launch.

I work with an RAF officer on an Air-sea rescue launch which operates just outside Alexandria Harbour, and when we draw alongside the ships, he calls to the bridge through a megaphone "What is the name of your vessel?" whilst I take a photograph. One of the purposes of the photographs is for recognition from aircraft – they are to be used by our pilots. (I heard later that the next volume of Jane's Ships also used some of the photographs to update.)

Whilst I am busy photographing the ships that are taking part in the invasion of Sicily, brother Bill has a very interesting job. He is in charge of the mosaic section where they are working on the production of photographic mosaic maps of the harbours, airfields, beaches and other military installations on the island of Sicily. These mosaics are especially interesting when viewed through a stereoscope, a simple device that enables one to see the detail in three dimensions.

I am billeted in a hotel, and now live by the sea front. I am hoping to arrange for Bill to come and stay with me for a few days, which would be wonderful, because everything is just about as good as it could be in the services. The food and sleeping arrangements are good. I do not even have to make my own bed. At night we sleep with the balcony door open, and let the sea breezes float right in. When I say we, it turns out that the bloke who shares the room with me hails from Birkenhead too. His name is Tom Finney and he lives in Well Lane, Birkenhead. I have quite a long tram journey each day, costing about eight shillings a week, but this is very pleasant, and taking all in all, I am living a life of ease, with no parades, and everything reminding me more of civvy street each day.

The day after I arrived I met Colonel Steffel's daughter, June, just near to my hotel, and I went with her to her friend's home. Lillian and her Mum were there too. I had met the family before in Cairo and I was invited to stay for supper. It was quite nice meeting them as they were the first people I had met here. I haven't been lonely though. A few days afterwards I met a couple of girls whom I knew from Cairo. I say a couple of girls but one is

There were many lovely villas, of which our HQ is one

above, They invited me to a party and I had a very pleasant time

a child of 16 and the other is Swiss. Bill and I call her Swiss Miss, she is 27 and works for a rich Egyptian family, looking after their daughter. Both girls dance very nicely.

They invited me to a party and I had a very pleasant time. It was held in one of those lovely big houses with panelled walls and rooms that are as big as ballrooms. There were a lot of soldiers there. Usually I am not fond of these gatherings where there are so many troops, I like something more personal, but, nevertheless, I did enjoy myself. It was the usual games, tea and cakes affair, and of course everything was in perfect taste, especially the cakes. We danced and played games and, if Bill comes, I will most certainly take him along with me to one of these parties.

Some odd things happen in this country. A rather interesting case is in the courts at the moment; A party are claiming £500 damages from the Egyptian State Telegraph Company. A sheik received a wire saying his sister had died and that her body would be arriving by train at a certain time. He made preparations for a grand funeral and informed all his relatives, numbering well over 100. He also employed professional mourners and the crowd thronged the station platform, the relatives moaning and the professional weepers with tears streaming down their faces. Suddenly, the body stepped down from the train with her face wreathed in smiles. Some of the women fainted thinking it was a ghost. Guess what? The clerk at the telegraph office had made a mistake in an Arabic word. Ah well, it adds interest to life!

It seems a bit odd being away from Bill but I guess I will cope. I must sign off now, have a shower, and get myself ready for dinner.

Lots of love, God bless,

Jack.

(This is the letter I sent home but I have added parts to the narrative that would not have been allowed during the war because of censorship.)

above, King Farouk's Ras El Tin Palace in Alexandria where we bribed the guards to let us in and we jumped on the Queen's bed

left, The United Forces Club where they must have known that we had come from the palace because they had the red carpet out!

44: The Three Palaces

We are in Alexandria, Egypt, and decide that as a change from the tent in the desert, we would visit a palace. Naturally, as lowly RAF lads we were not ever invited to a palace, but we thought that it would be interesting to see inside one and here is how we managed to visit and see how the other half lived:

We were on holiday in Alexandria, where King Farouk had quite a nice palace. In fact it was bigger than his huge Abdine Palace, which was in a very poor area of Cairo. We were spending a very pleasant week's leave staying at a Toc-H hostel and, as one does on holiday, we were looking for somewhere to visit when we came upon the King's Ras el Tin Palace. The most beautiful grounds surrounded the palace and the gate was open so we thought that we would take a look around. We could always say 'Sorry, we didn't know that visitors were not allowed.' It was a lovely morning and was just like an English Spring. Indeed, everything in the garden was lovely. Our Bill wasn't satisfied with just the garden and suggested that it would be very interesting to look around the palace.

A pal of ours from Bebington, who was sharing our holiday, suggested to Bill, "Why don't you ask one of the two policemen who are guarding the door what are the chances of us looking over the palace?" So off Bill went on what we thought was a fruitless errand. But Bill came back smiling and said that he had given one of the policemen some 'backshees' and he had said okay. We should mention that the police were so poorly paid that although Bill only gave him a modest sum, it was equivalent to a month's wages.

King Farouk's Ras El Tin Palace in Alexandria:

The rooms were very grand just like the National Trust houses that one sees in our country. The policemen were not too sure of our behaviour and one of them stayed with us to see that we conducted ourselves in a seemly manner, which of course, we did. That is until we arrived at the Queen's bedroom, which was all frills, when Ken and Bill decided to bounce up and down on the Queen's bed. I think they just wanted to swank to the lads back at the camp. The policeman was very annoyed shouting out, "Macnoon... macnoon" which is Arabic for ... "Are you mad?"

I guess that young people are a bit macnoon at times, which is as it should be. Our visit was a real experience and we were quite chuffed with ourselves. Looking back I'm quite sure that King Farouk would have been mad and I think that the RAF authorities would have had us on the carpet had they known what some of their lower ranks were up to.

The palace was unoccupied – no kitchen staff – so we had to eat elsewhere. Alex' is so well off for service clubs that we were spoilt for choice. However, we finished up at the United Forces Club where they must have known that we had come from the palace because they had the red carpet out.

Queen Farida's Palace:

We were actually invited to a palace, not so big as the royal palace in Alexandria, but a palace back in Heliopolis where Queen Farida had been in residence and here is how:

It was a lovely afternoon and we were quite excited. We had been invited for tea by Elise a young lady who lived with her rich uncle and so it was very special for us because it is not every day that one is invited to tea in a palace, during which the sense of occasion was heightened by the presence of a young man playing a Chopin waltz on a grand piano. You will, perhaps, smile when we tell you that the previous night we had placed our uniform trousers under the sheet on the bed and slept on them so that they would have a nice crease. This was, of course, something that many blokes in Blighty did.

On our arrival we had been greeted by a manservant who announced us. He didn't say 'LACs Jack and Bill Fairs' – just 'Two RAF men'. It was interesting that at the time of our visit we had moved from the swanky block in Heliopolis itself and we were now living in tented camp just on the outskirts of the town. To be seated in a palace, therefore, was like going from rags to riches, although going from 'rags to riches' was was just a play on words because we were reasonably turned out.

Our hostess and her cousin, Wilhelmina, made us very welcome. We were served afternoon tea with dainty sandwiches and strawberry cake with lashings of cream. Elise said that she would make us a strawberry cake to take back to camp and she was as good as her word. The following week she had made a cake for us and one of the lads asked whether it had been made by a princess! With Elise residing in the house in which Queen Farida had lived, it wasn't surprising that she could regale us with some anecdotes and this she did:

She said that young 18 year old King Farouk had set his eyes on a pretty young girl of 15 years of age. Her name was Safinaz Yulficar. She was from an important family of Turkish descent. Her father was a judge and her mother was one of Queen Nazli's ladies in waiting.

Farouk had driven his Alfa Romeo convertible to the girl's home and asked her to marry him. But she had said, I must ask my father." Farouk said, "Bring him." But Safinaz said, "He is on his way to Beirut for a 14 day holiday and is to board a ship at Port Said." Farouk had the ship stopped before it left port and the judge was ordered to return. The father was not too keen about the marriage saying that his daughter was too young, but Farouk wasn't having any. He made the judge a Pasha (Lord) and Ambassador to Persia so all were happy.

The next week was Safinaz's birthday and Farouk gave her a cheque for $50,000 and a diamond ring worth about the same amount and a new name 'Farida'. (Arabic for 'Only One') Elise also told us that Farouk's wedding cake was 12 feet high and 6 feet in diameter and that he surprised his new wife every day with a different present and did so for the first 12 months.

Strange really, the thing that remains in our minds about our visit to the palace was sitting in a conversation chair which we had not seen before. This was, in fact, two chairs side by side facing in opposite directions, joined together so that those seated are facing one

above, Queen Farida's Palace was now home to Elise a young lady who lived with her rich uncle

below, Elise with Jack on the balcony

another in close proximity. They are also sometimes known as 'loving chairs'.

We thoroughly enjoyed our visit to Elise and her cousin adding yet another section to the patchwork quilt of our overseas experiences. Reading a letter that we sent to Mum and Dad the following week I see that we wrote of our visit, sent a photograph, and mentioned that we had taken the two girls to the cinema.

King Farouk's Abdin Palace, Cairo:

There was quite a buzz in the unit today, a strange rumour that our tanks had surrounded King Farouk's Abdin Palace and burst in through the gates. This was confirmed later in the day as news trickled down from our Middle East HQ, although none of this was either reported in the newspapers or broadcast.

It seemed that a battalion of 600 British troops along with tanks and armoured cars had surrounded the palace grounds and then six burly officers, all over six feet in height, had approached the palace and one had shot the lock off the palace gates.

It was said that the king had refused to appoint a prime minister of our choosing and that he wished to appoint a minister who was considered decidedly pro-German. Sir Miles Lampson, our Ambassador, who disliked the young king, decided that he would have none of it and he made the decision to virtually storm the palace. The king had to back down. We saw nothing of this event in the press and so apart from those who witnessed the assault on the palace grounds, this very unusual event went virtually unnoticed.

The King's Palace in Cairo was huge. It had 550 rooms and a garage which contained over 200 cars. What he wanted this number for one would never know, but what was different is that he had informed the police that if they saw a red Cadillac Convertible, it was his and that, by law, only he would be allowed to have red cars.

Well, enough about palaces and royalty. We make our way back quietly to our tent in the desert and snuggle down for a good night's sleep. No marble floors for us – just sand.

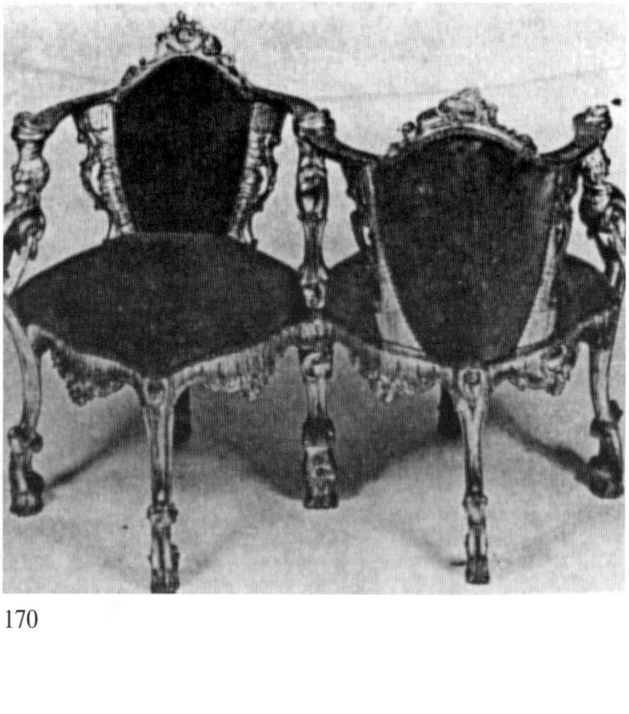

The unusual 'loving chair' at the palace

45: The Tura Caves

We were so busy at the unit that we were running out of photographic paper for printing the photographs so off we went to the Tura Caves, a huge supply depot in the Mokattam Hills a few miles from our unit. These were no ordinary caves. The Tura Caves were a few miles from the Pyramids of Giza and this was the place where thousands of Egyptians had toiled to hew the blocks of stone which were then transported across the Nile and used in the construction of the Pyramids. These wonderful artificial caves were now serving a most useful purpose – they had been converted into bombproof warehouses and workshops. It was here that I saw with amazement a mountain of photographic paper. I can think of no other way to describe it. Having worked for Kodak Wholesale in 1933 I had been used to seeing large quantities of paper, but this lot took my breath away – phew!

I learned that once again great numbers of Egyptians were working in these caves, not as an army of slaves as when building the pyramids, but now as paid labourers and without doubt, much happier workers. These vast caverns had been ignored for centuries and consequently a tremendous amount of work was required to bring them into use. Today's methods of working had not changed much from those early days thousands of years ago when the Pyramids were built. Yes, today the labourers had dug away at a hillside with small picks and shovels piling the rubble in wicker baskets for tipping further down the hillside whilst young children took the heavier stones on panniers fixed on each side of donkeys. The huge caves had been whitewashed and the floors concreted – very necessary because one of the

The Pyramids were built of stone from the caves

above, The Pyramids of Giza were just visible a few miles from the mouth of the Tura Caves

left, Three airmen holding the finished repaired propeller caves was being used as a bomb store. Others were engineering workshops for III RAF Maintenance Unit and I heard subsequently that another was used to store the treasures of Tutankhamun for the duration of the war.

The Arabs were suspicious of going into the inner recesses of the caves and it is said that our troops had come upon great lengths of plaited reed ropes which were extremely thick, left by the ancient Egyptian quarrymen of five thousand years ago, and that after the war the British Museum received many requests to buy the rope – probably just a tale.

On our return journey our driver called to see a pal of his who was an aircraft fitter. A sergeant and some local natives had set up a small engineering workshop. It wasn't the engineering shop that was the surprise, but the type of work that they had undertaken. They were actually repairing and reforming the blades of aircraft propellers, a job that was only considered possible with expensive presses and twisting machinery. The sergeant explained how they had purchased some second-hand presses costing about £25 each and a heavier press that had come from Turkey where it had been used for pressing grapes. Together with motor car jacks and scrap metal they had made a twisting machine enabling them to make a perfect job of straightening an airscrew. The unusual photograph taken from above shows three airmen holding the finished repaired propeller.

The sergeant said it all sounded very simple but when he explained that the airscrew had to be cleaned and stripped then annealed in a bath of salt liquid with heat until they are soft enough to be bent, then passed through a series of presses, immersed in molten salt, followed by a swift plunge into cold water to harden them, you will understand that it was quite a job! We learned that there were many such small workshops all over Cairo created by RAF technical officers who were dealing with the many hundreds of damaged aircraft.

Broadcasting Home:

One day Bill said, "I've got an idea, let's see if we can broadcast home. Mum would like that and we could save the cost of a stamp." He's the twin with a sense of humour! Bill is also the one with the ideas and he usually leaves me to carry them out. I told him that surely it could not be as easy as all that! However, off we went to the Egyptian Broadcasting Company, whom we understood had modelled themselves on our own BBC. Quite a smart young Egyptian fellow greeted us at the reception desk saying, "Good afternoon gentlemen." Wasn't that a nice greeting? I had told Bill that we should give our buttons an extra shine and that we must appear smart to make a good impression.

The outcome was that he said, "You have a good chance of sending a message". We were to prepare a script of about 150 words but we must bear in mind that they had a very long list and that we would have to be patient.

Later that evening when we were chatting about the day's events we glanced towards the heavens and saw that our lucky stars were shining and felt that to be a good omen. It was indeed, a good omen. Two weeks afterwards we had a call to present ourselves at the studio – well it wasn't really a studio but a courtyard – and on the floor was a gramophone and we said our piece into a microphone, our message being recorded on a vinyl record. One hundred and eighty words in all. Just what we said we cannot recall, apart from telling Dad to keep our tandem oiled ready for our return.

The whole exercise of our broadcast was a bit of fun really. The message was broadcast just before the news. Mum had been informed in advance and the local paper at home had mentioned the fact – fame at last!

above, Hello, soldier!

right, I'm in the RAF! Are you coming out?

below, The sisters' flat in Zamalek, with Ethelwyn, back left, and Sylvia next to Jack with some of their young friends

46: Some Very Interesting People

Two Sisters, Norman Shirley and the Atkinsons:

Bill and I had the good fortune to meet some very interesting people during our time overseas and such was the case with the two Broadbent sisters, Sylvia and Dorothy Ethelwyn. They were in their mid-thirties and I think Bill and I regarded them as one would an aunt.

Dorothy Ethelwyn was governess to King Farouk's sisters, the princesses Faiza and Fawzia and she lived at the palace. When we visited her and her sister, though, it was at their apartment in Zamalek, a suburb of Cairo. We were initially unaware of Dorothy's position at the palace, although she mentioned that she was a teacher and it was not until later that we learned that she was in fact governess to the young princesses and she enjoyed a friendly relationship with the young King Farouk. It seemed almost like Anna and the King of Siam.

When Bill and I were free on Friday evenings we would go to the apartment in Zamalek where the sisters had invited some of the soldiers who were on leave from the desert. There we chatted with the lads to make them feel at home and then handed out refreshments. At the end of the evening Dorothy held a prayer meeting. Both sisters were quite religious. On one occasion after prayers, Miss Broadbent disappeared into another room and through the door came the strains of two hymns played on the piano, 'Rose of Galilee' and 'Abide with Me'. She then pulled out an extremely valuable violin which she told us was a 'Amity' and on this gave a rendering of 'Humoresque' by Dvorak and ended with a Schumann lullaby.

On special occasions Dorothy would wear her old school blazer. At her school she had been captain of Leinster House first eleven hockey team and the blazer was splendid. It was white with gold trimmings and on the pocket the initials 'LHS' in gold filigree. On Empire Day or Armistice Day she would put on the regalia of a full-blown Ranger Girl Guide. This consisted of a uniform topped by a digger style hat, augmented with a whistle and a lanyard, a compass and a boy scout multi-purpose knife. Thus even a peaceful stroll through urban Cairo was inclined to take on the brave aspect of an expedition into the wilds.

Before we opened our account with Barclays Bank Miss Broadbent looked after our spare cash. I could hardly conclude without saying that Miss Broadbent had a passionate interest in flying. She passed all the tests necessary for her various licenses and over the years achieved her ambition to qualify as a multi-engined pilot. We learned later that as she had more or less grown up with the first generation of Egyptian air captains, they were always ready to invite her into the cockpits of their Viscounts and Comets when as an elderly lady she would travel back to England.

Our friendship with Miss Dorothy Ethelwyn lasted for many years. We felt that it had been a privilege to know her. We were still corresponding with her when she was in her nineties until she left for that better land where she would not need the protection of a multi-purpose scout knife. Miss Broadbent's father, E Hamer Broadbent, a small man with a goatee beard, and from a Suffolk vicarage, was a writer on religious subjects. We were told that he once earned the admiration of court officials by demonstrating with complete success the Malayan technique of shinning up a palm tree with bare feet, his toes clamping themselves to the knobbly parts. We learned also that he performed a small operation upon himself when engaged in a camel trek across the Gobi Desert. A most unusual man.

Norman Shirley:

For this part of our adventures we move forward almost 60 years to May 2000 in England. Bill and I were having our usual morning stroll chatting about yesteryear. We have an autograph book which we mentioned earlier and which we each hold for about six months then pass it over to the other. Bill said that the previous evening he had been scanning the pages and came across one with a photograph of Norman Shirley, taken in Heliopolis with palm tree in the background, with an inscription on the page;

'Not ships that pass in the night, but friends who please god will meet often, Norman Shirley, DFM'

We were interested to know why Norman had been awarded the DFM. It was a surprise that an LAC had been awarded a medal, usually the preserve of aircrew. I told Bill that I would try to find out where Norman was today. I seemed to recall that I had seen a photograph of Norman in a book 'Eyes of the RAF' written by Roy C Nesbitt who had written 14 books including 'The History of the RAF' and had served as a navigator in WW2. I wrote to him asking if he could give me Norman Shirley's address and he was kind enough to write back;

Dear Jack,

The work on 'The Eyes of the RAF' goes back a long way. I was asked by the Association of RAF Photo Officers to write the history and the subsequent work generated over one thousand letters. Working through all this correspondence I was able to come across an address for Norman Shirley but this was some 13 years ago. I suggest you ask Directory Enquiries. I do hope all goes well and that you have a splendid reunion.

Kind regards,

Roy C Nesbitt.

I obtained Norman's number through directory enquiries and phoned to see that he was there. He was, and very surprised to hear my voice after 56 years. I told him that Bill and I would like to know about his award and he wrote as follows;

Dear Jack and Bill,

Your phone call was a great surprise and here is a thumb-nail sketch of my life since my return to England from the Middle East:

I married the girl who had waited for me in 1944 and this was the most wonderful thing that happened to me. My working life has been almost entirely in University; my discipline has been

Metallurgy. Photography has been an underlying theme in Radiology and Crystallography. Still a photo man you see! I took anatomy and did some original research into metal inserts into the human body, such as hip replacements.

Now the answer to your query about the award – DFM: I had done 22 operational sorties before I arrived in Malta which, as you will recall, was under siege and there was a constant patrol of enemy fighters somewhere in the skies above and around the island. We arrived in a blaze of ack ack and dogfights, one of our pilots sailed down in his 'chute in front of us calmly lit a cigarette and just strolled away. That was Luqua in Malta.

I went on to complete 13 more sorties, number 13 with F/Lt White and we were shot down by an Me109 whilst landing. We had been attacked prior to this and although I tried to persuade him to remain airborne as we were faster at sea level than a 109 (I had learned a lot from F/Lt Warburton), White decided to land. As I expected they came in about halfway through our approach, I saw part of the rudder fly off and a piece of the wing then a terrific bang in front when the armour plate of the Very Light Box exploded and I was hit in several places including the left lower abdomen, which was painful.

Norman Shirley, DFM

I was also hit in the teeth and spitting blood, quite unable to talk to my pilot. White landed well considering but I was busy putting out fires caused by the exploding Very Lights. I was about to leave when I saw that the air intake behind him was ablaze and he was sitting in his seat staring at it and not moving so I went along the plane put the fire out and shoved him through the cockpit sidelight. When I tried to get out myself my legs wouldn't work so he pulled me through. All wasn't over then. The 109s sprayed both of us and also the first aid rescue services whom I thought were marvellous.

The Beaufighter did not explode and I was able to receive some treatment on the ground beside the plane before being rushed by stretcher to the Medical Room and then by ambulance to hospital. I was in a hospital bed with my legs sand-bagged apart unable to see clearly. I had just had surgery to remove a splinter of cannon shell from my left eye and my right eye was weeping in sympathy, neither could I speak properly through swollen gums and the stumps of my departed teeth.

Through the haze and pain I saw a group of officers at the foot of the bed. One of them pinned a medal on the front of my pyjamas and I was told that I had received the immediate award of the DFM. Apparently it has to be awarded within three days of the incident and is the same as the King awarding it in the heat of battle. I do not know how true this is but as you can see there is no death and glory stuff about this incident, I give it to you straight off the cuff.

I apologise to you both for the rotten typing and for the presentation. I feel that we are not of this 'e-mail' generation.

Sincerely yours,

Norman.

Well, we have done what a great many people would like to do asking ourselves 'I wonder what happened to so and so'. We have, with a little diligence, gone back and found an answer – the answer to 'What happened to Norman?'

The Atkinson Family:

I think it would also be appropriate to mention the Atkinson family. Reading our letters home we seem to have taken the girls out on several occasions:

The Atkinson family lived in an apartment, not a house like we do in England, and they had kindly invited me for a meal (Bill was out with his girl friend, Anna). The girls had been educated at the English School in Heliopolis, their mother was Italian, and their father, although English by birth, had a strong foreign accent, probably through living in India for many years. The mum was quite young, played the piano well and she came to our church dances, not so much as a chaperone, but because she enjoyed them. We took both the girls out on their own, indeed, Bill and I would not have taken any girls out if they had been chaperoned! Their brother, Sidney, had listened to our stories of photography in the RAF and had joined locally although he did not serve on our unit.

A pleasant lunch over, the girls decided that later in the week we should go on a picnic, and our picture shows us setting out, although not planned it would seem that together with our letters home and our pictures we had virtually an illustrated diary. We had promised Mum and Dad and sister Gladys that we would keep them fully informed of our life overseas and this we were doing in very full measure.

Back to the Atkinsons: Iona had quite a sweet voice and she sang on the Cairo Radio, and her sister Doris, who was a good looking girl, was a member of a local dramatic society and we saw her at The Opera House one evening. Not so exciting, but we mention the family because they are another patch of the qulit that we are assembling of our life overseas.

Off for a picnic, Ruby, Jack, Doris, Sydney and Iona, with Bill behind camera

47: The Birthday

And so it came to pass that on 25th August 1918 the midwife called at the home of Mr and Mrs Fairs for an important event.

It was to be the birth of a son, a bonny child weighing 8lbs 2oz, but lo and behold, the midwife made a special announcement, "Mrs Fairs, I have a surprise for you, and some bad news, I'm sorry to tell you that there is another one". It was almost unbelievable that mother was unaware that she had been carrying two 8lb babies, nevertheless she assures us that this was true.

So the identical twins, Jack and Bill Fairs, make their appearance, and we bet that mother was glad to get rid of us; remembering some of the stories that she told us of when we were young, we are sure that there were many other times when she would have been glad to get rid of us. Dad used to tell us that there were times when he would come home from his work and find four of us all crying – mother, our sister, who was just three years older than us and Bill and I.

We are pleased to say that 24 years have passed, and mother has become quite fond of us, anyway she intimates that she has. It was in the early years when we were a handful (that's putting it mildly) mother used to say that she wouldn't wish twins on anyone.

Included in this chapter is a letter (N°25) that Bill sent home, which tells how we spent our 24th birthday.

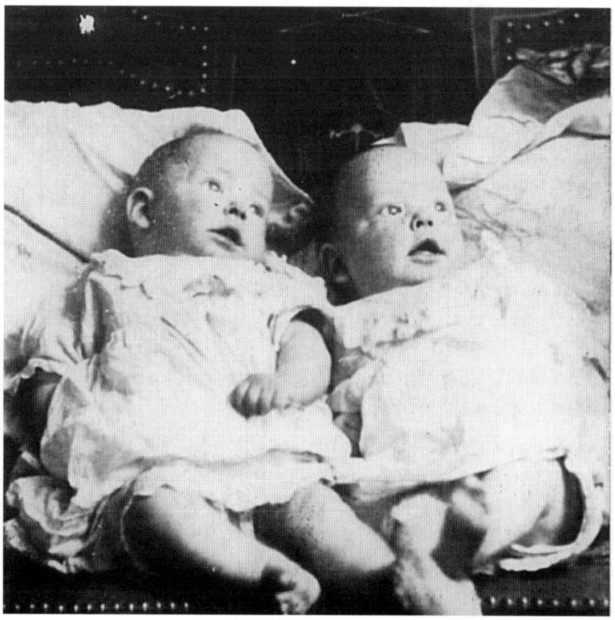

Jack and Bill in their younger days

25th August 1942
75091 LAC Fairs W
MEIU
MEF

'Our Birthday'

Dear Mum and Dad,

Well, here we are, almost one quarter of a century old. I thought it would be an idea to write today, although I might not be able to fill this card. I think you would like to know just how we have spent the day, so here goes;

We rose about 8.30am, cleaned our bedspace, a shower, and off to the Victory Club. There was Peter waiting for us, very precise is our Peter. He stood up and shook hands, wishing us all the best. We had met Peter at the Gezira Club. He was dressed in hospital blue – he had been wounded in the desert and because the army base hospital was nearby, the walking wounded were allowed out for recreation and we had formed a friendship.

It was our Toc-H job to make hospital visits, this was something similar, although we had just been sitting at adjoining tables and got into conversation. We then ordered eggs, sausage, chips and coffee. This we followed by peaches and ice cream, and yet another coffee. This meal took some time, and when it was over we went to our paper shop and collected the 'Parade' magazine, which incidentally, I hope you are receiving fairly regularly. Then according to plan, we caught a train to the Big Club. Here we decided it would be fruit salad and ice cream, together with lemonade. It was very quiet indeed at the club today, we like it like this, we aren't ones for crowds.

We spent a couple of hours reading and talking. Peter again in style doing most of the talking, this suited us though, because it was rather hot. On our way back to camp, and again according to plan, I called on Anna's friend, and here we received a present for Jack and one for myself. Guess what? For each of us six very large excellent quality handkerchiefs, each with an initial in the corner. The initials were embroidered and were extremely well done by Anna herself. We won't use them until we get home, as we are well supplied with hankies. The main reason, though, is because the laundry do not use very good soap and they would rot after some time

We celebrated today by using one of the Lever's easy shaving sticks you sent out. Oh boy, what a difference from the ones made locally. Incidentally, Mum, we both have complete kits, we want for nothing, and most of our clothes are nearly new. We have laundry done four times per week. You see, out here things need washing very regularly, our working clothes are done by the RAF.

Just in case you have not received our previous letters, we received your cable of birthday greetings. Thank you very much, and we sincerely hope that next year we will be able to save the price of a cable. As a matter of fact, we have just risen, you see we are on nights tonight, so we always have a few hours sleep before going on duty. Jack has just asked me to hurry up and get ready to go for a stroll, this being our usual procedure, just as you and Dad go down Lever's Causeway. Well, as I want to post this today, I'll close.

Bye for now, Your loving sons,

Jack and Bill.

The Fairs Folly:

With the tremendous increase in demand for photographs, it was realised that a change was required in our method of production. Our boss being well aware of our enthusiasm for

above, Flt/Lt J Telles-Langdon, the officer in charge of recreation on our unit, with the two pretty girls we accompanied

right, The girls pose close to the Sphinx and the Great Pyramid

Mena House Hotel adjacent to the pyramids where we entertained the girls was the meeting place of the big three – Roosevelt, Churchill and 'Uncle' Joe Stalin

nnovation and improvement, called us both into his office and said, "You two are full of bright ideas, I want you to draw up plans for a new darkroom."

We were thrilled that we had been given this task, and spent the next few days carefully observing the flow of work, and making sure that the materials required were always close to hand. At MEIU our department was concerned with the production of photographic prints, enlargements and mosaics; the interpretation and model making, although in the same building, were separate departments. There was very little red tape on the unit, nd although it was somewhat unusual for a couple of LACs to design a darkroom, Bill and I thought it was a good idea. We must mention that some of the lads referred to the new darkroom as 'The Fairs Folly'. The boss, Flt/Lt Langdon, though, was pleased with the plan. The works and bricks department were called in, and, hey ho, there we were with a nice new darkroom. We had arranged six identical printing machine positions and three enlargers, with the developing dishes within easy reach. It all worked out very well.

We were called into the office a week or two later, and the boss said, "I've got some good news and some bad news for you. The good news which will please you is that you have both been put forward for a mention in dispatches, the bad news is that the unit has used up its allowance of honours." Bill and I were, of course, pleased. We had no idea that a mention in despatches could be awarded for anything other than bravery on the field of battle, and though it had come to naught it was gratifying to know that our efforts had been appreciated.

Some weeks earlier I had designed a colour coded system for the film library. We had thousands of tins of film which needed to be easy to retrieve from the library. There were 14 different sections in the library, and each required a different label on the end of the tim. Bill had been asked to design a leaflet giving instructions for making photographic mosaics, and I guess that the boss had considered our endeavours when he proposed our mention.

A·Photographic Sortie:

I was developing some buckshees (private photographs) when the boss, Flt/Lt Langdon, happened to pass, looking over my shoulder he watched as the image of a couple of our girl friends gradually appeared in the dish. He seemed very interested and said, "Fairs, what do you say to a little photographic sortie this afternoon?" "It's OK with me, sir," was my reply. So a little later, camera at the ready, we made our way and it came to pass that my bright star had been shining. Although we had not chosen a target for the day, a chance encounter with two pretty English girls completed our formation. It was strange really, I cannot recall how we met. Usually we met girls in service clubs, but officers and other ranks do not, of course, use the same clubs. The girls, however, were keen to join our little expedition.

My lucky star must have been shining because there were literally tens of thousands of servicemen in Cairo, who would have given a week's pay to escort these two pretty girls on a tour of the sights of Egypt. Talking about a week's pay, we took the girls to the Mena House Hotel adjacent to the pyramids, where the rich people eat, and I had the honour to pay the bill, the cost being a little more than a week's pay! We had quite an interesting chat during lunch, the boss telling how the Nile fed by the far off Abyssinian rains, the river running for 500 miles and then being diverted into canals like arteries, and then into lesser veins. The water is then lifted by water-wheels and by the peasants with leather buckets to provide the water for the fields of maize, cotton and tomatoes etc. We actually saw the leather buckets being used, and also a water-wheel. The girls were quite thrilled with the opportunity of exploring scenes far away from the city and seeing sights that had not changed for five thousand years.

We visited a village on our way from the pyramids. The girls had not been to one before, and they were shocked at the poverty. A little ragged girl whose clothes were just a series of patches stitched together, and mud hovels that were falling to pieces. The boss told us an interesting fact. The Royal Society of Agriculture had erected on their model farm a village with small well-built houses with concrete roofing. The Arab peasants, however, would not use them, they much preferred their mud huts, because they were warmer in winter and cooler in summer, and so the traditional way of doing things had proved the best.

We visited the Pyramids of Giza, the Sphinx and the Citadel. I found it all very interesting, it is usually when one is showing friends around that we go visiting ourselves and learn a little too. I let the boss lead our tour, which was a wise choice, for he had been leading tours for the airmen, and was quite knowledgeable about the sights. We also visited mosques, and climbed the inside of the minarets where the Mueddin, usually a blind man, calls the people to prayer. I had no idea how the boss usually passed his off duty hours, but I do know that he was chuffed with the day out, and he said so, and during the next few days we printed a nice set of photographs for the girls to send to their families. I should add that Flt/Lt Telles Langdon was the officer in charge of recreation on our unit, so important to servicemen, and this expedition of course came under the heading of 'recreation'.

A little ragged girl whose clothes were just patches stitched together carries her baby sister oblivious of the flies

above, Canada House, like Toc-H, was superior

top left, Jack and friends on the back of the truck

left, We had a pleasant walk along the sea front for about 13 miles

left, He steered a big laundry iron with his foot spraying by mouth

48: Night of the Big Fish

It all happened during our ten day's leave in the Egyptian Port of Alexandria, with a friend, Jack Crimes from Bromborough. Jack worked for the RAF 52 MT Company (motor transport) and his job was to arrange deliveries and so what better than that he should arrange to deliver Bill and I, and himself of course, to Alexandria on our holiday. This he did even to the extent of arranging to collect us from our camp gates on a huge American Mack Truck.

Arriving at Alexandria we presented ourselves at Toc-H where we had previously written to book rooms, but found, to our disappointment, that our letter had not arrived and there was 'no room at the inn'. We had, however, heard that Canada House, like Toc-H, was superior and we were fortunate to find that they could accommodate us – Oh Boy! What a place – it was a huge palatial house originally owned by a rich Syrian. It had been converted into a hostel for the Royal Canadian Air Force for all ranks, although 75% of those present were officers. It was a super place, our bright star was certainly shining and it was quite refreshing to find that the barrier between officers and men was almost non existent. Later that evening at ten o' clock a F/Lt knocked on the door and asked if we would like to go to a party, apparently someone had phoned with an invitation for six. We had nothing special to do, in fact we were just about to retire to bed, so we cancelled our order for sandwiches and accompanied the F/lt and two warrant officers to the party.

The door was opened by a young lady in a long evening dress and there were six other girls all dressed for the ball. The rest of the motley throng was composed of a captain with a monocle, a naval officer and three Egyptian men, two of whom had obviously been educated at public schools in England. Boy! Did they speak far back! It was fortunate that we had our pal Jack with us as he had worked with the Civil Service in London and was able to interpret for us.

We talked and danced and sat. We were rapidly coming to the conclusion that it wasn't really our sort of party – that was until we sat down for supper. Then we felt very much at home. On the table was the most lavish array of food that we had ever seen, apart from in pictures in American magazines. Yes sir! It was fit for a king. In fact it would not have surprised us if King Farouk himself had walked in. He didn't and we marvelled at the big fish that seemed to stretch the length of the table. It was on a silver tray with olives for eyes and dressed for a banquet, surrounded by shrimps, parsley and what have you....

We proceeded to uncover its backbone and managed very well. Our next trick was to cause part of the turkey to disappear and then we started on the rest of the table and did ourselves handsome. it was one of the nicest fish that we had ever seen and was the outstanding thing about the party.

It took us until about 2am to clear the rest of the table and after a taxi home, a wash and a couple of indigestion tablets we were in bed with that satisfied feeling that we had experienced a memorable night... 'The Night of the Big Fish'. Quite unusual and it left an indelible impression upon our memories.

The next morning we had a very pleasant walk along the sea front which stretched for about 13 miles. It was full of interest and we admired many lovely villas owned by the rich who had without doubt made their fortunes from cotton. We found Alexandria to be quite European compared with Cairo, no doubt due to being a port there were many Greeks, Swiss, Italians, Syrians and Armenians there and it was much cleaner than Cairo. Whilst on our tour we came upon an excellent photographic studio. We went in and introduced ourselves to the owner telling him of our intention to open a studio in England when we returned home. He was kind enough to spend time showing us his studio and workrooms not only that but he took a photograph of Bill and I and said, "If you call tomorrow I will give you the results." We called and he gave us without payment the photographs and the negatives. We were quite surprised and naturally very pleased. Mum was too, when she saw how her sons were looking at that moment in time.

I am jumping ahead a little. Still on the tour, Bill walking ahead called out, "Just come and see this Dhobi wallah." (laundry man) Not quite the same as at home. He was steering a big laundry iron with his foot and skilfully spraying the ironing with his talking orifice. Yes! He was taking a swig of water from a bottle and spraying the clothing with his mouth, so skilful that it was a joy to watch, that is unless one felt unhappy about him spitting upon your laundry. Bill was chatting to our pal Jack saying how lucky we were not just because we were enjoying ourselves on holiday with such a variety of scenes full of interest, but also because we had the good fortune to be working for a unit that enabled us to play a part in photographic intelligence gathering. Yes, working at our own profession and enjoying every minute of it, well, almost. There were odd times when we were cheesed off, but very few and we only remember the good times ...

49: The WAAFs

We are off today and the sun is shining, but we have a parade at 09.30 and it's rather special – a unit photograph of MEIU, yes! Someone has built up a little empire and they want a photo for the album. Bill and I had not realised the unit was quite so big because with working shifts, quite a number of personnel would be resting. Even so we were quite surprised that the unit had grown so big, and this was just the photographic production side together with interpretation. When one added the squadrons of reconnaissance aircraft it was quite considerable. On the unit photograph Bill and I are among the group of six at the extreme right. So for those who thought that we would be near the centre – no, we are shy and retiring!

A short while ago we met up with some WAAFs, to be exact there were four and they were all Scottish wireless operators. So we co-opted another member to our party, Archie, a Scottish lad, and there we were – a group of eight. The girls newly arrived from England, were thoroughly enjoying themselves. We chaperoned them (!), visiting some of the wonders of Egypt, and they were bubbling over with excitement. We had wanted to ask them about conditions in Blighty, but we didn't get a chance and we had to leave that for another meeting.

'someone's little empire' – ME1U – I never realised how many we were. Bill and I extreme right

The four lads and the four WAAFs sat overlooking Cairo from the Citadel with the Sultan's Hassan Mosque and the Mosque of El Rifai in the foreground

We determined to give the girls an afternoon that they would remember, and so we took them on a tour of some of the sights of Cairo. The Mohammed Ali Mosque and the Citadel, which stood on the verge of the eastern Desert looking over the slopes of the Mokattam Hills with a super view across the city with its minarets. This was our first stop, and putting on the unbelievers' overshoes, we stepped inside. Suddenly there was coolness and silence. We were all impressed with the simplicity and dignity of this huge open space where hundreds of Muslims were kneeling and bowing towards Mecca.

We stood for a few minutes marvelling at the scene that met our eyes. I was standing next to Bill's girlfriend and she leant over and whispered, saying that she could not help but be struck by the differences in our places of worship at home. Here there were no family pews, no altars, no candlesticks, no statues of saints, just space with rush mats covering the floor. Pat was quite right, she wasn't just a pretty face.

Our next visit was to the most spectacular of the mosques, the Mohammed Ali Mosque, which is one of the largest. There were many oohs and aahs from the girls as we gazed around this fabulous building. I mentioned that my boss Flt/Lt Langdon had told me that Mohammed Ali had been one of Egypt's most intelligent rulers, but most important, it was he who had introduced the growing of cotton to the country. He was Albanian and could not speak a word of Arabic, he was a man who thought nothing of murdering his enemies, and who sold as slaves any Europeans who fell into his hands.

We were tired and ready for a rest after the heat of the day, because it certainly was very hot as we made our way for tea to the big Gezira Club where we sat eating delicious sandwiches carefully prepared by the lady volunteers. It was very pleasant sitting there at the tables under the trees, and quite a change chatting with girls from our own country. Conversation flowed so much easier, we had not realised this until spending a few hours in the company of girls. It was all so very relaxing, seemingly without a care in the world. Oh boy, was our bright star shining!

Tea over, we took the girls home to their tented camp. They were stationed a 40 minute train journey outside Cairo. The girls had good voices and we indulged in some community singing on the train, mostly Scottish airs, with the rest of the carriage joining in. We were mystified with some of the singing, particularly a song sung with a Scottish accent, which went: 'Maiz-e-doats and doeze doats and little lambs e-divey, a kidle-e-divey too, wouldn't you?' If the words sound queer and funny to your ear – a little bit jumbled and jivey, just say – ''mares eat oats and does eat oats and little lambs eat ivy'. It was a new song, just out in the UK, but we had not heard it before.

We had a good laugh the other day. In 1940 I would possibly have taken a box of Black Magic when meeting a girlfriend, here in 1943 I was taking a box of louse powder! I should explain, however, it was for the WAAFs, and they had asked for it because they were troubled with 'creepy crawlies' in their tent. We enjoyed the company of the girls, meeting on a number of occasions. Each day we would choose a different venue, and looking over our photograph album I see that we went to the Pyramids and the Moorish Gardens. We also visited Cairo Zoo, a beautiful garden of 56 acres of tropical vegetation where the animals are kept in open pens similar to Regents Park. Passing the zoo offices we managed to engage one of the officers in conversation, asking him when the zoo had been established. We were told the gardens were once the property of a very rich Pasha, who, it was said, built the suspension bridge over an artificial lake in answer to his wife, who once asked what a suspension bridge looked like. Apart from the animals, giraffes, hippopotamus and lions, all in splendid condition, I think that the girls were mostly taken by the little Egyptian boys about 10 years of age and dressed in European clothes, with the exception of the little red tarbush on each of their small heads. Egypt is one of the greatest egg producers, and it seemed the zoo was no exception. They were selling ostrich eggs in the ticket office for two pounds each.

Off course we printed a set of buckshee photographs for each of the girls to send home to their families, and 57 years later chatting to Pat, one of the WAAFs (now a grandmother living in Leeds) she tells me that she still has those photographs among her souvenirs. Looking back to those far off days, those light-hearted romps were a rather special patch in the patchwork quilt which we made of our Middle East experiences.

We also visited Cairo Zoo

I guess that we should mention that we have been promoted to Corporals, in fact, we have been running shifts, and taking charge of the production section for some time. It means a little extra pay, and we have the use of the Corporals' Mess. Strangely for a couple of lads who want to progress in life, we have never sought promotion in the services. I think that we considered as LACs we would more easily be able to stay working together, and this was more important than climbing the ladder. Most of our stories describing our off duty hours picture them as a collection of pleasant experiences, and undoubtedly they were. So what, you may ask, were we doing to win the war?

Well, when on duty our work work was extremely secret, and as these stories are compiled from letters home, if we had made mention when writing what the squadron was doing the censor would most certainly have 'sorted us out'. As a matter of note, each day we would climb to the flat roof of our building and light a fire to burn any surplus or damaged photographs.

We doubt very much whether our daily tasks would be of much interest, but we will tell you a little; Arriving at the unit at 8am, we would check the jobs that the night shift had completed, for instance, reading an order which said 'Print negatives 145 and 146 of Tobruk film A67'. We would carefully check that the correct negatives had been printed and then rewind the long roll of film back onto its reel. The next job might be a mosaic where a number of photographs taken in what we call line overlap, are carefully cut with a razor blade, stuck on a card and then re-photographed. Both skill and experience are required so that, say, ten different photographs are made into one picture without the joins showing.

This was in the production department where we were checking the night's work, and the most interesting thing in the department was the notice on the front of the desk, so typical of the boss:

'The DIFFICULT will be done without delay, MIRACLES take a little longer!'

Yousef's Well was built by Crusade prisoners

50: Kan El Khalili

It is 30th September 1943 and we wake early and take a shower. Phew, the water sure is cold – our shower building is a bit primitive, it is constructed of corrugated iron, but it is just a stone's throw from our tent, so in two minutes we are back, a brisk rub with the towel and we are dressed.

Our tented camp is on the edge of the desert. It seems amazing that on the outskirts of Egypt's cities it is possible to step straight into the desert. Yes! Where the irrigation ditch, the grass or the cornfield ends, the desert begins – it is so sudden – there isn't even a no-mans land of part soil and part sand. For hundreds of miles along the Nile you can stand with one foot in lush grass and the other in dry sand.

However, a pleasant twenty minutes walk to Heliopolis from our camp and we are tucking into bacon and eggs, and marmalade butties at our unit cookhouse. Then it is off to Cairo where we have been invited to visit a bazaar by a friend Sylvia Broadbent. She is an English lady and a teacher and what is more she speaks Arabic fluently – very useful for our visit.

The Kan El Khalili is one of the biggest bazaars in the world and something never to be forgotten – it is an immense conglomeration of shops. We wander through the narrow streets and find craftsmen and indeed craft boys carving and sewing and making all manner of things. We ask if we may take a photograph and are a bit surprised when they say OK and don't ask for any money. A young lad is carving monkeys out of ivory, 'Hear all, see all, say nowt!' He shows a technical skill that we understand has always characterised the Nile Valley, so we give him a few piastres and he thanks us in Arabic saying, 'God be with you.'

The bazaar is also known as the Mousky and this is what the troops call it, after all, 'Kan El Khalili' is a bit of a mouthful. It is most enjoyable browsing through this market of narrow alleys, most just wide enough to permit two persons to walk side by side. It has sections reserved for particular merchandise. There is an amazing display of gold and gems both real and artificial. We haven't ever seen so much gold on display – what a city of contrasts when just a few yards away a native is so poor that he will collect and value a rusty tin can.

On one stall we saw them dropping odd bits of silver, broken teaspoons etc into a crucible, heating it until it was liquid and then making small ingots. Merchants beckon from

above, Villas beside the sea at Alexandria

left, We made ourselves very comfortable on the lorry, amongst the load was a case containing blankets

52: Cleo and Alexandria – May 1944

Now what does one do when as an NCO you find an airman asleep on duty? Well, when you are Cpl Jack Fairs and in charge of the shift, you wake him up and say, "Surely it's not very comfortable sleeping on that wooden bench?"

Romeo Psaylor, the sleeping airman, was Maltese and the reason he was asleep was because he was working on his own in a very hot room, feeding many hundreds of wet photographs onto four heated chromium plated glazing drums to dry them, and it certainly was conducive to sleep. It was the night shift and, probably like Jack and Bill Fairs, he had been out during the day enjoying himself. I told him to be more careful. Most of the photographs he was drying could be described as boring, but one was different, and our photograph shows where the Germans had ploughed up a forward landing field – it was quite picturesque – but a complete waste of time on their part, here is why:

The CO set one of our squadrons to work on the adjoining ground removing rocks,

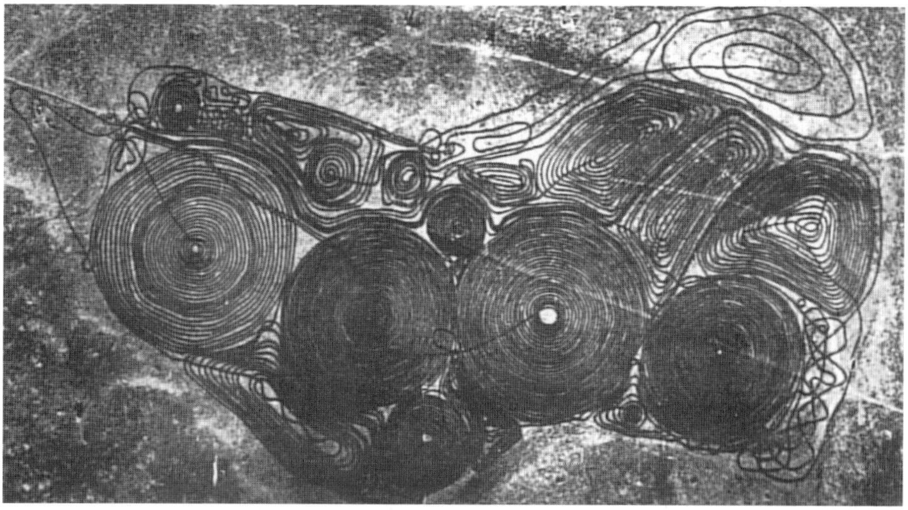

The Germans had ploughed up the landing field – it was quite picturesque!

pulling out the tussocks of grass, and with some levelling it was possible in a couple of hours to use it as a new landing ground.

That was yesterday and today we are off on leave to Alexandria. We have decided to hitch hike, it is approximately 140 miles. To reach the road to Alexandria we decided it would be better to take a taxi for the first few miles. Our taxi driver made up his mind that he would travel as slowly as a donkey and, unfortunately, not having learnt any Arabic swear words, there was little we could do about it. We stopped at a police post where they could not have been more helpful. They arranged a lift for us on a lorry. You can see from the photograph, that I am seated contentedly with a pal from Bromborough, and the driver. Bill as usual is not in the picture, he is taking the photo. We were very comfortable because amongst the load was a case containing blankets, so we borrowed some just for the trip.

We arrive at Alexandria. What a pleasant change. It was so much cooler with a fresh breeze blowing in from the sea, much preferred to the heat of Cairo. A most agreeable place with a series of delightful beaches, there are hotels, a race course and one room tenements next door to palatial villas stretching a mile or so from the sea. It was a real hotch-potch but made all the more interesting by being so. Cairo is a cosmopolitan city but Alexandria leads it easily. While the main population is Egyptian, there are large colonies of French, Italians, Greeks, Syrians, British and Jews. Much of the commerce of the port is under foreign control. Alexandria is one of the largest Greek cities in the world. Greek cafes are everywhere – you can sip a glass of ouzo or retsina and read a Greek newspaper. Bill and I liked the Greek cafes because we could try our few words of Greek. Looking at many of the signs over the shops written in Greek one could almost imagine that one was in Athens, its character and pace being set by the Greeks and foreign merchants.

Our digs are quite a change. We are staying as paying guests at the house of an English lady. It is very comfortable and she has a phone. We just had bed and breakfast there, eating mainly at Toc-H hostel.

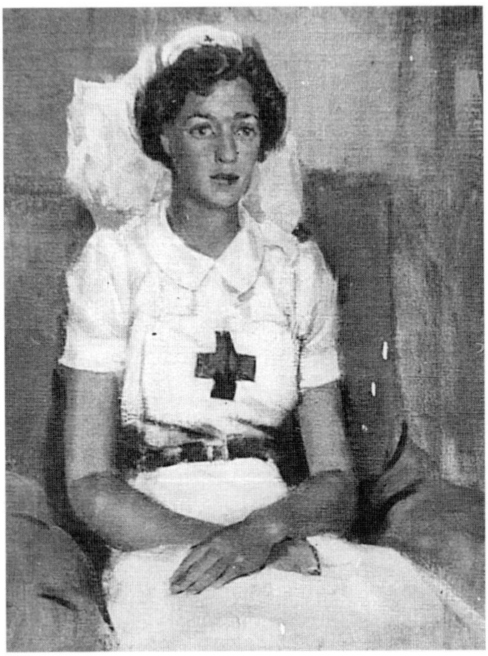

A painting of Cleo in her nurse's uniform

One of the highlights of our visit was lunch with Cleo, short for Cleopatra. Her parents own a big hotel. She is Swiss and 21 years of age. We spent an afternoon in the hotel grounds and we had been invited to dinner the following day – thank you bright star! We had the good fortune to meet Cleo on a previous visit when we were entertained at a garden party which was held in a large villa in its own grounds owned by a Swiss lady, Mrs Kupper. She had invited a number of young ladies, also Swiss, to entertain the lads who were so far from their homes.

Bill, our pal, and I played a game of hockey. It was RAF against the Navy. They beat us hollow – I think they had played before! Bill did not play, he was too interested in taking photographs for Mum and Dad to see what we were up to and who we were meeting.

In a letter home Bill mentions that after tea we sat chatting with two of the girls, Cleo and Doris, and had some good laughs. Both girls were well travelled and we talked about Greece. He also mentions that if possible when we are again on leave, we must repeat the entertainment, and so here we are ...

Cleo outside Beau Rivage Hotel

He also wrote that we had very small sandwiches, a slice of cucumber and a slice of egg, very dainty and 'Buckingham Palaceish'. I cannot help but think that it was most unfair that we should be so fortunate being with such pleasant companions and eating like kings. If it had been possible to swap with a couple of army lads from the desert we would willingly have done so ... but I'm afraid life isn't like that.

What a contrast to a fellow townsman, Arthur Evans, who had the bad luck to be a prisoner of war in Stalag VIIIB Lamsdorf in Upper Silesia. Arthur worked for Lever Bros in the soapworks at Port Sunlight, but now his breakfast consists of warm acorn coffee, which they also use for shaving occasionally. At 12 noon, an issue of mangel or birdseed soup with two or three potatoes boiled in their skins to conceal the rotten parts, and at 4pm about four ounces of black bread with some unidentifiable smearing or stinking cheese – aptly named – it smells absolutely foul and that is their food day after day.

So when we write about a lucky star, we are certainly not kidding!

The following morning we visited a workshop where the smith was making a lovely wrought iron bracket to hang a sign. Bill said, "we must have one of these for out studio after the war. We made a note of this in our Blue Book and sure enough in 1947, those who are old enough to remember and who had passed our studio in Dacre Hill, would have seen an oak post on the front lawn with a wrought iron bracket suspending a sign bearing the words' WILLIAM FAIRS – PHOTOGRAPHER OF CHILDREN'.

The week passed all too quickly and here we were on our journey home to Cairo. It took just three hours hitch hiking once again.

We found the trip most interesting. The land was flat and low lying with crops of maize and sugar cane and there were groves of date palms. It certainly was a land of sunshine and with the Nile soil it would have not been possible to stop anything growing – indeed, here with some produce, it was possible to grow two or three crops in one year. What a marvellous experience this was with its unforgettable scenes. We were not with Thomas Cook, of course, but were fortunate to have booked our trip with the Royal Air Force travel agents.

recco unit was requested to take a series of shots from 35,000 feet at 11.45am so that they could assess the height of the buildings. During the first 10 days of February fourteen sorties had been flown over Amiens and district for the purpose of obtaining photographic reconnaissance. Just as soon as the photographs were taken the modelling section was asked to produce a scale replica of the prison to simulate what the crews would see from a height of 200 feet four miles away. The model was made of paper mache and wood.

The model was treated like the Crown Jewels and placed in a wooden box under lock and key in the AOCs office. Although Bill and I worked for years in a building with a model making section, we were never allowed in such was the secrecy desired. Even in our already well-guarded building there was one occasion when there was an extra RAF guard on the doorway to brother Bill's mosaic room – during the planning of the North Africa invasion.

The Air Ministry insisted upon the model of the prison being carried out by our Central Interpretation Unit to cut out 'red tape' as they called it, knowing that our unit was used to being on constant call to prepare 'hit-quick notice' targets. The detail of the building that was obtained was surprising. The local resistance movement even obtained the architect' original drawings of the prison. The aircrew were able to examine the model and by viewing it at eye level were able to observe it in miniature, as if flying over the original at anything from 50 to 500 feet. By selecting a combination of easily recognisable landmarks, a target approach route could be clearly defined.

It was decided to use semi-armour piercing hard-nose bombs to break through the outer wall and medium case bombs to explode on impact with the inner walls. A strong escort would be provided by Typhoons, but there were still a lot of ifs:

If the weather permitted?

If there was enough outside help for escaping inmates?

If the pilots could place the bombs in the correct positions?

These and many more questions were raised.

Some hundred locals outside and some 16 prisoners inside were in on the secret that the raid would be made any day but they had only been told that it would be at midday and to prepare themselves. There was an incredible amount of arrangements to be made for the proposed raid by those in the prison and in the vicinity. For instance, about noon each day 10 large trucks, a butcher's and baker's delivery van plus several private cars, made a point of being in the area, which was certainly not easy as they must not be seen hovering around too long so near the prison. The cycle repairer, too, played his part by providing a supply of bicycles in nearby houses for the use of the escaping prisoners.

A Madame Vignon, who had been nicknamed 'Wardrobe Mistress of Amiens' had been requested to supply a consignment of clothes of all types, shapes and sizes, male and female, for the escapees. She lived in a large house next to the military barracks and her house resembled an overstocked second-hand clothes shop. Many an American and British airman had said thank you to her for saving their lives.

Nineteen aircrews were chosen; eighteen attackers and one photographic. They were composed of a mixture of British, Aussies and New Zealanders, with one Canadian and one Frenchman. It was decided to aim a number of bombs at the base of the prison walls. Their explosion should throw doors out of alignment making the locks ineffective damaging the prison walls and enabling the prisoners to escape into the yard. Shortly before 5am in the darkness of 18th February the crews of three squadrons were told to report to the briefing room. They found very strict security with RAF police checking each man's identity disc and ticking off his name on a long list. Security men had been specially drafted into the airfield and its surrounding neighbourhood to cover local pubs and cafes as a precaution against leaks. Phones were tapped and letters censored. From Signals Section the men were given a list of codes for the day, printed on rice paper, so that if they were shot down the list was to be eaten.

Snow and sleet were falling over the sea when 18 Mosquitoes of Nos 21, 464 and 487 Squadrons set of on 18th February 1944. It was filthy weather – low clouds blanketed the route. The operation would have been called off had it not been for a last moment desperate appeal from the French underground. They said that more than 100 people collected from prisons all over France were facing execution in Amiens Prison. By the time the planes had risen a mere hundred feet the pilots could see nothing except a soupy driving mist of swirling snow beating against the perspex of their windows. Four were soon helplessly lost and found it difficult to get back to base let alone struggle on to the target. Others also had problems and the attack was down to just 12 aircraft. Six were detailed to breach the walls by flying virtually at ground level as the walls were only 25 feet high and if the bombs were misplaced they could bounce over and blow everyone to smithereens. records show that a pilot, Black Smith, dropped his bombs from a height of just 10 feet. Lightened by the loss of the load the aircraft bobbed up violently and then flattened out and hurtled along almost at street level causing passers-by to throw themselves flat or rush into doorways. Another, John McCaul yelled to his gunner, "We've scored a direct hit on the guards' quarters," and was told that two aircraft had breached the northern wall in two places and that the western wall had also collapsed.

Tony Wickham of the RAF Film Unit spotted and focused on the escapers, men in dungaree type outfits running through the gaping breaches in the outer walls and stumbling across adjacent fields. They looked like tiny ant-like figures, contrasting with the whiteness of the snowy landscape. Some of the prisoners had dressed in German soldiers' uniforms which had been stolen from those killed in the bombing. In one instance two prisoners in German uniforms marched eight of the others with rifles pointing at their backs to safety away from the prison.

A message sent by the Resistance to London in March 1944 read;

'I thank you in the name of our comrades for the bombardment of the prison. We were not able to save all, but thanks to the admirable precision of the attack, the first bomb blew in nearly all of the doors and 150 prisoners escaped with the help of the civilian population. Of these 12 were to have been shot on February 19th. In addition37 prisoners were killed, some of them by German machine guns, and 50 Germans also were killed.'

There was also another immense benefit. Escaped political prisoners identified more than 60 of the Gestapo agents and collaborators responsible for their imprisonment.

above, We were very content, it was a pleasant camp near to a town
below, Bill with two companions and the bamboo pole before beetles got at it!

54: The Tented Camp

Everything in the garden was lovely. Well, it was until someone at Middle East Headquarters thought to themselves 'let's upset things just a little bit'.

And so the powers that be decided that the lesser fry, that was us, did not deserve the luxury of apartments in Heliopolis and so we were directed to a tented camp in the desert, just twenty minutes walk from our unit. Not quite the luxury that we had been used to, we started the day with a cold shower in a corrugated iron ablution block, we did not have wash basins, just a board bench with eight cast iron taps.

I write these details not as a complaint but just to paint the picture. Indeed we were very content and lucky to be on such as pleasant camp near to a town. The photograph of Bill and two of our companions shows our new abode which was sent to Mum and on the back we have written... 'The Hole in the Ground' which was, by the way, four feet deep. We wrote, too, that it was very comfortable, note the mosquito nets. Jolly good job that it didn't rain or we should have had a different story to tell. The bamboo tent pole, was the pole in question, and when you ask what question? The answer is, another question. What was the slight rasping noise that persisted all through the night? Here is the answer, or rather we found the answer when the pole collapsed: It had been eaten away by a wood-boring beetle, it was quite a surprise.

Another question is what is a bint?

The answer in an Egyptian girl and it is seeing photographs of the tented camp that brings this to mind. The average Egyptian peasant had so little that I guess it was only natural that he desired some of our possessions, and to stop them helping themselves a barbed wire fence had been erected around the perimeter of the camp. Guards were detailed to patrol the fence at night and some of the lads had found themselves Egyptian girls to share their duty, and the girls were called 'Bints', I only heard about this, I do not think they were good girls, and I did hear that the lads used to give them sandwiches.

No! Jack and Bill did not hand out any sandwiches, our guard duties took place at the Unit HQ. I cannot recall anything ever being stolen from our camp, although it was common knowledge that the natives were experts at stealing. Stories were told that when the lads were sleeping in the desert they would sleep with their heads on their kitbags to protect them, and in the morning when they awoke their kitbags had been stolen and something else substituted. Yes! Their pillows had been exchanged without them being wakened.

In the Canal Zone it was quite a different matter, raids on the camp occurred almost nightly. It was a tremendous place to guard – with a fifteen mile perimeter fence, sixteen miles of railway, twenty seven miles of roads – and 450,000 tons of supplies. This was one of the bases which supplied the North African Campaign. The number of guards needed in some camps was so large that even volunteer German Prisoners were sometimes employed. There were belts of barbed wire; armed guards and patrol cars; dogs – mostly Alsatians and Boxers. In spite of all these precautions losses averaged in cash about £4,000 per week. Some prisoners were taken and once or twice a week a man would be killed.

Well, our built-in restlessness has taken over, we must always be doing something and so we are off. As a start we visit the tent of the camp dhobi wallah, laundry man, who stands at a trestle table covered in bundles of clean dhobi. We count our bundle of socks, yes! They are all there, eight of them and surprise, surprise... they are all ours. The native hands them over tied with a piece of string, and we say, No! we are going to town and you must wrap them in brown paper. He says that he hasn't any but we find some beneath his bench and come away satisfied.

Twenty minutes walk and we are sitting on the Metro wending our way to Cairo when a rather stoutish fellow of about fifty sat opposite. I guessed that he had seen service with the army and could speak English although he was obviously not British. I was surprised to see him open an Arabic newspaper because I did not think he was Egyptian. Whilst I was scrutinising him he looked across and asked whether we were twins and thus we entered into a conversation, and I found that I was correct he had seen service with the British forces.

We learned he was a Physician, and he invited us to his consulting rooms, where he showed us many press cuttings of articles he had written. It appeared that he was quite eminent in the Arabic world and he had lectured in America, Syria, Hungary, Paris and Berlin. He was Lebanese, and he was a friend of General Allenby, he showed us one or two letters that he had received from him.... odd whom one meets on the tram isn't it!

We met Farid el Gindi the film producer in Soliman Pasha Street and he asked where we had been staying. He had not seen us and thought that we had been posted

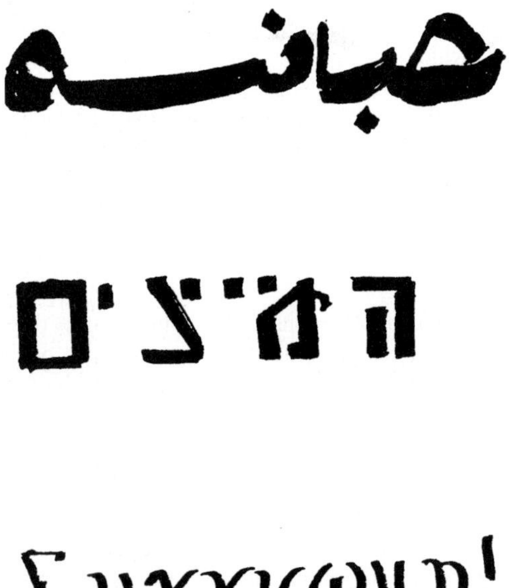

top, Greek script
middle, Israeli script
bottom, Arabic script

away. We told him that we had been very busy, and during our conversation we asked him what the word was for twins in Arabic, saying that in each Country we had learned the appropriate name. Greece – Theethema.. Palestine – Tvilling, and Germany – Svillinger, Farid told us that in Arabic it was 'Fee Batna Wahida' and that it meant two in one belly... we thought 'Oh!, we will forget that one.'

Scripts:

We were finding life most interesting, we had lived in three different countries, each with its own distinctive script, all quite dissimilar in character. Although we had not tried to learn to read even one word Greek, we had however learnt one or two Arabic phrases, one of which proved very useful when we were being pestered by the shoe shine urchins, when they said 'shoe shine mister'! we would reply 'Awia bukra fil mish mish' and translated it meant 'Yes, tomorrow when the apricots grow' in other words 'Get Lost'!

Whilst on the subject of languages we should mention that our friend Colonel Steffell was not only fluent in Arabic, but he could write it as well which we thought was very good. Upon reflection it is perhaps interesting that Bill and I at no time felt out of places amongst officers, indeed at a recent wedding there were eighteen officers and just four other ranks including Bill and I. I guess that it was because we ourselves felt at ease, and we were never short of conversation.

The Corporals' Bar – the desert was really not such a bad place!

above, This 'fellah' had not heard of progress, with his buffalo he ploughed as his forefathers had done for thousands of years

left, We were amazed that the women could carry and balance the heavy containers on their heads

55: Ali Shaltoot

Today is 11th September 1944 and it is our day off. We had just had a pleasant twenty minute stroll from our tent in the desert to our cookhouse which was an apartment in a neo-Moorish villa – quite posh and not a bit like an average cookhouse. We were sitting enjoying our bacon and eggs when one of our oppos from the unit told us that our photo officer, Fl/t Langdon, wished to see us when we had finished our meal. Now what is coming we wondered?

A knock at the office door and a request, "Come in". "Good morning Sgts Fairs," says our chief, "Yes, I have some good news for you – you have both been promoted to Sergeants." "Thank you very much, sir," we said in unison. We were very pleased – it would seem that the well-known song, "You'll get no promotion this side of the ocean, so cheer up my lads, bless them all" was not true in our case. The news was quite unexpected, but very welcome. It meant more pay, improved food and, no doubt, better accommodation on the troop ship home.

Thinking about the boat, which was quite often in our minds these days, we realised that our holiday in the Middle East was rapidly nearing its end. Sad in some ways with the continual sunshine and a very active social life – ah well, all good things come to an end. We decided that we had better learn a little about Egypt, apart from the cinemas and the girls that we had met.

Bill suggested that the best way was to visit one of the villages and the next day, after we had called at the camp tailor to have a third stripe added to our sleeves, we set off by Metro tram for Cairo. A short walk to the Giza Road and then we hitch hiked until we were about four miles from the Pyramids of Giza. Turning left we travelled along a path running parallel to a canal. We came across a little group of water-carriers and we were amazed that the women could carry and balance the heavy containers on their heads, even a youngster of about twelve years of age. Not so Hassan – he was a wise old bird and he was using a donkey to do his carrying. It would seem that water carrying all over the world is woman's work. Proceeding on our way, we arrived at a typical country village called Talbaya, It was a poor-looking place. Visiting one of the mud houses, we met the occupants, Abu and his wife and their three children. The house was windowless although it did have an aperture and it was sparsely furnished.

The main room had a raised dried mud platform with a rush mat on top which was used as a bed, a large wooden box containing their belongings, only a small oil stove for making

Just look whom we picked up today!

On our way from the village we met two young Egyptian girls and got into conversation with them. We learned that they were secondary school girls who were employed by the Typhus Commission and that they visited the village every day. Their names were Gamila and Fathia. We chatted with them for a few minutes, they were not well versed in English, which was not surprising, this was indeed the first time during the four years that we had been in Egypt that I can recollect speaking to an Egyptian girl, apart from our friend Farid el Gindi's sisters.

We took the photograph with the girls more or less to pull the legs of the lads back at the unit, saying, "Just look whom we picked up today!" (a complete fabrication of course!) It's grand to be young!

56: Dishforth

Hardly a story from the Middle East, as Dishforth is in North Yorkshire and was where we spent most of our first 12 months with the RAF. However, all will be revealed as this tale unfolds:

The postman had just delivered three letters, one of which has a Nottingham postmark. It is from a young lady called Vera, and brings back memories of a very pleasant interlude, so here we will flash back in time to 14th April 1940. I am at home on leave from our heavy bomber station Dishforth and awake at the unearthly hour of 5,30am. And here is why:

It is eight months since we were called up to serve our King and country, and at our camp we are living in a wooden hut which houses 22 airmen. We have made some good friends and one especially, Eric, is an air gunner with 51 Heavy Bomber Squadron, travelling in the rear turret of a huge Whitley Bomber. Eric was showing me a sketch that was drawn from a photograph by his girl cousin. It was very well done and I asked him whether he thought that perhaps she would make a similar sketch of a girlfriend of mine. He said, Why not write and ask her?"

Well, I did just that and so we started corresponding. She wrote and suggested that I spend a couple of days with her family, so here I am off to Liverpool to catch the 7am train to Nottingham. Alas, I find that train is not running. I guess it might have something to with it being wartime! Nothing left but to hitch hike, and here I was

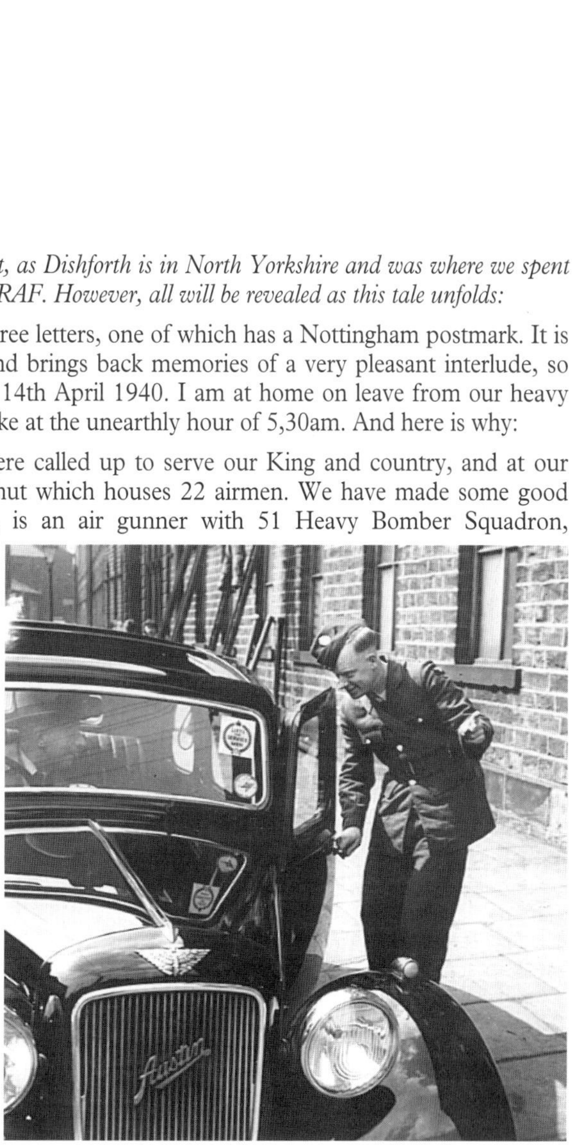

Bill as an AC plonk thumbing a lift home

fairly lucky. I did not have a map, but found that the drivers were most helpful, especially the truck drivers. They suggested the best places to wait and connect with transport heading for the next town on my journey.

With my mention of hitch hiking I will digress a little as it brings to mind just how much we used this method of travel during our first 12 months with the RAF. We reckon that our journeys must have covered at total of over 2,000 miles in just 12 months, starting when we were in Debden, Essex. This was our first station and we were fortunate enough to work in the Operations Room and to be able to plot our sortie home by cutting strips from maps of our route to Birkenhead. The distance covered by our hitch hiking was not perhaps surprising when I tell you that our Bill had met a very nice young lady whilst dancing at the Tower Ballroom, New Brighton. Bill said, "May I take you home?" The young lady said, "Yes, I live in Sunderland, 137 miles away." Fortunately, Eleanor was staying with her aunt in Liverpool. Bill did become serious with her and he did hitch to Sunderland several times.

When we found ourselves in a large town we would make our way to the central bus station and with the help of the inspector we were soon on our way by bus to the outskirts of the town on the road where we had been advised the traffic would be heading in the direction of our home. In those wartime days the drivers were wonderful. There were 'lifts for servicemen' labels on some of the cars and the photograph shows Bill as an AC plonk thumbing a lift home to see the family and friends and, almost certainly, to go dancing. What more could one ask?

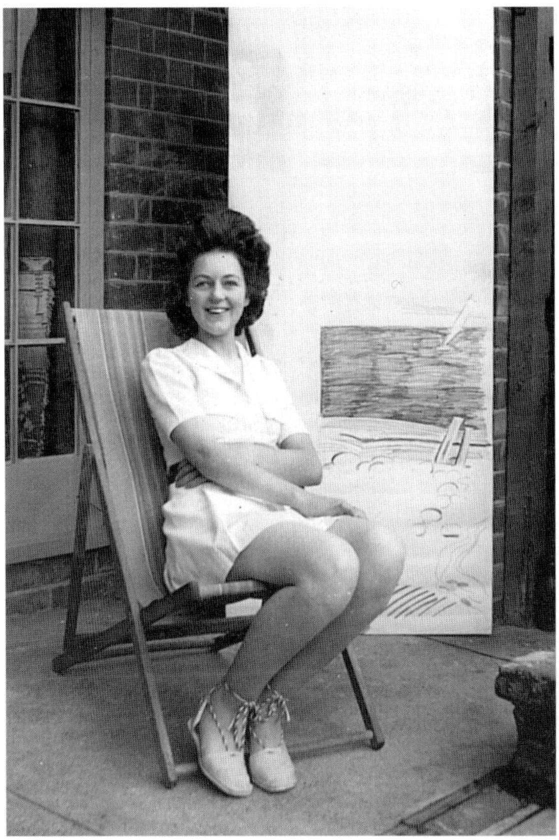

Vera was a lovely girl, just 19 years of age

On more than one occasion the driver offered us a ten-shilling note. We protested strongly saying, "We are not short of money," but we realised that it was far better to accept their kind gift and say "Thank you", because they obviously wanted us to take the money.

Anyway, back to the story.... I arrived safely and Vera and her family made me very welcome. We went out for walks and to the cinema where we sat holding hands, it's great to be young. I thought that Vera was a lovely girl, she was 19 years of age. I made a note in my diary to say that she was unspoilt. I think I was her first boyfriend, and I considered that she deserved someone nicer than me, if I was honest – and I am honest! Vera's father, Mr Frettingham, was a lace designer at a textile factory, and without doubt it was from her father that she inherited her talent for drawing.

The leaflet drops gave Jack and Bill ideas for their Christmas greetings

However, back to the leaflet story...

Eric told me what an awful job it was and what conditions were like. He said, "The fuselage was crammed with large parcels of leaflets wrapped in coarse brown paper and tied up with thick twine. We were flying at 15,000 feet, the outside temperature was fifteen degrees below freezing, we were so cold I think my teeth were chattering. We had to disconnect ourselves from the oxygen supply to be able to place the bundles in the flare chute, so that on emerging into the slipstream they would scatter immediately."

"Freezing! The aircraft used to ice up, and on one occasion touching the knife to cut the twine the knife stuck to my fingers. There was no doubt we were subject to intense cold and inadequately prepared. We had to wear layers of clothes to avoid freezing, and now you know why I am smiling as I sit here in Hut Eleven recounting this story to you in front of a blazing stove."

After describing the conditions, LAC Eric said, "That's the bad side, and now the good side. Air Ministry have decided overnight that all other ranks flying as aircrew will be made up to Sergeant, and have the advantage of the Sergeants' Mess".

Leaflets were not the only thing the aircraft delivered, they also dropped bombs and tea. What an odd thing to drop you will no doubt think! Here is the story:

As a crew member, Pilot Officer John Brewster had carried out several operations from RAF Dishforth on 51 Squadron Whitleys, but now he was to be captain of his own aircraft. Why then was he told that he was to go on a 'nursery trip'? He was aggrieved, it was as if he had never flown on operations before, but orders were orders. "Your aircraft is going to Rotterdam", he was told in the operations room. He had just reached the door when 'ops' called out, "And you will drop your tea in a residential area". Brewster hesitated, about to ask about 'tea', but decided not to show his ignorance. "I am either daft, or 'tea' must be some sort of code that I don't know about. Perhaps it's another name for 'razzle'" he thought, and decided to ask a corporal fitter about this 'tea' stuff. "It's tea alright", said the corporal, "Three barrels of little bags with tickets on them saying 'a present from the East Indies'."

Brewster was glad they also carried bombs to drop on the Rotterdam docks. Bombs gone he banked the Whitley to fly over the residential area while the crew went back to tip the teabags out through the flare chute. The inevitable happened – the teabags blew back and they were flying everywhere, inside the fuselage as well as outside. At that moment, flak burst all around the aircraft, and Brewster threw the Whitley through its normal jinking routine as the crew members staggered about trying to gather up the flying teabags. When the crew decided to call it a day, two and a half barrels of teabags had been poured into Rotterdam's night sky.

The homeward flight was uneventful until the moment the Whitley touched down at Dishforth. The lights went out, the flare path was doused, and impenetrable darkness surrounded the still rolling aircraft. "The miserable B's", Brewster swore under his breath, "Why did they do that?" Calling the second pilot to fetch the Aldis lamp and opening the top hatch so that they could alert dispersal, Brewster had his answer. An aircraft passed over the Whitley 'going like hell'. Later the group captain told him that everyone had been on tenterhooks for the half-hour the German had been following him in over the North Sea.

Another Whitley was sent on a similar lone 'nursery' flight a few nights later. Next morning Brewster saw the ragged pieces of a Sidcot flying suit in the locker room, and outside the wreckage of a Whitley. A cannon shell had passed over the head of the tail gunner, shot past the navigator and wireless operator and then between the second pilot, who was sitting on the step and the captain. At that moment the captain reached for the throttle and the shell neatly took it off. The Whitley 'piled in'. "Great God" Brewster thought grimly as he looked at the wreckage, "All for a packet of tea."

Two months later, after being shot down on a raid on Dusseldorf, Brewster walked through the main gate into Dulag Luft POW Camp.

The story of Pilot Officer Brewster and the teabags and the flare chute recalls to mind a little incident that happened to Bill:

It was decided to experiment with night photography by dropping a strong flash from the aircraft. One of the squadron's two engined Whitley bombers was used, and Bill was chosen to make the trip. After a good take-off and ten minutes airborne, they reached the target area. Bill opened the shutter on the camera and pushed the flash down the chute. Great flash and, hopefully, a successful sortie, so back to base to develop the picture. On the return journey Bill was looking through the window at one of the engines which sounded very rough and after a few minutes it decided to die. Bill said he was quite concerned (really meaning that he was scared stiff) but his bright star was shining and all was well. They were two minutes from another aerodrome and the pilot made a successful landing with just one engine.

Looking back to our days at Dishforth, it is surprising what a small part this occupies in our memories, and upon reflection, we cannot help but be grateful that we spent so much of our time overseas, where life was exciting and so full of interest. We do recall the friendly atmosphere amongst the lads of Hut Eleven, they were like ourselves, in the main new to the RAF.

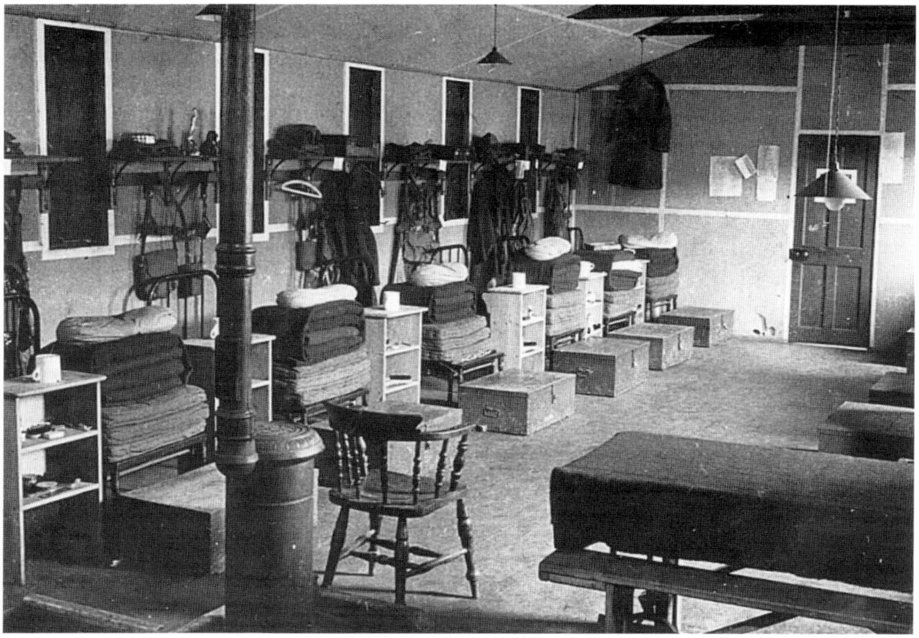

Our 'home' – Hut Eleven at Dishforth

Of Dishforth we remember the awful guard patrols around the airfield on freezing nights, often with snow on the ground, we hated them. The hitch hikes home. Bill's girlfriend in Harrogate, he kindly loaned her to me on the odd occasion. The photo training, which was interesting.

An old Irishman, a reservist, approached me in the hut once and said, "Would you write a letter to the CO for me. I am not very good at writing. I would like some compassionate leave because I have heard that my wife has a new fur coat and I did not buy it for her!"

I think perhaps we had better return to the Middle East and Cairo ...

above, Fl/Sgt Steve Waring working in the model section at Medmenham in 1943
below, Model of Palermo, Italy, constructed from photography at 35,000 feet

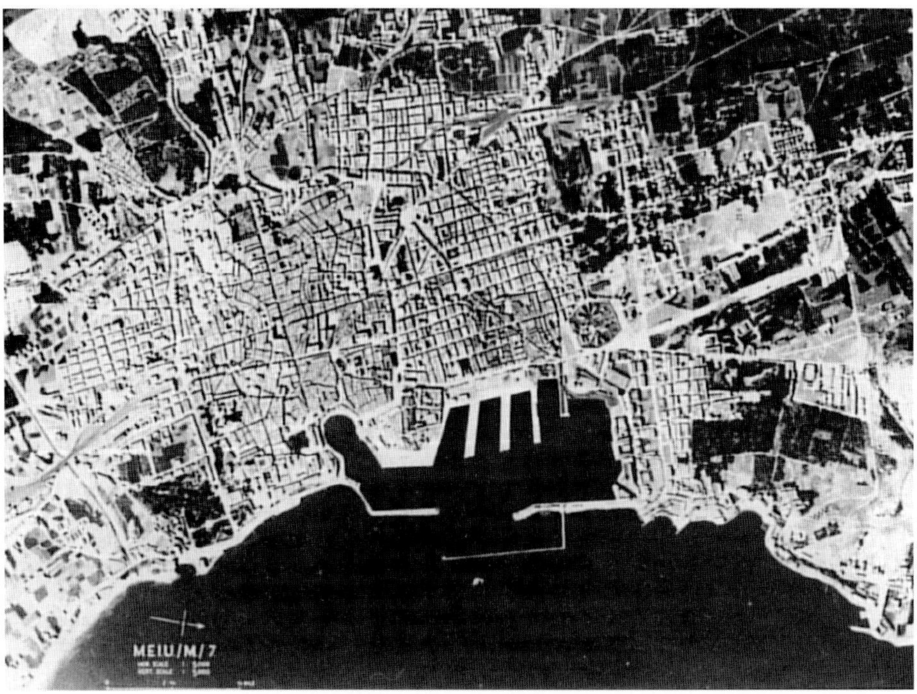

57: Eyes In The Sky

We have in earlier chapters told a little of the part we played in photographic reconnaissance in which Bill and I had the good fortune to serve during our very interesting six and a half years with the RAF, but feel that we should add to the story:

Photography from the air was not new, it was taking place over 100years ago. In the first instance the cameras were fixed to the baskets of balloons. A French pioneer took many excellent photographs by this method. It was even attempted by the attaching of a very small camera to a homing pigeon. The camera was German made and took 30 photographs. It was not very successful – we guess the pigeon had a problem reading map references!

Early attempts with a pigeon and small camera

Even in those early days, 1918, at the end of the First War, the importance of photography had been taken very much on board. There were as many as 4,000 cameras in the front line, in addition to another 5,000 in use at home for training. This number was drastically reduced when the squadrons themselves were cut in numbers from about 200 to 33, and it was not until Winston Churchill, together with Lord Trenchard, took on the job of revitalising the RAF that photography was given the high priority that it deserved.

You will have gathered that our unit was far from a military 'spit and polish' organisation. The personnel were carefully selected. Most of the lads on the unit were photographers pre-war, and there was a very civilian atmosphere in the section. The interpreters were almost all chosen for their academic background. For instance, Claud Wavell, a brilliant mathematician, who had worked on the survey of Rio de Janiero before the war. Bill Wager, Professor of Geology at Oxford. Hamshaw Thomas, whose speciality was the study of fossil plants, and it was the same patient approach and deductive reasoning that brought him success in studying photographs of the Nazi war industry, which was his speciality.

It was interesting to hear from the interpreters just how by studying aerial photographs they were able to discover answers to activity on the ground. For example, new telephone lines – betrayed by the shadow of each post, and the pale circle of newly turned earth at its foot – indicated where a local headquarters was installed, and the myriad of tracks of heavy lorries converging on a special area left little doubt where ammunition and stores were being hidden.

We were intrigued to learn how our units kept their eyes on German U-boat production, and here is how. An interpreter named David Brachi, who specialised in German shipyard operation hit upon a clever idea. German shipyards were regularly photographed, and one day David detected what appeared to be the keel of a submarine in the shipyard of Blohm and Voss. The next sortie taken a month after the keel had been laid showed that the midships portion of the hull was just going into position and a camouflage cradle was being put over it. A later photograph showed how the camouflage cradle had been lengthened because the hull had been extended to its full length. Yet another pair of photographs were taken six months after the laying of the keel, which showed where part of the cradle had been removed so that they could finish work on the conning tower.

On one of the photographs that David was examining he detected a slim grey splinter with a dark grey knob about halfway along. That splinter was in fact a newly launched 500 ton submarine. David had a measuring magnifier, a small precision instrument for counting the threads in textiles to check the regularity of the weave, with a metal scale that was calibrated in tenths of a millimetre. Writing down a figure, then with his slide rule he was able to check the length of the sub – 250 feet. Having watched the German shipyards from month to month, he knew that the 500 ton subs were usually off the slips in eight months, fitting out took another two or three months, and so it was possible to estimate the time for the building of a submarine from the date the keel was laid.

The production of U-boats based on David Bachi's figures suggested that 10 could be produced this month and 20 next month. These figures were carefully checked, and were regarded as so alarming that they were sent to the Chiefs of Staffs, and the new production estimate was sent to the Prime Minister. It was little wonder that our Chiefs of Staffs were alarmed. During the year 1943 the Germans had over 400 U-boats in action, and it was not unusual for them to set a pack of 20 to attack one of our convoys, resulting in appalling losses.

Much of the photographic information required by agents and other services was supplied by photographic mosaics or models. Brother Bill was in charge of the mosaic section, and he worked on the mosaic which was used for the model of Palermo for the invasion of Sicily.

Model making was a very specialised job, and it was interesting to know that this section was composed of artists, sculptors, wedding cake makers and wood machinists. The results as shown on the mosaic of Palermo were quite amazing.

The mosaics were composed of a number of aerial photographs, which were taken line overlap, and perhaps two or three runs in parallel. A tough job for a brave pilot, who would possibly be subject to enemy fighters and anti-aircraft fire at the same time. It was our job to paste these photographs onto a cardboard sheet and re-photograph them, and these mosaics were then passed to the model section if required, or to the service that had requested them.

We have not referred to German photographic intelligence in any earlier chapters, and so we must make brief reference to what the Luftwaffe were doing. There is no doubt that the Germans were the finest camera makers in the world. Their precision engineering was outstanding; the Leica and the Contax cameras were a joy to behold. The RAF bought all the Contax cameras that were available at the beginning of the war. The detail and clarity of many of their aerial photographs was outstanding, BUT their Air Inspectorate for Photography, which was formed in 1942, was given a low priority. Indeed, the majority of their interpreters remained as NCOs, and strangely their photographs were seldom used for the systematic gathering of intelligence or for high-level military decisions. The Germans did not develop high performance photo reconnaissance planes like our Spitfires and Mosquito, and although their cameras were of excellent quality, they were far too heavy for very high altitude work.

The aircraft that carried the cameras were eventually outclassed by the new allied fighters. To sum up, German Photographic Reconnaissance can be classed as disastrous. We were very fortunate that this was so, because in almost all other fields the guns and their tanks were not just superior, but very superior.

Referring to Bill making tests with aerial flash photographs, we have to say that the bomber pilots hated these photo flashes because the crew had the job of putting them in the flash tube, and the pilot had to fly straight and level when they ought to be weaving to avoid flack. The photographs were taken at the time the bombs were landing to help with damage assessment, but their value proved to be of much more importance, bringing to light errors of navigation. It is a sad fact that examination of the flash photographs and statistics taken over a period of three months showed that a high proportion of the bombs fell a long way from target areas, and a study of these photographs gave the realisation that it ws imperative to do something about it.

New bomb sights were designed, and our bombing results improved tremendously, which of course meant if a raid was successful another trip was not required, and without doubt less of our aircrews were lost.

It is interesting to learn of the steady demand for very detailed interpretations of just what lay on the other side, so that agents who were going to land by parachute or by boat could be properly briefed. They needed a lot of facts that a map could not give them, the height of a hedge around a farmhouse, the position of a barbed wire fence, the low line of a creek – knowledge of these could easily mean the difference between success and failure.

One of the WAAFs who worked in this section was Dorothy Guard, who had been Professor of Archaeology at Cambridge, and was an eminent authority on the subject. It was second nature to her to search patiently. She was just one of the many who contributed to the success of the Photographic Reconnaissance Units.

above, We say goodbye to the WAAFs at their new services club in Cairo
below, Jack and Doris, Bill and Evaline at their last St Michael's Church dance

58: The Last Letter

Dear Mum and Dad,

It won't be long now, boat home and our family will be together again and then we shall see whether Blighty is able to offer the same interest as the Middle East – we rather doubt it!

It seems strange to think that this may be the last letter that we will send to you from the Middle East, we have completed our four years tour, in fact we have done a few weeks over our time. The overseas tour is three years for married men and four years for single men.

There is much talk among the boys on the unit about 'The Boat' and no doubt we will be coming home via the Mediterranean which will be a much shorter journey than our outward cruise of six weeks via South Africa. Many of our thoughts recently, when we have been walking around the block or sitting at the Gezira Club, have been concerned with the discussing and planning of our business after the war. Dad, we have in mind that when the studio is established, you will join us, it matters not that you haven't any photographic knowledge, mounting photographs and framing are just the sort of thing a handy man can take in his stride. We have firmly decided that we will establish a studio run by Bill. I will return to work until such a time that the business can support us both, giving help when I am not at work.

We received a letter and some leaflets from the Canadian Immigration authorities the other day, we still have Vancouver very much in mind, but it will have to wait until we are settled, one thing at a time.

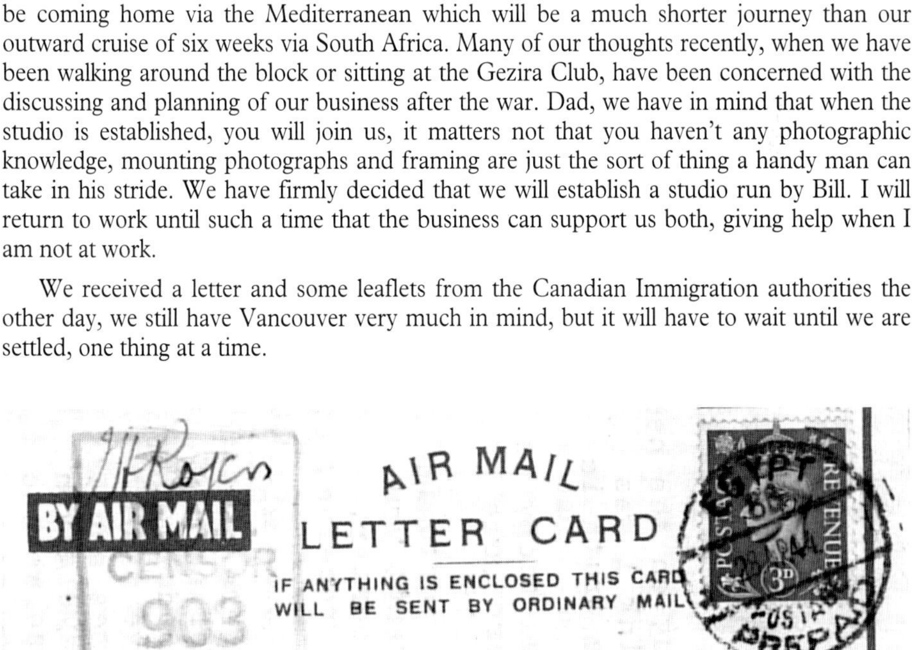

Farid el Gindi; We felt we had to say farewell to Farid el Gindi, the Egyptian film director we had the good fortune to meet on our first day in Cairo.

We had met him at the Misr Film Studios, and finding that we had a few free days, Farid had kindly volunteered to introduce us to the city. We formed a friendship and visited the Zoo, the University, the bazaars and, especially, his home where we had meals and were warmly greeted by his family. When Farid was out on location we met him on the set and took his photograph to remind us of our friendship.

Although we said goodbye it was not to be a final meeting because Bill and his wife met Farid twenty five years later when they were on holiday in Egypt. They had no difficulty in tracing him – they just called into the Egyptian Film Studio and Farid met them at their hotel later.

Bill found Farid a little more portly, but Farid was delighted to see them and took them on a short tour of Cairo just as he had done with the two of us twenty five years earlier.

When Farid was out on location we met him on the set

Cyril Ritchard on stage after 'The Merry Widow' said "We hope to play in Rome soon!"

The Royal Opera House: It would not be possible for us to say goodbye to Cairo without a mention of the Royal Opera House where we had spent so many splendid evenings. It was beautifully decorated inside with rich crimson hangings and gold brocade. What pleasant memories this recalls to mind. It seems hard to accept that we should be able to take our girlfriends by car and chauffeur and book one of the best boxes. We really lived it up – and on many occasions.

The boxes, too, were splendid. They had rich crimson curtains and were furnished with armchairs and a sofa – proper posh it all was! Here we were, often with a box of chocolates – yes, during the war – not a bit like cinemas that we were used to at home. The Royal Opera House was built in 1869 and only took five months to build. It was constructed of wood and was said in design to be strongly influenced by the Paris Opera House. The first performance after its construction was a great success. It was said, however, that the audience provided a greater spectacle than the show itself. In the royal box sat the Empress Eugenie, Emperor Franz Joseph and the Khedive Ismail. Here we were, Jack and Bill and our girlfriends, living for a short while in a land of make believe, very lucky to have the experience for, regrettably, the Opera House was burnt down a few years later.

F/Lt Langdon: Whilst we were still on duty, one of the lads said that 'he' wants to see you. We guessed 'he' was F/Lt Langdon, right, and he gave us a very pleasant surprise by handing us a letter.

This was most unusual but was typical of our boss, that he should take time to tell us of his appreciation of the extra help that we had given.

Middle East Interpretation Unit
Royal Air Force
Middle East
5th November 1944

Dear Fairs,

Just before leaving I want to thank you both for your loyal co-operation over the past two years. I cannot tell you how highly I valued your services at MEIU.

When I took over the photographic section in 1942 the situation could only be described as chaotic – the 8th Army was advancing rapidly and our small contribution to the success of the campaign depended on the rapidity with which we were able to reproduce the demands for photographic material. Your many helpful suggestions and your untiring efforts throughout the early period of re-organisation enabled the section to fulfil the most exacting demands.

Later on when the volume and intricacies of the work increased with the planning of the Sicilian and South of France landings and the re-entry into Greece it was very gratifying to me to feel I had two NCOs on whom I could depend implicitly. You shouldered the many responsibilities I placed on you in an exemplary manner and with sound commonsense. The quality of our photography and the speed of our production was, on more than one occasion, the subject of very favourable comments from the highest authorities.

I will also take this opportunity of wishing you both every success when you return to civilian life, and in the meantime a Happy Christmas and a prosperous New Year.

Yours sincerely,

J Telles Langdon F/Lt

We sat chatting, mostly about our impending departure on the boat, the boss reflecting upon some of our achievements in the department. How we had planned the darkrooms, developed a colour coded storage system for the easy retrieval of the tins of filed films, and how I had built a printer for printing the larger rolls of negatives – fourteen days of do-it-yourself and scrounging bits. It was seventh heaven! We shook hands and said that we had been fortunate to work for an officer who was so helpful and understanding (I think we were remembering those evenings when we were able to swap duties and attend dances!) And so it was goodbye Middle East Interpretation Unit.

A Friendly Place: Cairo to Bill and I had been a friendly place where we felt very much at home. I would suggest that this was because we were 'Base Wallahs' actually stationed in Cairo. We know that many people did not share our experiences of the place and had very different views:

On one occasion we were having a meal at the canteen on Gezira Island when we got into conversation with a soldier. He had every appearance of a 'Desert Rat'. (A strange name, that, for men who had served in the Western Desert with the 8th Army.) Our assumption was correct, he was on leave and went on to describe his experiences. He had been serving in the forward areas of the desert and had evidently been in the midst of the battle. But here was a welcome period of leave. By coincidence his company had come to the Beni Yusef camp, the same base where we spent our first twelve days in Cairo as guests of the army. He told us that his CO had addressed the men on parade telling them how to behave in the town. Then with pockets of back pay they boarded a three ton truck and made their way into Cairo.

As soon as they alighted from the truck they were battened onto by a horde of locals arguing among themselves as to who should escort the visitors to a 'hotel'. The most persistent escorted them to a tall building called the 'Kitchener House Pension' where he and his pal booked for seven nights at a cost of twenty piastres (about four shillings for bed and breakfast) He had not slept well. Instead of the luxury of a real bed, it turned out to be rather hard with just a single coverlet which failed to produce much warmth. The other occupants of the room (there were six beds) rolled in about midnight with much raucous chatter and boot dropping – not a good night.

He had lunch at the YMCA in Rue Soliman Pasha and sat for an hour or two reading Blighty magazines and then spent some time browsing in the Internationale Library. He had been on a visit to the Citadel but he considered that, outside the central cosmopolitan area, the place was dirty and ramshackle, full of squalor, flies and smells and diseased looking people. These were his words. I think perhaps that Bill and I wore rose-tinted spectacles when we went visiting. But he was impressed with the Ali Mohammed Mosque.

The centre of Heliopolis in 1943 with hardly a vehicle in sight. The MEIU headquarters was on the right hand side of the square and Jack and Bill's apartment was on the left hand side

The previous night he had been with his pal to a bar in the Rue Foud el Awal where he said the beer wasn't bad and that they had rather more than a drop. On the way home they had called at the notorious 'Berka'. His conclusion on the leave was that it was rather disappointing. If you enjoyed beer and cinemas you were 'quids in'. But there wasn't much contact between the ordinary soldier and civilians.

If it had not been for the service clubs and canteens he would have had a very lean time.

So we can appreciate that life on leave for those many thousands of servicemen was not as we have portrayed ours. In many cases it was as experienced by our unhappy mealtime companion.

Talking of the YMCA, it is sad to relate that in 1946 when the Egyptians were angry at Britain's continued occupation of their country, a terrorist threw a bomb into the courtyard of the YMCA injuring seventeen people.

Bill considers buying a couple of rabbits off a local street trader

The YMCA in Cairo, which was to be a scene of destruction a few years later

60: The Boat

The Boat – two simple words but to the lads overseas they meant that soon they would be homeward bound, and how they looked forward to their return, after a tour of three or four years.

However, before we climb the gangway to board our troopship, the Stirling Castle, and because our stories of the Middle East will end with this chapter, we will digress and tell you how the British were eventually to say goodbye to Cairo:

This would occur approximately seven years after our return home. During this period the war would be over, tens of thousands of troops would be withdrawn, and the huge sums of money that the allies had been pouring into Egypt would cease, putting 300,000 out of work.

The hundreds of millions of pounds that Britain and the allies had spent in Egypt, had been going into the hands of the rich rather than the poor, and this naturally led to great discontent which was further stirred up by the Soviet Union. For years the Egyptians had wanted to get rid of the British, and we guess quite rightly – they asked why should they be virtually ruled by a foreign power? They had every reason to wish to be rid of us, the writing was on the wall for many years pointing to the end of our occupation.

A number of extreme nationalist groups were becoming stronger, one of which, the Muslim Brethren, had its own newspaper which denounced the king and government for its failure to relieve the plight of the poor and suggested that the British be thrown out. Another trained its members in the art of terrorism and assassination. Meanwhile, the upper crust carried on, with their heads in the sand, the British still sipping their gin and tonics on the terrace of Shepherds. There was still polo at the Gezira Club, and dancing at the Auberge des Piramides.

Then it happened – Black Saturday arrived – the date, 26th January 1952. Gangs of arsonists appeared from nowhere. They were well dressed young men who knew exactly what they were doing. They had brought petrol and iron bars with them and they moved from building to building and soon four or five were blazing fiercely. They invited the bystanders to join in and they did so willingly whilst the crowds cheered. Soon every cinema, bar and cabaret in the city centre was destroyed. Barclays Bank, the BOAC, W H Smiths, the British Council Offices and the American Roof Garden where we had spent so many happy hours, were all

The American Roof Garden where we had spent so many happy hours

burning. The crowds of arsonists made their way to the Mena House Hotel at the foot of the Pyramids and the hotel was only saved because the camel drivers and the peddlers begged the gangs to spare it saying that their livelihoods depended upon it.

The Gezira Club and the Garden City were left unmolested no doubt because of a strong active police presence, whereas in the city the police had just stood by, even encouraging the gangs in their work of destruction.

At the well known Shepherds Hotel the gangs burst in and started ripping down the curtains and smashing the furniture to make a bonfire whilst the terrified guests rushed to escape. Within twenty minutes the Moorish Hall with its coloured glass dome had crashed to the floor. What a sad end to such a famous hotel!

There we have it – that is how the British, the French, the Swiss and many other nationalities said their goodbyes to Cairo!

Happily, our friends the Steffell family had long since left Egypt before the troubles began and had made their home in Kenya.

Bill and I are sure that many older readers who were in Cairo during the War will be interested to know what did happen to the city.

Back to the Boat home: When we came out to the Middle East in 1940 it was our first trip abroad and travelling on a 20,000 ton liner was tremendously exciting, with visits to Lagos, and Durban in South Africa, which we thought was like fairyland compared with the blackout conditions back home. But this trip was so different. We passed the Rock of Gibraltar which, of course, we found of interest, but otherwise it was just a trip and, upon reflection it almost seemed a non event.

Our boss F/Lt Langdon held a small photo exhibition in the saloon and we were able to assist him during which we got into conversation with an Army captain. We were discussing photographic reconnaissance and he suggested we continue our talk in his cabin. Our boat was a dry boat – no intoxicating liquor – and when we arrived in the cabin the captain opened the wardrobe door to reveal quite a stock of whisky and other drinks. “What will you have?” he said. “Two lemonades” said I. He was somewhat surprised and, I think, a little disappointed. Once again we had the opportunity to drink and so it had been throughout our service career on so many occasions when others would have been so pleased to have the opportunity. Ah well, that’s life!The clarity of the remembrance of our life overseas is so clear that it seems almost remarkable and yet this most important voyage to our home after four years away is practically a blank. Oh, yes! We do remember that the eggs on board were twice the size of the Egyptian eggs.

One fact that we should mention is that we were fortunate not to have the knowledge that four of the sister ships of the Castle Line had been sunk by U-Boats. Had we known this at the time I doubt whether we would have slept as soundly in our beds as, of course, the war was still on in Europe.

Hurrah! We are home sailing into the Mersey estuary – and there they are – Wallasey, New Brighton, Woodside, and there is Cammell Lairds in the distance – Liverpool too – the Liver Birds – now we are excited.

But, hold on, what is happening? The tugs are turning our ship around and we understand that we are to sail back down river. It’s almost beyond belief! But it happened, although not before Bill had called to one of the men on the tugs and asked if he would get a message to Mum to tell her we were home – well almost. He said OK and Bill threw our address and a packet of cigarettes.

Off we sailed we knew not where. Then we found ourselves in Bonnie Scotland and we did not return to Liverpool until six days later – why? We never knew!

But here we are again approaching the Mersey bar and our pilot has arrived in a small boat and climbed aboard by means of a rope ladder to take charge of the navigation – very necessary because he must navigate the boat up the channels between the sandbanks. We were not aware at the time just how big the Pilot Service was and we learned later that there were three hundred pilots and apprentice pilots which we suppose was understandable when Liverpool was the largest port in the world.

Coming alongside the landing stage, we had our fingers crossed that we were going to tie up. One of the dockers whose mate was handling a rope shouted to him, “Throwirover” and he replied, “Itscumin!” Yes! We were home in the land of scouse.

We were home to be reunited with our family, Mum and Dad and our sister Gladys. We haven’t mentioned her until now. She was a wonderful person, we were very close and although we shouldn’t say it, she thought that the sun shone out of our eyes. It was Gladys who saved the hundreds of letters that form the basis of this book.

“Home come the conquering heroes”. Well you would have thought we were,

The Stirling Castle, our 20,000 ton troopship

and no doubt some of the lads who had fought in the Western Desert deserved the recognition for there was quite a reception. A band, no less, and a real welcome from the volunteer ladies of Liverpool with cakes and cups of tea – and with that strong Liverpool accent from the ladies, I must admit that our eyes were quite moist.

Although we were just two miles from home as the crow flies, we weren't crows and so we boarded a train for our reception camp and to experience once more life in England and to await our next posting ...

61: Home and Tain

Home on disembarkation leave – how pleasant it is once again to be seated around the table, Dad and Mum, sister Gladys and Bill and I, just like the old days. During our first meal we did not discuss our Middle East experiences because through the medium of our comprehensive letters and photographs there was little more to say...

We chatted instead about the Fairs family at war, Dad telling us how Cammell Lairds, where he worked, were building a ship every twenty days which was phenomenal, and of which he was justly proud. Sister Gladys was on war work at Arthur H Lees tapestry works in Birkenhead, where she worked supervising girls who were splicing wires for the Halifax bombers. The tapestry works, which were world famous for their elaborate tapestries where

Mum and Dad, with sister Gladys

the girls worked with delicate coloured threads, was now splicing wire – what a change!

It is appropriate at this stage to show a photograph of Mum and Dad to whom we sent all these letters about our Middle East experiences and sister Gladys who conscientiously kept over 300 of our letters and made all this possible.

Bill and I of course were serving in the RAF. But Mum probably had the hardest job, like all mothers at that time, having to provide meals with the pitiable rations that were then available. Fish, although never rationed, was almost non-existent during the war, although tuna and whale meat was available. Those were the days of egg powder, sugar was very scarce, and as a substitute, saccharin was introduced, although many considered its taste awful.

The days flew by during our disembarkation leave. We went dancing of course and renewed some friendships. We wondered where our next posting or change of unit, would take us. This, though, we would find out from the Orderly Room after returning from leave – and we did. Unbeknown to Bill and I, Corporal 'Soddit' at RAF station Insworth in Gloucester was sitting at his desk leafing through a sheaf of postings. His job was to despatch personnel from one unit to another. When he came upon a letter asking that the Fairs brothers be posted together, he noted that they had been lucky with a 'cushy' billet in Heliopolis and a duty in Iraq, where he himself had served. He remembered that it had been so hot that aircraft fitters had been able to fry an egg on the aircraft fuselage, left.

On his desk were three filing boxes of the different units. He decide that a complete change was in order, so, choosing from the 'Not So Good' file he chose north east Scotland. As it was January – that should cool them down after Iraq! RAF Tain and RAF Banff should be just the job!

He certainly had not got his mind on the job because these two stations were 105 miles apart, no chance for us to even cycle over and see each other. So it came to pass that Jack found himself at Tain and it was cold! I recall one occasion when there was a blizzard – I had not experienced one before – I had seen one on film when penguins in the Arctic were bunched up together to keep warm, whilst the snow whirled around them – we could have done with bunching up at Tain especially with a few of the WAAFs! I was facing the wind at the time, walking to the billet and simply had to turn around and face the other direction leaning backwards against the wind to remain on my feet I was wearing a balaclava at the time, which was not surprising because there were nine inch icicles hanging from the gutters of our hut – something which I do not recall ever seeing before!

There was not much work on the unit and not much social life either. Very few girls and strong competition to partner any of them, especially from the Polish squadron. However, there was a dance at the village hall on Saturday night to look forward to. Saturday was cold and snowy, but nice and warm in the hall, and I was enjoying a few dances, when I met up with a pleasant young lady who told me that her father was a fisherman. Now, remembering that Mum had told me that fish was almost unobtainable, I thought what a good idea it would be to send some home. I asked my partner whether it would be possible to send some home and she said, "Most certainly". I gave her Mum's address and money for postage and Mum had a nice surprise – a parcel of smoked haddock through the post!

After an enjoyable evening our RAF bus was waiting to take us home to our hut, to the land of dreams. Well, we had not gone far when we came to an incline and our bus started to slip on the icy road and we slithered to a halt. "All out," shouted the driver. A bit of pushing was the order of the day or should I say, of the night!

Eventually, to bed which was a bit on the cool side! Even with a greatcoat and jacket on top of the blankets – but sleep came – that is until 3 o'clock in the morning when there was a call "All out". This time it was to clear snow off the runway for the returning planes to land. Well! In retrospect it wasn't so bad and it was very important that the returning aircrew should not be faced with any hazard after an exhausting fifteen hours or so cooped up in the aircraft. We were well wrapped up and soon wide awake, with almost the whole camp working together we found that we quite enjoyed it and were soon able to return to our beds.

Tain, however, could be quite an exciting place to be at times:

An incident occurred when Squadron Leader Terry Bulloch was on patrol from Tain. He was in a huge Liberator, a rather ancient machine at that time, flying in and out of cloud at about two hundred feet over the North Atlantic. Suddenly they came upon a U-boat dead ahead, which opened up immediately with cannon fire at about quarter of a mile range. It hit both starboard engines, N°4 bursting into flame and N°3 disabled with an oil leak. This wasn't all though, the starboard fin and rudder were also shot away – they were taken totally by surprise. They had to fly back to Tain on the two port engines, indeed, somewhat dicey. The crew threw everything they could out of the plane to lighten it, guns, ammunition and anything of any weight.. They flew straight over the Naval Base at Scapa Flow and wondered why the Navy didn't shoot at them – they were always known to be very 'trigger-happy' at Scapa! They were very lucky, though, and were able to make a successful landing. Worn out after a near 16 hour sortie, they modestly said it was 'quite exciting'. This was clearly evident from the holes in the fuselage and the missing fin and rudder!

Squadron Leader Bulloch was subsequently asked to take over command of the squadron but he wanted to keep flying, and this he did until the end of the war, achieving

The huge Liberator, a rather ancient machine at that time

4,500 flying hours.

Serving with Coastal Command was certainly no picnic – between September 1939 and May 1945 over 8,000 crewmen were killed or taken prisoner whilst mine-laying, anti-U-boat patrol, photo recce, anti-shipping and attacks on land targets. They also lost over 2,000 aircraft.

The Germans had a flotilla of U-boats, based in the northern Norwegian ports, which were attacking and sinking allied convoys bound for Russia. The battleship Tirpitz was also a constant threat to our shipping. A strong force of three carriers, battleships, cruisers and destroyers had carried out a bombing attack on the German battle ship which had fled to the safety of a deep fiord. It was the job of Flight Lieutenant John Cruikshank, another Liberator pilot from 86 Squadron Tain, to attack the U-boats which were gathering in force to threaten our fleet:

Patrol Lofoten Islands – F/lt Cruikshank; 'We took off in perfect weather and, after five hours reached the patrol area which was covered by dense sea fog and visibility was poor. After three hours patrolling the radar operator reported a contact at fifteen miles and, on closing in, this was identified as an enemy submarine. We attacked at fifty feet, but because of faulty mechanism the depth charge failed to release. The submarine was still visible so I ordered another attack and told the crew to prepare. As we came in we encountered heavy flak from the submarine which began hitting our aircraft and exploding inside. But we pressed home our attack – the aircraft tracked over the submarine and this time the depth charges were released. I then climbed into sea fog.

It was apparent we had suffered casualties from the flak, including myself, and a lot of damage to the aircraft, as well as a fire aft. The submarine was never sighted again so we set course for base. I handed over controls to the second pilot, Garnett, and retired to the rear of the aircraft to have my wounds attended to and to rest, so that when we neared Sullom Voe I would be able to resume control for landing the aircraft.

Some six hours later we arrived over the base, but it was still dark and we continued to circuit the base until first light in order to ensure a safe landing. Whilst we were circuiting the crew jettisoned all unnecessary equipment. I returned to the cockpit to assist Garnett to land the aircraft. We came down about two miles from the shore-line, taxied in and beached the aircraft on the shore. That's all I can remember. The medical team took hold of myself and the other wounded and we were driven to hospital.

Our attack showed that the depth charges on our second run had exploded within lethal range and, much later, we were credited with the sinking of the U-boat.'

These stories are typical of the difficulties experienced by the aircrew, the long hours cooped up in the aircraft, and the extreme danger from enemy gunfire. So, Jack Fairs, when you are called out at 3 o'clock in the morning to help clear snow off the runway, go with a willing heart and be thankful that you are not aircrew!

The days were passing and neither Bill nor I were happy at being apart and so Bill applied to his CO for posting to my unit. This was granted, the RAF were good at keeping brothers together. So, Bill was posted to Tain. But, guess what? The very day Bill arrived, I was posted which meant that more letters were required, making a serious interruption in the war effort. But, I guess it was worth it if it meant that we were to be together once more.

Our lucky star was shining once more, and we found ourselves at a station called Benson, in the pleasant county of Oxfordshire ...

62: Benson

We arrived at RAF Benson and, if any unit was qualified to say that it had 'eyes in the sky' Benson certainly was; It had four squadrons of Spitfires and Mosquitos, each with 12 planes able to carry 3 cameras.

(We have borrowed the name "Eyes In The Sky" from Roy Nesbit's book of the same name; an excellent book telling the story of photgraphic reconnaissance. Roy Nesbit has kindly given us permission to use any of his photographs, and in his letter wished us luck.)

Benson was the largest and most important unit of its kind in the world; it was the HOME of aerial photography, and the pilots who flew alone and unarmed to their targets, often from five miles high, were very special.

What a complete change there was at Benson: As sergeants we had been used to supervising the lads at Heliopolis, but here we were supervising a team of WAAFs. I was

The Spitfires were equipped with three cameras, two forward facing

going to say that they were 'manning' huge automatic photo printing machines, but I guess 'womanning' should be the word! The girls were most efficient and did a very good job. They worked a shift system through the night. They had excellent singing voices, very melodious. I recall one of the songs which went something like this; "Come inside you silly so and so's, come inside." The scene was a lunatic asylum where the inmates were looking out through the railings, telling those outside to come in where everything was free, they were fed and waited on and lived a life of bliss. The song was amusing and unforgettable.

"Guess who I met today?" said our Bill, "Harry Blackmore." Harry had served on our unit in North Yorkshire, and we had met again in Egypt, and yet again here at Benson. We had lots of tales to tell, and here is one of them;

When in Cairo, Harry had worked on an Airgraph Unit. In the UK airgraph letters were photographed on to narrow rolls of film which were sent by air to Egypt where they were reprinted and it was Harry's department where this was done. It was very confidential, of course, but he told us how he saw many "Dear John" letters, which unfortunately, were well known overseas. What were they?

The long separation between wives and sweethearts, sometimes for years, inevitably caused many to transfer their affections from the men overseas, and they would write saying, "Sorry, it is all over between us."

It was the practice in Iraq, called Mesopotamia, to refer to these letters as "Messpots". They were all male camps, and they did not have the niceties of camps where ladies were present. The letters were pinned on the wall and the lads would eject their saliva at them. I was going to say 'spat' but this is a high quality book!

One, for example, from a wife to her husband in Iraq, told of a strange visit to their home by a young girl who thrust a little baby into the wife's arms and had then run off. She did not know who the girl was and so, she had decided to keep the baby for company and hoped her husband didn't mind!

Harry was saying how he was walking out with the pub landlord's daughter, Joyce. When there was a delivery of beer by the drinks lorry, those in the know would give a special knock – two knocks, pause two seconds, and two further knocks – and the door would open. There were some very nice watercress beds in the stream in the village and the previous evening Harry had given the required knocks on the door, and was making his way home on his bicycle. A little unsure of his way in the dark, he mistook the watercress bed for the road. He hadn't tasted watercress before and now was his chance. He was wet through, and, as he didn't like to trouble the station policeman in the guardroom, he returned to camp through a gap in the hedge.

Mum had been so pleased with the fish that we had sent from Scotland that we thought it would be a good idea if we sent some eggs, and so we made a tour of the farms and did quite well. We used to wrap them in small rolls of corrugated paper and then pack them in large film tins. They arrived almost all unbroken, and we sent a tin home each week. Harry told us recently, we are still in contact with him, that we had givenhim six eggs for his future mother in law to make his wedding cake. No, he didn't marry the landlord's daughter but a WAAF who used to give him a ride in her van.

Benson – the altercation: I guess everything in life cannot go swimmingly all the time and that there must be the odd blip. So it was that we ran into a little trouble. Can you imagine us interfering with the running of the section? Perhaps you can, and, perhaps you are right, but only so far as our making helpful suggestions.

We had been on the station about three weeks, and I was working in a room drying large

The girls were very efficient, on the table are the large film tins we sent the eggs home in

rolls of film on hot air machines, when I came across an electrician drilling holes in the wall. I considered that dust from the drilling may fall upon the film, causing marks on the negatives. So I asked the electrician if he would mind working at the other end of the room, and he said "Okay".

The next day the Squadron Leader in charge of the section called me into his office, and said, "Sgt fairs, you and your brother are interfering and are having too much to say." Although I explained about the problem of the dust, he was not satisfied. He said, "I am going to separate you, one will work on one shift and one on another at the film library," which was in a bomb dump about half a mile away. Calamity, how could anyone wish to separate Jack and Bill, we had always worked together.

The officer was an unsavoury chacter (a nasty piece of work would be an apt description). I considered that his action in separating us was unjust and, knowing a couple of things about him, decided to fix him.

Later that afternoon I went to the Orderly Room and asked whether it was possible to see the Air Officer Commanding. He is over a number of RAF stations. I thought if I complained to the Station Commanding Officer he may be friendly with the Squadron Leader. I think that I was wrong in that regard.

The Orderly Room said that yes it was possible to see the AOC providing I made the correct application. I wrote an application to the CO and took it to the Squadron Leader. He said, "You cannot see the AOC." I said that I had been told at the Orderly Room that I could. The Squadron leader then asked me what I wanted to see him about. I said, "It's about you, and I am not going to tell you. I will mention just one thing and that is that you said your NCOs were imbeciles." "I never did", he said. "Oh, yes you did, and I have witnesses," said I. He then said, "You've got me cold, what is it you want?" I replied, "To go back on shift with my brother." He said, "Okay," and I turned just before leaving the room and said, "And don't you dare try any victimisation." Looking back on this episode, I

do not know where I got the nerve from, although the other complaint was of a very serious nature ...

So all was well, our bright star was shining once more:

The Warrant Officer in charge of our section asked Bill and I if we would assist at a local fete at the village of Ewelme where he lived with his family. He had decided that the RAF would help by providing photographs of the villagers at no cost. Bill and I were pleased to give our services, and this proved to be a very good move as it was here that I met up with Betty, right, who came to have her photograph taken.

Looking back, what a wonderful time it was in those days, being young and fancy free. Betty and I struck up a very pleasant friendship, cycling along the country lanes hand in hand, there was very little traffic in those days.

She was a refined young lady working as a land girl. She lived in a bothy (a small dwelling) on the estate of the Christie family, famous for their hats (they still make them today). Betty told me that the lady of the house said she did not take her butter ration (a quarter of a pound a week). Betty said she had no need, she sent two pounds of butter from her farm to her house in Scotland each week.

Bill was not entirely left out, Betty had a sister who came to visit her, not quite so demure, but wow, Bill quite liked her visits! Betty's boy-friend at the time was a rat catcher, so I had to watch my step!

Bill also met Hazel – a vicar's daughter, who worked as a nanny, left.

63: London and the BBSU

(British Bombing Survey Unit)

Two weeks have passed and the Squadron Leader with whom we had our row considered us a threat and, accordingly, decided to remove both of us from the station. So we are posted – goodbye Benson and goodbye Betty and Hazel.

Before taking our leave of Benson it would be quite wrong not to say a little about 'RAF Medmenham' which was a large Tudor style mansion called Danesfield, a huge house of whitish-grey stone with castellated towers on a magnificent site high above the Thames between Marlow and Henley. If Benson was the 'eyes' where the photographs were

WAAF personnel working on the multiprinting machine at Medmenham

above, Danesfield at Medmenham had expanded rapidly as the development of photo-reconnaissance and interpretation techniques advanced. Photo courtesy of Aerofilms

below, We had the use of our own Avro Anson at BBSU in London

produced, then Medmenham was the 'brains' where the photographs were interpreted describing what the eyes had seen. They had a special department to watch and report on enemy shipping and the devastating effect of this was admitted by a leading Italian Admiral in 1943, when Italy surrendered. He was asked why his navy had made such a poor showing. He replied, "The Allied Navy knew the exact position of every unit of our fleet at all times, but we never knew where they were."

There was not only the mansion but it had a grown a crop of mammoth sized huts needed to house the many different sections. In one of the huts two of the interpreters were looking at photographs taken after a bombing raid and they noticed a regular pattern of German fields with dozens of bomb craters giving the appearance of bombing raids gone wrong. Studying the photographs through a stereoscope they saw what appeared to be four large buildings, or rather, the foundations with walls about five feet high. They were able to judge the height of the walls by the length of their shadows. Inside these rectangles were what looked like square bundles of straw. They deduced that these buildings were decoys and that if the straw was set alight, from the air they would look just like burning buildings causing our pilots to drop even more bombs.

Another of the huts at Medmenham housed the aerodrome section. As early as 1942 Bomber Command attacked the German aerodrome at Rostock and, after damage assessment interpreters had examined the photographs, which were beautifully sharp, (they had been taken with a 36-inch lens) they had discovered the first twin jet aircraft in the world to fly. This important discovery made them decide to put on a flying programme to cover over fifty enemy airfields where prototype aircraft were likely to appear. I guess the tremendous amount of work entailed is the reason why Medmenham was so extensive.

Medmenham was visited by an American General, and it is hard to believe that prior to Pearl harbour, the USA did not have a single photographic interpreter. The United States Navy sent three of their officers over to Medmenham where they were welcomed and, after they had spent a few months there, they went back to the States and started up a school of photographic interpretation.

However, back to our posting: RAF records at Gloucester was a unit whose function it was to post personnel to where they were required. One day two clerks were talking, they were responsible for the photographic postings! One said, "Here are those two again, the Fairs brothers, they haven't spent very long at Benson. Remember when they came back from the Middle east we decided to give them a real change, so we sent them to Northern Scotland during the winter as they had requested being together? Well, we sent them both north of the border, one to Tain and one to Banff, miles apart. Unfortunately, of course, these mistakes do happen so let's give them a break this time shall we? A real cushy number and no doubt right down their street, let's post them to BBSU."

And so it came to pass. Hostilities were finally over and our bright star was shining. We were posted to London to a very special unit – British Bombing Survey Unit. Had we been able to choose a posting ourselves we could not have done better. This unit came into being when the powers that be decided that it would be a good idea to check on the photographic interpreters' reports of the bombing of targets compiled from aerial photographs over Germany, to confirm or otherwise, whether the damage reported was correct, and with the war now over, why not go and do a ground check?

Our section of BBSU comprised a few dozen personnel with its own small plane, an Avro Anson. Our new offices were in Whitehall, the officers were friendly and it was almost like civvy street. Reporting to headquarters we were taken to our billets by an airman. We found it hard to believe our eyes – they were luxury flats with centrally heated bathrooms, very unusual in those days. What a contrast to the usual RAF camp and to the tent and corrugated tin shower in the desert outside Cairo.

A WAAF interpreter working at Medmenham using a stereoscope

The next morning we reported to our new workplace, which was quite a large complex of three underground levels (including a very nice canteen). There did not seem to be much work in progress, fortunately, being well acquainted with 'Parkinson's Law' from our pre-war days when we worked for Commercial Solvents, we could pass the time quite pleasantly.

One doesn't hear much of Parkinson's Law these days when staff levels have been cut to a minimum, but for those unfamiliar with the term, it is to make the work fill the time available, ie; to stretch half an hour's work to fill a morning.

We thought it was too good to be true – the luxury flats we mean. Sorry to say, but after just four days it was suggested we move. We were fortunate, however, to be able to find a room in a Toc-H Hostel just opposite the Houses of Parliament.

One day, after we had been kicking our heels at the unit, the officer in charge said, "Would you two like to go over to Bad Nenndorf in Germany, we have quite a nice HQ over there?" our answer was "Yes, please." We had been looking at an aerial photograph which our unit had taken of Bad Nenndorf and it seemed a small town set in the country and our headquarters was a large building set in its own grounds and it looked pretty good to us.

Once again we found it hard to understand why we should be fortunate to be asked would we like to go! And not just told to report to the Orderly Room and be given orders. Mind you, we did not have an Orderly Room, we did not have any parades either – our lucky star was definitely shining!

Transport was arranged the following day to collect us from Toc-H and take us to the airfield where we boarded the unit's Avro Anson and flew to Holland. There we were refuelled and then took off for Hanover. Arriving at the 'drome, we were taken by a small truck on a twenty five mile journey to the Hotel Kassal which, today, would be described as five star.

64: Bad Nenndorf

We are on our way to our new headquarters in Germany travelling west of Hannover, passing through some lovely countryside with woods and meadows and small farms all looking very peaceful.

After travelling for twenty five miles we stop outside a handsome three storey building set in its own grounds. It is BBSU Headquarters. We learn later it is the Kassel Hotel or rather it was before the RAF decided it would make a splendid residence for our unit. It was all very grand, indeed, luxurious. The bedroom had fitted white furniture, almost unheard of in those days when we were used to mahogany and oak wardrobes and chests of drawers.

The next morning we were made welcome in the Photographic Section, and told that we could wander around the village and familiarise ourselves with the surroundings. So off we went for a walk around the block. It was not really a block but an attractive path on the edge of the countryside.

The Kassel Hotel was all very grand, indeed, luxurious

above, Not really 'round the block' but an attractive path on the edge of the countryside
below, One or two of the lads had a key and took their frauleins to the Shooting Lodge

First, we walked through the grounds of the hotel asking, "What is that building over there?" We were told it was the Shooting Lodge. It was not being used now though, because the shooting had stopped. The airman who told us said that it wasn't quite true that the building was not being used as one or two of the lads had a key and they took their frauleins in during the evening, just out of the rain of course! We were told by the lads that there was a good deal of fraternization and the locals did not seem too unfriendly.

The hotel was just on the edge of the country and we found some lovely paths to wander at will. It was quite lonely and we wondered once or twice whether any of the Germans might have made a swipe at us, annoyed that the Englander had consorted with his fraulein, however, we walked without hindrance.

What was interesting about Germany at that time was that we did not require currency to buy anything – one just bartered cigarettes and we did. We obtained a large box of 100 sheets of Agfa photo paper 16 by 10 inches and what a wise purchase, or barter, that turned out to be.

We were to find when we returned home, that sensitised paper was in such short supply, that unless one had an account pre-war, it was virtually impossible to obtain supplies. Because we had the good fortune to obtain this large box of paper we were able to operate our new studio for three months. We say good fortune but perhaps it was opportunism because we also obtained a small retouching knife and a tiny sharpener. (Looking at the retouching knife recently I see that the blade is almost worn away, so much was it used.)

We were fortunate that being non-smokers we could use our ration of cigarettes as currency.

Back at the hotel for lunch, the large dining room was very posh with damask wall covering similar to the great country houses in England. Lunch was served by German frauleins, a fish course and to our surprise the knives and forks were in the shape of fish. I said to Bill, "Not bad, eh? Better than corned beef in the desert?" Naturally, he agreed.

The hotel's claim to fame was not only that Jack and Bill had stayed there, but that Napoleon had stayed there too. He was recuperating after an illness and recovered well.

We learned that there was a German Hospital nearby and we went to visit and took some of our cigarette ration which was very well received.

We noted on Daily Routine Orders that we were to join a small team and journey to Hannover to interview a railway engineer regarding one of our bombing raids.

So far we have dealt only with the pleasant side of our visit, but when our team went on this short visit to Hannover, we stopped our car a little distance from the city. Not only the car stopped – but my heart almost did as well. The complete devastation was so appalling that tears came to my eyes. The futility of war, a dreadful waste of life and material cost too. So much could have been done to improve the world with the hundreds of millions that we were wasting on armaments.

Our interpreter was German and Jewish. He had managed to leave Germany just before the war. We wondered how he felt amongst the people who had perpetrated such awful deeds upon his fellow countrymen, or in fact, what thoughts were going through the mind of a German engineer as he discussed the horrific destruction of his railway with the representatives of the RAF. Strangely enough, the proceedings were conducted on a quite friendly basis.

above: The complete devastation was so appalling that tears came to my eyes.
He discussed the horrific destruction of his railway with the representatives of the RAF

65: The Teams

Today our team is visiting a chemical factory that our bombers had put out of action. I think the Germans would have said that the factory was 'Kaput'.

All the team wore basically the same uniform the only difference being Bill who would wear a forage cap and of course his sergeant's stripes denoting he is an NCO. He also wore a medal ribbon, nothing special, just a Middle East campaign medal. We had four more but haven't ever worn them since. If there had been a medal for employing your off-duty hours in an enjoyable manner, I think we would both have merited that!

However, we will skip the levity and be serious for once.

Bill would wear a forage cap and of course his sergeant's stripes denoting he is an NCO

With the war over, there was a determination on the part of the allies to plunder Germany of her industries. We were unaware at the time just how many teams were touring Germany or, inded, what they were up to. It was not until much later that some surprising facts became available.

There were many hundreds of teams sent by the allies whose job it was to plunder the factories and seize documents and plans from the research departments.

To understand the significance of the next part of our story it will be helpful to appreciate a few facts of life:

1. We have to acknowledge that the Germans had technical superiority in almost every aspect of their armaments.
2. The Americans and ourselves were led by people, many of whom were obstinate and arrogant, and who thought they had all the answers. We did of course have clever far-sighted military leaders, engineers and civil servants, but in so many cases they were over-ruled by higher authority.

Of the organised plunder teams sent to Europe, one specialist group was sent by the Americans whose mission it was, not only to seize the documents, but also the personnel, who had secretly developed synthetic fuel. This part of the plundering was to protect the USA's Texas oil industry.

One battle was over and another had just started. This was the battle between the Allies, the French, the Russians, the Americans and of course, ourselves. Unfortunately, for this battle we were poorly armed and badly led.

An example of this was pre-war in 1936 when one of our most brilliant engineers, Roy Fedden, was invited by the Germans to visit one of their new aircraft factories, probably to impress him. Upon his return Fedden put in an eyewitness acount of 110 pages saying that Britain would be in peril unless drastic action were taken. Typical of his suggestions was that the Spitfire should be fitted with a 20mm Oerlikon or Hispano cannon. These were not fitted until four years later, in the meantime our planes were under-armed and this, no doubt, led to many unnecessary deaths. His report was considered alarmist and no action was taken.

This disgraceful state of affairs, I guess, could be expected when a retiring treasury chief, Sir Warren Fisher complained that for some years we have had from the Air Ministry, "Soothing syrup and incompetence in equal measure."

Similarly, it seems incredible that the Spitfire, the Hurricane and the Mosquito, Britain's three most successful aeroplanes, were all built as private or semi-private ventures without Air Ministry support. Yet, even the success of the Spitfire in the Battle of Britain concealed that it was under powered compared with the German fighters.

Typical of the mistakes made by our authorities is the following: Before the war Britain had been totally dependant upon imported clocks and watches from Germany and Switzerland. Embarrassed by the lack of vital timing mechanisms for mines and bombs, a war cabinet committee recommended the creation of a new industry in Britain. A plunder team subsequently reported that in Southern Germany there were factories magnificently equipped to manufacture clocks, in fact they were over-equipped. But the British left it too late – the French had already seized 70% of the best machines and they refused to release the remainder.

By December 1945 over 200 tons of equipment had been shipped back to Britain. This was in contrast to the 8,000 tons which had been shipped to America. An investigation by

above, I think the Germans would have said that the factory was 'Kaput'

below, This shed was a noticeboard for people seeking information about their relatives

the army discovered that a substantial amount of equipment destined for Britain had mysteriously been diverted to America.

Tom Bowers, author of the amazing book, 'The Paper Clip Conspiracy' leaves no one in any doubt that in obtaining reparations from Germany, or 'plunder' as it may be called, those concerned, our military leaders and our Whitehall warriors were totally inept – which is putting it politely!

Well, after that serious interlude, perhaps we should lighten it up a bit! Just what were Jack and Bill doing regarding the German frauleins? Nothing, is the answer, through lack of opportunity, no doubt. So, to brighten this piece we have taken from our autograph book a picture of a German fraulein we photographed in 1938. We note from our book that she married a German officer in 1939. I often wonder what happened to them both in the ensuing chaos.

Fraulein Rita pictured in 1938

The days were passing leisurely by – no war. Although we were quite enjoying our holiday we would have liked a little more to do – we were not used to inactivity. However, we read on the Daily Routine Orders that there was a small team going to Hamburg and Berchtesgaden. Bill read this and he came to me and suggested that it would be most interesting and we should see if there was a possibility that we could go along ...

It was said that this huge block was not bombed so that it could be used by the Allies later!

66: Berchtesgaden

We have mentioned previously about Daily Routine Orders which were for the whole unit and were posted on the notice board each day and everyone was directed to read them.

One day, they stated that a small team was to go to Berchtesgaden on the German-Austrian border. Now, that sounded very interesting, Hitler's stronghold, and just the sort of place that Bill and I would like to visit. Bill thought it would be a good idea if I went to see the officer concerned.

Fingers crossed, I went to see our section commander and suggested to him that if we went along on the trip we could take a series of photographs and if our party needed any meals prepared by the roadside, we were just the boys, having been camping before the war. No kidding, that is just what I said and, reading earlier chapters, you will realise that we were a bit naive!

Our officer said they were tight on transport, but that he would see what they could do. It was to be a nine day trip and a little later on in the day he came back and said, "Okay, you can come." Our little team had a saloon car and a small wagon to carry our luggage. Oh boy, were we lucky to have the opportunity to go on such an exciting trip! No war on either.

After lunch we retired to the Sergeants' Mess and there we listened to records; Richard Tauber, Strauss and one of Lili Marlene, a tune which was very popular when we were in the Western Desert, and was familiar to everyone who served in the Second World War. We were seated very comfortably and after a good meal we felt very content.

Lili Marlene had been recorded before the war in Berlin by a woman called Lale Anderson and when the Germans captured Belgrade it was used as a fill-in on one of their radio programmes. Thousands of German soldiers wrote begging to hear it again. We were even able to pick up a postcard which was issued to German soldiers.

We were off, all packed for our short holiday. Our first stop was at the railway station where we photographed the damage. This photograph was typical of the many dozens that we took on our journey.

We had to smile when we thought of our suggestion of making meals by the roadside. Our bright star was shining and we found ourselves in the American Sector where we were made to feel very welcome. We fed like kings and once or twice we ate our meals with an orchestra playing.

In one small town which had been badly bombed we entered a house out of interest. It

above, We were even able to pick up a postcard which was issued to German soldiers

below, The house had evidently been evacuated in a hurry and had been vandalised

had evidently been evacuated in a hurry and had been vandalised. What a spectrum of pictures we were to see during our time in the services!

On a more serious note we made a most remarkable discovery:

Whilst our team were making their way to Berchtesgaden, another team were slowly driving along a forest road towards the small village of Volkenrode. They discovered, cunningly camouflaged under one thousand acres of dense trees, a large complex of low stone buildings. They found workshops, laboratories, parts of aeroplane engines and huge mounds which they later found were wind-tunnels. They soon learned that they had arrived at the Herman Goering Aeronautical Research Institute, the most sophisticated and advanced of its kind in the world. It was discovered later that, although the institute had been established as long ago as 1935 and was operational at the start of the war, due to a failure of allied intelligence, we were totally unaware of its existence. What a failure! So much for our research!

A USA test pilot, Colonel Donald Putt, who was leading a 'search and plunder' mission, was amazed. Walking through the complex he realised that he was probably amongst the most magnificent and lavish research establishment facility ever constructed. The sheer abundance and extravagance of the instruments and testing equipment was awe-inspiring. Supersonic wind-tunnels; the engine section was equipped with a camera that could take a thousand pictures a second, to study the growth of flames. He discovered high altitude test beds where jet engines were run at full speed normal flying conditions instead of the cumbersome allied practice of testing engines on flying planes with all the attendant risks.

There was a desperate battle amongst the allies to encourage the top brilliant German scientists to come to the west. The Russians, too, were promising them well-paid contracts to settle in Moscow with their families with good food and villas. The Russians and the French took on anyone, regardless of their crimes. Many of them were top Nazi scientists.

The Russian's successful launch of their space rocket and Neil Armstrong's landing on the moon in 1969 were due to the German experts. Von Braun's rocket team had used slave labour to build the V2 rockets. However, in 1945 it was considered more important to use the scientists to gain the secrets of the Third Reich than to consider their possible crimes against humanity.

Towards the end of the war six German Messerschmitt fighters had attacked a raiding party of huge American 'Flying Fortresses' with devastating effect; within minutes fourteen 'fortresses' had been destroyed with a new missile, the R4/M. The scientists who designed these missiles offered their services to the Americans who spurned the approach. It was not until five years later, at the beginning of the Korean war, that the Americans realised their mistake and quickly recruited them and spirited them to the USA. However, by then some of the team had already equipped the Russian Mig fighters with the world's best missiles and aircraft guns.

The British Air Ministry had decided to launch a plan called 'Operation Surgeon' to cut the heart out of the German aviation industry. As the German Aeronautical Research Institute at Volkenrode was in the British Sector it was the place to start. Thirty five scientists were flown out from Britain. Valuable equipment was to be packed and transported to Britain. The German scientists were to write detailed reports of their research and the best of them were to be brought back to Britain. Search parties were sent out to bring back former staff who were promised food and pay in return for their knowledge. One of our scientists sent there was Ralph Maltby who worked at Farnborough. The nearest he had got to shooting was service as a corporal in the Home Guard. He was kitted out in an officer's uniform bought at Harrods and sent to Volkenrode. His task was to get the low speed wind-tunnel working again. Maltby said afterwards that he felt too young and inexperienced to interrogate the German pioneers and he felt that a lot of information was missed.

Farnborough was the centre of British aero research – the 'think tank' that led our nation's aircraft manufacturers – where it was felt the key to the future was in Volkenrode. Hundreds of reports by both German and visiting specialists testified to the superiority of German scientific achievement.

Operation Surgeon had been completed and was succeeded by Operation Spanner-Hammer for the transfer of equipment to Britain. Much of the surrounding forest was felled to make packing cases, and the plant was transported in hundred ton trucks to Hamburg and on to Farnborough where the equipment was reassembled. Thus Britain gained an ultra modern aircraft research centre.

Twenty six Germans at Volkenrode were offered contracts to work in Britain with the long-term possibility of British citizenship. One of the scientists, Dietrich Kuchemann, a thirty five year old pioneer of propulsion dynamics, was one of the most successful designers in post-war Britain. He became a much admired and loved British citizen, designing the world's only supersonic commercial airliner, 'Concorde'.

We have dealt with the aeronautical side of search and plunder and there were in fact

Our first stop was at the railway station where we photographed the damage. This photograph was typical of the many dozens that we took on our journey

After lunch we retired to the Sergeants' Mess and there we listened to records

many teams from different aspects of manufacturing, some successful but, sadly in may cases, the French, the Americans and the Russians, too, ran rings around the British. Between Russian stealth and American resourcefulness, within two weeks of victory, British interests were already being squeezed. Even two months prior to the surrender, the American Advanced Communications Centre had already established a daily train dubbed the 'Toot Sweet Express' to carry plundered equipment to Paris and then across the Atlantic to USA.

above, All that was left of the dummy trees at Berchtesgaden after an RAF raid
below, In a room next to Hitler's lounge we saw two full size film projectors

67: Hitler's Chalet

As we approached Berchtesgaden it rained, and how it did rain! Our photo shows what was left of the dummy trees after an RAF raid and it also shows just what the weather was like when we arrived. However, the next morning was beautiful.

There it was – the 'Berghof' – Hitler's Chalet. Although, I must make it clear, it was all that was left of it after the RAF had bombed the complex in April 1945. They had created a great deal of damage, however, we were able to go into the ruins of the lounge and look out of the 27 foot wide picture window commanding a magnificent view of the Bavarian Alps and the town.

Like the summer residences of Bavarian Kings, Hitler, too, had chosen this superb landscape and on the Obersalzberg about one thousand five hundred feet above the town he had built his chalet. So, too, had Herman Goering, Martin Bormann and other Nazi leaders, their chalets linked to the town by a cable railway. (The American Army also appreciated the beauty of this countryside and used the less damaged buildings for recreational facilities right through until 1955.)

In a room next to Hitler's lounge we saw two full size film projectors. We were in the American Sector and strict instructions had been issued not to collect souvenirs. There was just nothing that could easily be removed from the projectors unless one had a spanner and we did not have one, so no souvenirs! We understand that Hitler had no interest in watching movies unless they were official German newsreels when he would watch the progress of the war and censor any passages that were not to his liking. He had told his secretary that, "The war is on and I cannot afford to watch films. Besides, I have to be careful of my eyesight." Although, it is said, that his mistress, Eva Braun, did manage to persuade him to watch 'Gone With The Wind'.

Bill and I did manage to remove a window catch, but it has long since disappeared. We went into the dental surgery which was below ground and had not been affected by the bombing. But it had been damaged by the yanks – they had taken everything that was small enough to pocket – leaving just the dental chair and a number of large machines.

We were not able to visit the 'Eagle's Nest' which was Hitler's private retreat. This was connected by an elevator which was cut into the solid rock – a vertical shaft of over four hundred feet. It was here that in mid-September 1938 Hitler had met with Prime Minister Neville Chamberlain when they discussed Czechoslovakia.

Allied intelligence had had information that Hitler was to leave Berchtesgaden on 25th April 1945 and, in an effort to destroy him, had planned a huge raid using sixteen Mosquito aircraft and sixteen Lancasters. The targets were Hitler's chalet and the adjacent SS barracks. Unfortunately, the raid failed to kill Hitler as he was in Berlin at the time. The SS barracks, however, were completely destroyed and much of the rest of the complex was severely damaged. Two aircraft were lost in the raid. Ironically, although the raid failed to kill Hitler, his reprieve was short-lived. He took his own life just five days later as the Russians neared his headquarters bunker in Berlin.

We took a few more photographs and left for our return journey staying overnight at an American Air Force base where we were invited to a concert. It was held in a huge palatial hall in the nearby town, which was quite undamaged by the bombing. It had wonderful chandeliers and plush seats, all very posh. But, the thing which sticks in our memories is that up on the balcony where we were seated, an American soldier was operating a machine making hot doughnuts – they were very nice!

We passed towns quite undamaged by war and others which had been severely damaged. Travelling along the autobahn we had to make a detour around a collapsed bridge. the photo shows Bill surveying the damage which we think was caused by dynamite rather than bombing. Back at headquarters, the Kassel Hotel, we resumed our pleasant routine and during our morning walk Bill suggested that we should return to Britain saying, "We are so near our release date that it would be better if we were at home."

The next day I approached our officer with the suggestion that we would like to go home and he said, "Just leave it with me, I will see what can be arranged." Sure enough, he called us into the office and said that he had arranged our return and it would be better if we went by the unit's Anson plane as the rail and boat were fraught with delays. We were very lucky to be going home by plane. We liked the Anson, it seated eight passengers and was comfortable. The Anson was of course, quite a small plane made of wood and covered in canvas. We did wonder whether it may even have been serviced or repaired at our local aerodrome, because Martin Hearn, a small company, were firmly established at RAF Hooton and were responsible for repairing and servicing hundreds of these planes.

We were saying goodbye to the Kassel Hotel and to Germany. We collected our kit bags and settled back in our unit transport for a pleasant journey to the airfield which was about twenty five miles away. Off and away! Quite an interesting trip because we were flying fairly low. We were passing over Holland and could see the dykes and huge stretches of water. It started to mist up a little and then we landed to refuel. We were held up for about an hour and the fog was really thick. Our pilot was pacing up and down and he said, "You know, the sun is shining brightly up there, just above the clouds, I think we will take off." Bill and I would have rather waited but we were not in charge and so we said a little prayer and with our hearts in our mouths and before you could say 'Jack Robinson' there we were in the lovely sunshine!

Before getting back to Britain, this chapter gives me an opportunity to report one or two facts that I have subsequently learned: When we were in Egypt we had written home to Mum and Dad saying. "There is no doubt that British is best." I think that we were comparing our soap with the local Egyptian soap at the time. Yes, we really did assume our nation was a leader. Sadly, it seems we were very wrong;

For example – tanks:

John Fuller, a conventional but rebellious British staff officer had fumed during the First War at the blinkered attitude of his superiors towards the use of tanks. Twenty years later

Hitler's dining room in 1938, well before the RAF got at it!

below, The beautiful mountain village of Berchtesgaden from a pre-war postcard

he found that little had changed and the War Office committee refused to endorse his views that tanks would play a major part in any future battle. As a result, British tank crews were hopelessly out-gunned by Rommel's tanks due to our tank manufacturers who were described as 'inflexible, inefficient and inept'. To back up this statement the following is a good example; In one battle in the Western Desert, out of one hundred and forty of our Matilda tanks, just five survived, resulting in a tremendous loss of life.

John Fuller reported that at the field trials of our tanks, they were overweight, underpowered, inadequately armed and built of badly machined and unsuccessfully welded armour. What a pity it was that those responsible did not go into battle in these tanks.

Another example – engineering:

Newspapers were partly to blame for our apathy in the gathering of intelligence because they had been praising British engineering to such an extent that we did not think that we could learn much from Germany...

The arrogance of the British and, indeed, the Americans in considering that much of German technical superiority was a myth shows how out of touch our military and our government were with the real state of affairs. The scientists who subsequently developed the American and Russian space rockets were German, without whom neither of those countries would have had the scientific knowledge to put a man on the moon. German scientists and engineers designed the Mig 15s plane for the Russians and another German team designed the Americans F86 Sabres. It paid dividends when those countries attracted the Germans to emigrate.

Civil servants and military chiefs were largely ignorant and even disdainful of those pressing for technical innovation. The proof of German technical prowess is overwhelmingly established in the hundreds of reports that were subsequently written describing their astonishing achievements and superb inventions.

Sorry this chapter is so down beat, but shortly we will be commencing the great adventure of creating our own business and we are determined to accept advice from others, realising that we have so much to learn.

Bill surveying the damage to the Autobahn bridge which caused their detour

68: Demob' Centre

Well, here we are back in Blighty. We have arrived at the Demobilization Centre where we are to be kitted out for civvy street. We are on 'Clothing Parade' for the last time, but this time it is different – no uniform, but civilian attire.

A corporal takes our measurements, and calls these to his oppo' who walks to a huge stack and selects a grey pin-stripe suit, and then a trilby. He throws these over and we make our way to the shoe department. There were, of course, many of the grey pin-stripe suits in evidence in civvy street. They were known as 'demob' suits' and millions must have been manufactured by the thirty shilling (£1.50) tailors and Burtons.

Now that we are nearing the end of our service career we cannot help but be profoundly grateful for the fact that although we are just 'two little cogs' in the vast machine of Photographic Intelligence, we have had so many interesting experiences. During our time we have visited 11 different countries and met so many kindly people. To use RAF slang, at times it has been a bit 'dicey' but on the whole it has been a 'piece of cake'.

A large part of the work of our unit has been concerned with the results of our bombing. We have not dwelt upon the results of the raids themselves or the experiences of the aircrews, but have deliberately written of the lighter side of life in the RAF recalling times that gave us a great deal of pleasure. There is a considerable amount of sadness in this world without our adding to it in our writings

Yes! We have arrived home.. Jack will return to his work at Commercial Solvents (Great Britain) Ltd, an American company that produces methylated spirits and acetone, amongst other chemicals. Solvent's, what a good company to work for! There was a friendly attitude amongst the staff which numbered just over two hundred. I rode to work on my bicycle, almost everyone travelled by bicycle in the 1930s and 1940s, even our accountant, so few owned cars.

Looking back on those days, work seemed almost leisurely. I helped prepare the wages and did the invoicing, no pressure! There weren't many invoices, we sold in large quantities, usually thousands of gallons at a time. Our accountant, who had worked for various companies, said that Solvents was the best company that he had worked for and I, too, felt that they were the tops, especially considering that they paid half my salary whilst I had been serving with the RAF.

Our walks often took us along Bebington Road past the Regal Cinema

I had better mention Bill. He had decided not to take up his job with the commercial photographer, Leonard Card, with whom he had been working until the outbreak of war, but to set his mind on preparing for our new studio.

We had decided to recommence our business of photographing cricket teams. The place to take team photographs was Arrowe Park. There were a number of cricket pitches and we were able to take four or five teams in one afternoon. We could not afford a car in those days, and we rode out on our tandem. We recall photographing Oxton cricket team, and one of the members saying we must get ourselves a car – so we did.

The mention of cricket teams brings back memories of an amusing occurrence. A man called to have his passport photo taken which was urgently required. To hasten the drying of the 5x4 inch negative I held it over a gas flame. It was just on low, but to my horror, I saw the emulsion melting and the face sliding to the bottom corner of the negative. Catastrophe! What could we do? Ah, I remembered that we had photographed this man in a cricket team some weeks previously, and hey presto! With a little manoeuvring we were able to produce a very satisfactory passport picture (our bright star was still shining for us).

Although we had not yet obtained premises, we had decided to place display cases showing our photographs at Rock Ferry, Bebington and Central stations, and Bill set to work constructing these of wood with glass fronts. We had both been quite proficient at carpentry, and when completed and painted dark blue, they looked very professional.

It was a Saturday evening and we had just been finishing some work on our darkroom when we went off for a stroll 'around the block', which is what we called our 'morning' walk. In the Middle East it had meant different things: On the troopship a walk round and round the deck, in Egypt, around the avenues in Heliopolis, and when in the Western Desert, a walk around the perimeter of the camp. These strolls were taken in the morning to avoid the heat of the day, or before duty. But, now that we are home our 'walks around the block' were usually later in the evening when our work was finished.

Our walks often took us along Bebington Road past the Regal Cinema, now Tesco's, and then around Egerton Park, which has not changed too much during the last 50 years, apart from a few new blocks of flats.

Home, and it was work with a vengeance. We worked most days until 10pm generally having Sunday off. We would finish making our photographic enlargements by 10pm and they just had to wash for an hour to take away the hypo fixer. We would walk up Dacre Hill and over the last few days we had stopped on Bebington Road and stood on the window ledge of Martins Bank, a Georgian building which was on the corner, and was unoccupied having been closed for the period of the war.

Inside the bank we saw lots of handsome mahogany panelling and some huge safes. It was all very posh and Bill said, "I think this would be just the place for a photographic studio". The next evening we called on the family who were resident, living at the rear of the bank, to ask them to whom we should enquire with regard to the premises. They

Martins Bank, on the corner of Dacre Hill and Bebington Road, was unoccupied

suggested we get in touch with the Premises Manager at Martins Bank Buildings in Liverpool.

We wrote and received a reply from the Premises Manager, Mr Holmes, who arranged an appointment. We sat in his office and he asked us about our business intentions. We were pleased to see that he was wearing a British Legion badge and hoped that he would be helpful to ex-servicemen.

One of the questions Mr Holmes asked was, "Can you keep the business going without making a profit for the first year?" Our answer was "Yes, we are both living at home and one of us is a wage earner." "Leave it with me, I will be in touch," he said. Sure enough he wrote arranging for us to call at his office in the grand Martins Building in Water Street next to Liverpool Town Hall, when he said they were pleased to offer us a five year lease.

We will digress a little here to say that apart from Martins Bank Building being one of the most modern and impressive buildings in Liverpool, it had two claims to fame: One was that it was the birthplace of Jack and Bill's business, the other was concerned with gold: When France collapsed in 1940, there was a great scare that we would be invaded.

Martins Bank Building, Water Street, Liverpool

The government decided to remove Britain's gold reserves from London and to store it in the vast strong rooms of Martins Bank Building, prior to it being shipped to Canada. Some of it was also stored in the cellars of Thornton Hall in Thornton Hough.

Isn't it surprising how these odd snippets of information surface!

And so now our preparations began – to open a studio 'William Fairs Photographer of Children'.

69: The Studio

Before starting this chapter I have written some notes regarding the setting up of the studio. Looking back on it today, it looks a formidable task. However, in those days of 1946 I don't think we considered that it was so daunting – we were so bursting with energy.

At this juncture perhaps we should tell you a little of our preparations;

We had just been reading our 'Blue Book', the book in which we had written reports on those studios which we had visited in the Middle East, setting out how they were furnished, the cameras and lighting layout and many other things that we considered would be useful when the great day came and we would be designing our very own studio.

We had been told that we could take possession of Martins Bank sub branch building in two weeks time when they had removed some safes and the furniture. There was so much to think about; carpeting, office desks, seats, typewriter, stationery, mounts, studio lighting, notepaper, just a few of those items listed in the Blue Book – in total there were thirty one!

It sounds as though finding a location for our studio was easy. But, it was not so. We had searched for weeks in Birkenhead and the outlying areas without success and looking back it was a combination of diligence and our lucky star that presented us with these lovely Georgian premises at 64 Dacre Hill – that is before the powers that be decided to rename it Old Chester Road!

When we examined our new studio, the bank premises were just one large room on the ground floor, and a basement and from these we had to make a reception room, studio, a workroom on the ground floor, and in the basement we would build a darkroom where we could also make tea – most important! In the basement there was also a room which was just like a wine cellar having an arched brick ceiling and it was here that Bill and I would build a workshop with a wooden bench complete with wooden vice, fortunately, we were both competent wood-workers having had excellent tuition at school.

We were very lucky that Cammell Laird's shipyard had just embarked on the job of converting the liners back to their peace-time use and were taking out a good deal of wooden fitments used when they were troopships. These were very handy for us to construct the partitioning for the studio and the workroom. I recall with some amusement Bill walking some of the wood from Laird's to the new studio on the pedal of his bicycle.

In one of the studios in Cairo, owned by a famous photographer called Korchid, he had the walls of his reception room covered in picture frames which were unusual inasmuch as they were 12 by 10 inches and 3 inches deep. We made twenty of these and stippled them matt black – they looked most effective when they were eventually filled with child studies.

I also noted in the Blue Book that Weinberg's Studio in Cairo mounted their photographs by brushing the back with shellac and then applying the photo to the mount. In England we used ADM, which was Ademco Dry Mounting tissue – this was a tissue paper coated on both sides with a very fine adhesive which was placed between the back of the photo and the mount and then heated causing the enlargement to adhere to the mount. In those far off days there were available huge heavy iron letter presses which had been used for copying letters. We bought one of these and by placing a gas ring underneath we were able to make a hot press for dry mounting with adhesive film.

Jack had to start practising the art of retouching negatives; a very small spot of retouching solution was most carefully applied to the emulsion side of the negative with the end of a finger covered with a well-worn handkerchief, and when dry this imparted a fine matt surface to the emulsion which accepted the lead from a sharp pencil. The negative was carefully retouched until the wrinkle or blemish matched the surrounding area. Fortunately, children do not have wrinkles, but sometimes mums required a little retouching.

When I worked for Kodak before the war I had obtained a lamphouse and large glass condensers for a professional enlarger and Bill and I decided to construct an enlarger which could accommodate negatives up to 6 inches by 4. It stood as high as six feet from the floor. The lamphouse and glass condensers were very heavy and, incorporating a negative carrier, they moved up and down in wooden channels. WE smile now when we recall that the lamphouse was so heavy that we had to counterbalance it on pulleys with sash window weights.

We thought that it would be a good idea to hide the cameras from the children and so we hid them behind the painting of a toy car. Each of the wheels was, in fact, a camera lens. We had decided that the studio should be for children only, although fairly soon we were able to change this to include weddings.

The days flew by and the great day arrived for us to welcome our first clients. We were fortunate to have a number of friends and relatives to keep us busy for the first few weeks and we were able to have what we call a 'dummy run'. All went smoothly and we had some favourable comments about our work.

Things were made easier because Bill operated the camera whilst Jack amused the children. We were blessed with much patience and in some cases we sure needed it! We were determined to be professional about running our business and we ordered Hypo Fixer in 1 cwt kegs. We also ordered two stainless steel sinks, one for fixing and the other for washing the photographs, these were both connected to the drains.

Our lucky star was still shining – at the bottom of the front lawn was a large oak post which Martins Bank had used for their sign and we were able to make use of it for our new studio sign. It was hung on a distinctive wrought iron bracket which was made by a blacksmith in New Ferry. It was almost an exact copy of the one in our Blue Book which we had noted from the blacksmith in Alexandria.

How different things were in those days. We had just been allocated a telephone, our number was Rock Ferry 3634. The local exchange was staffed by girl operators who asked "Number please." I was amused one day when the operator asked, "Is that Jackie or Willie?" She had evidently recognised our voices.

The months rolled rapidly by and we were now into 1947 and our studio 'William Fairs Photographer of Children' had been successfully launched. I was getting itchy feet and was thinking of emigrating to Vancouver.

It was whilst in the Middle East that Bill and I had considered emigrating to Vancouver and now we had just received a letter from Frank Sheepwash suggesting that if I decided to go, that he and his wife Laura, would be pleased to put me up for a few weeks whilst I was in Canada. You may recall that Frank was the ship's radio officer on the Empress of Canada, the troopship that took us to the Middle east in 1940, when we had become firm friends. He reminded us in the letter that he had given each of us a Canadian dollar saying, "Spend this when you come to Vancouver." He thought that now was the time and included with his letter were a couple of photographs, one of the avenue where he lived and the other a general view of Vancouver. Frank was suggesting that I take a trip out to Vancouver to investigate the possibility of setting up a studio there.

It was teatime and we as a family were seated around the table, an excellent time to discuss thing. Our topic was 'Going to Vancouver'. Bill led the discussion by saying that he had recently read a classic geography book a section of which mentioned the climate in Vancouver and British Columbia which stated that the summers that follow the cold but invigorating winter are dry as well as warm, which sounded pretty good. He read also that British Columbia had more sunshine than any part of Great Britain, Germany, Holland or Northern France. I said to Bill that I thought he had been reading a tourist brochure!

I raised one or two points and observations; Neither Bill nor I had made any ties regarding friends, girls or others, sufficiently to keep us at home, although we would not consider going unless our family were to follow shortly. Dad said he would leave his job and join Bill in the running of the studio. I was much more comfortable with this arrangement. I had felt a little guilty at the idea of leaving Bill on his own.

Frank Sheepwash had sent us this photo of his home in Vancouver

above, I was fortunate to be able to book a passage on the SS Aquitania

below, I was bowled over by the opulence of this liner. Some idea can be gauged by this picture of the first class restaurant taken before the war

70: Emigration

We were home from the war, the year was 1947, our studio, 'William Fairs Photographer of Children' had been successfully launched and the decision had been made that I should go to Vancouver with a view to setting up a studio there whilst Bill looked after our studio at home...

I was in Liverpool one day where I met with an old pal, Ron Miller. He had spent a couple of years with the RAF in a town called Calgary in Canada where he had become friendly with a Canadian girl. It was his intention to emigrate there. Of course, I was full of questions about his time in Canada and we decided that we should travel together if possible. I told Ron about the letter I had received from Frank, my Canadian friend, and that he had suggested I could stay with his family for a few weeks. So we decided to make enquiries about booking a passage and to get in touch with the Canadian immigration authorities to see whether they considered that I would be welcome in their country.

Ah! Another cruise was in sight and so Ron and I went to the Cunard Buildings at the Pier Head to see whether passages were available and what they could offer us. We were told that passages to Halifax in Canada were available but we could not choose, we would have to wait until we were notified. We were very impatient and called on Cunard every other day. Our persistence paid off and I was fortunate to be able to book a passage on the SS Aquitania, a huge four funnel liner. Unfortunately, mine was the very last berth available but Ron was able to get onto a cargo ship, a Liberty Ship, which was sailing to the Canadian city of Quebec. The ship was sailing empty and would take about two weeks for the journey.

The mention of Liberty Ships gives me the opportunity to tell a little of their amazing story: Built by the Americans, it is hard to believe, but they actually built more than one ship per day producing over 2,700 between 1941 and 1945. They were cargo ships generally around 4,000 tons. Under the leadership of Henry J Kaiser, the revolutionary assembly plants produced these ships much like our car factories operate today. To make each ship over thirty thousand components were needed and these were produced in thousands of factories across the States. The reason for this phenomenal success was due to them not always using conventional methods of shipbuilding and because they approached the task with open minds and a determination to get things done quickly. As for the workers, well some of them had never even seen a ship at close quarters.

Back to Cunard – When I was in their offices I picked up a brochure extolling the virtues of travelling by Cunard and was bowled over by the opulence of the liners. Some idea can be gauged by the picture of the first class restaurant taken before the war. No doubt rich mine owners and mill owners travelled in this, the height of luxury, whilst the miners in dreadful conditions hacked away at the coal deep in the bowels of the earth, returning black as the coal they were digging to wash in a tin bath before the fire.

Ah well! Back to the story. My berth was 'tourist' or perhaps it was called 'steerage' and the fare was £40. (Five week's wages in those days). However,I wish my bright star had been shining to tell me that for just £55 I could have travelled first class. But then it's fine being wise after the event! Pouring over the atlas to see what the route through the Rockies looked like, I thought it might be a good idea to make a detour whilst on the journey and visit our cousin Charles. He had emigrated to America just before the war and to us he was a local boy who had made good. Looking at the map, Detroit, where Charles lived, seemed only about 3½ inches away off my route (as the crow flies of course). Well, it was a small scale map and eventually proved quite a detour!

Strange that as a result of a chance meeting on a troopship in 1940 here I was, seven years later, contemplating a journey of three thousand miles by sea and three thousand miles by rail to British Columbia. So, off I went to Liverpool to buy a large cabin trunk, the type that one saw in the films when a person was making a long romantic journey. It was quite beyond my wildest dreams that I should ever be doing so. I remember thinking how wonderful it was when I was told that a horse and cart would call at home and collect the trunk which would be transported to 2831 West Thirty Second Street in Vancouver without my even seeing it on my journey.

The weeks rushed by and the day arrived to say goodbye to my family. The good thing was that it was somewhat different from eight years ago when we had both left home for the Middle east. That must have been a very difficult time for our parents sending both boys off to war. As I climbed the gangplank to board the SS Aquitania, Bill was there to see me off wishing, I think, that he too were going. A steward showed me to my cabin. It was a big one with twenty two-tier bunks. Our accommodation was male only, the ship having been used as a troopship, and although austere, it was comfortable enough. After exploring the ship it was quite evident from the splendour of the dining rooms and lounges that those who had travelled pre-war had experienced a level of luxury that most of us only ever saw in films. The food was excellent and our dining room quite palatial and so I came to the conclusion that I should regard my trip across the Atlantic as another cruise, although, in retrospect I can remember little about the crossing other than it taking about six days.

This was a very different experience from my last four sea journeys which were taken during wartime. Now I was able to sleep confident that I would have a peaceful night without the constant threat of submarines. At dinner in the evening we had a posh printed menu on the table, which also gave the weather report. One particular day it stated 'precipitous seas'. I was not surprised when, during the afternoon chatting in the lounge, I had excused myself saying, "I won't be long I will just go on deck for a few minutes."

There was a cinema on board and also a library but I spent most of my time chatting with other passengers in the lounge. Some of their stories were very interesting, a number of brides telling me how they met their husbands and, of course, they wondered whether their new life would be what they had been promised. And so, we steamed into Halifax, Nova Scotia, and another great adventure was about to begin ...

71: Halifax & The USA

Halifax – strange really, on the way out to Vancouver I can recall so little about this city. It was an important port for convoys and one of Canada's principal ice-free ports.

Leaving the ship and passing through immigration and customs went smoothly, and it was not until I boarded the train and passed through huge tracts of forests and farmland that I began to have a little understanding of just how vast Canada was and, compared with England, how under-developed it was.

Here I was on the start of a journey by train of over three thousand miles, on a line that was one of the greatest engineering achievements of its time – stretching from the Atlantic to the Pacific – built not only through mountains but over mile after mile of deep wet swampland swept by bitter winter blizzards. The achievement that appealed to me most was the fact that I could sit in such luxury, travelling Pullman with meals provided, observing the wonderful scenery thanks to my lucky star which was still there even on the other side of the world.

I was soon chatting away with the other passengers, learning more about the country, and, before you could say 'Jack Robinson', I had arrived at Quebec. It was here that I experienced an amazing coincidence. I met up with the pal whom I had decided to emigrate with, Ron Miller. My voyage on the Aquitania had taken six days and Ron's, on the Liberty ship, had taken fourteen, but here we were meeting by sheer chance in the railway station at Quebec. It was hard to believe and we stood there looking at one another laughing.

Looking back on my decision to pop in and see cousin Charles on my way to Vancouver. I guess I had not quite taken into account the great distance. It was certainly a long way, but the countryside was full of interest and when I crossed into the United States it was a lot noisier and everything was on such a bigger scale, especially the advertising signs vying to outdo each other and grab your attention.

The great moment had arrived, Detroit Railway Station and there was cousin Charles, whom I had last remembered delivering bread by horse and cart for the Co-op, standing there 'dressed to kill' with a big fat cigar and with a limousine no less – or so it seemed to me who rode a bicycle!

America – well it was just like the glossy magazines had portrayed, even more so, and in Detroit, so different. Everything seemed so big, even Charles' house was No 20292 Bloom Avenue, Detroit, whilst in England we lived at No 31 and few of our roads seemed to have

Aunt Maggie, Uncle Bert and cousin Charles with their huge 'limousine' outside their holiday bungalow down by the lake

more than a hundred houses. (Charles has since told me that the house number did not always indicate the number of properties in a road.)

I was most impressed with America; Charles took me to a football game at the University of Michigan Stadium, which held one hundred and sixteen thousand people. Before the game started the teams put on a show and Charles explained that the idea was that one of the teams was going to parade and show how to make sausages of their opponents and then to eat them. This performance was accompanied by two bands and attractive girl cheerleaders whirling about – quite different from Tranmere Rovers!

Charles' home was very swish and even in those early days his kitchen was fitted with the lovely worktops and wall cupboards that we know today. It had a large refrigerator and sets of stainless steel pans, unheard of in most English homes in those days of 1947. Charles said, "Let's go get some food." He took me to a huge store which astounded me. At home our local shops were John Irwin and the Maypole, just small grocery shops with their marble counter top complete with bacon slicer and a huge block of New Zealand butter with its two wooden spatulas for patting out half a pound. "Just help yourself." said Charles. Strange really, I can remember I was so moved that I felt like bursting into tears when I considered our ration of a few ounces of butter and cheese and very little sugar. Rationing in England was quite severe in those days even though the war had been over for a couple of years.

Being an opportunist I did buy some sugar and other scarce goods and asked Charles whether he would kindly send them home to Mum, which he did. I had seen the Pyramids, Table Mountain, and the Acropolis, but nothing moved me as much as the sight of the mountains of food that was available without coupons in this gigantic store which we now know as a supermarket.

Charles took me shooting, just like the gentry in England. I was dressed the part too. I would like to say that I shot a duck but I am an honest fellow, we did not see anything to shoot and so I loosed off a couple of shots at the topmost branches of a tree – I missed them too.

A vivid impression I had of the USA was the number of small modern factories, metal clad, just like those which have sprung up recently in the business parks of our own country. Before the war Liverpool was one mass of brick-built factories as old as the hills. I suppose it has taken about fifty years for us to come up to date and copy them.

My Uncle Bert's son had one of these factories and he was engaged in the manufacture of small parts for cars. I was invited to his home. It was so posh and swanky that I was afraid to sit down in case I disturbed anything. I smile when I recall at home we used to keep papers under some of the cushions and sometimes, when it was cold during the winter, we would put a house brick in our cast iron oven, then wrap it in and old pullover to keep us warm in bed. Ours was indeed a very happy homely house.

Uncle Bert and Aunt Maggie took me to see their holiday bungalow down by the lake where I stayed overnight and I was introduced to great friends of theirs. The husband's name was Art and he worked in a car factory where he was on the night shift for years and he did not wish to go back on days as he so liked the peaceful nights.

I was impressed with the basements which, unlike British cellars, were bright rooms, dry with light grey floors, making another floor to the house. I wondered why we did not have them.

Uncle Bert took me to one of his restaurants for breakfast and I remember saying how unusual it was. He said many of the workers were used to having their breakfast this way.

However, I must tell you more of cousin Charles: When he first emigrated he worked for Uncle Bert who owned two restaurants, one a hamburger restaurant, the other Chinese. Charles, however, had always been avid about education and it was not long before he was working for General Motors rising to Director of Controlled Material. Then, after taking a BSc in Mechanical Engineering, he obtained a position with the Wyandotte Chemical Corporation, his present company, where he was Corporate Purchasing Manager. He recounted the following story which I thought quite amusing.

One of the Wyandotte factories had been destroyed by fire and had been rebuilt. However, there was a problem; they required a certain type of reactor pump and without it were unable to start production. They had been informed by the suppliers that they could not improve on three weeks delivery. Charles had been sent for by his Managing Director who suggested he pay a visit to the supplier to see if he could improve things. Charles took a trip over to see the machinery manufacturer and spent an hour or so with the boss but was told, "Sorry, we can't do any better for you." Charles then noticed a pamphlet on the desk portraying an electric organ and the boss mentioned that he was having a problem playing the organ. Charles, who had a degree in Music from Victoria College in London and played the organ himself, suggested that he could perhaps help. Before long they were playing at the gentleman's home.

Yes! You've guessed it – after all it was possible to let Wyandotte have delivery at once. That's not the end of the story though. The next day when Charles was on his way back to his own factory, he passed the van delivering the pumps. When he was called into the MD's office and asked how he had got on he was able to say that not only had he got them but he had brought them back with him and they were just coming into the yard!

My short stay in the USA was an unforgettable experience, but my destination was Vancouver. Cousin Charles bid me farewell at Detroit Station from where I would make my way to Fort William where I would join again the Trans Canada line.

72: Vancouver

It was fifteen days since my departure from England and, having spent those few days with cousin Charles in America, I was over here to consider the possibility of opening a studio and our family emigrating to Canada.

My American holiday over, I made my way complete with hand luggage to the outskirts of Vancouver to 2831 West Thirty Second Street, Kerrisdale. I had arrived at last at Frank's home and my mind went back to that day on board the Empress of Canada when we were having tea in his cabin and he had said, "After the war you must come to my home in Vancouver." Little did I dream that day would arrive .... but here I was.

His house was in a lovely quiet district and, in appearance, was not unlike those in England. However, I noticed that it was roofed with wooden shingles and not the usual slates we are used to at home. The Sheepwash family, Frank and Laura and their two children, made me very welcome. Laura was a super cook – it was quite evident my lucky star was still shining.

I was very fortunate to find that Frank was home on a few days leave and he was able to take me on a short tour of the city. What a beautiful place it was. With the backdrop of the mountains, many of the beautiful properties in the suburbs looked just like film stars' homes.

Frank Quarrier Sheepwash told me that he was one of eleven children and they had originally been farming in Alberta before moving to Vancouver. Living with this family and chatting during mealtimes was a delightful experience. I recall that in Frank's house, as in most others in Canada and the USA, there was a full size basement. Frank was fortunate, his plot was on a slope and the basement had windows at the rear peeping out just above the level of the ground. In it was a workshop and a central heating room where the boiler was strangely fed with sawdust. This was automatic and very efficient. British Columbia was a huge exporter of timber and had mountains of sawdust which was, consequently, very inexpensive.

Oh yes! I was supposed to be investigating the possibility of setting up a studio and this I did by visiting sixteen studios which I had found. I introduced myself by asking if I could do any work for them by colouring their photographs in oils, and I showed them examples of my work. It did not take me long to realise that there were many dozens of studios

Whilst I was staying there I did this drawing of 2831 West Thirty Sevond Street, the home of the Sheepwash family

already established and many more being set up by returning servicemen. The competition would be tremendous!

I think it was at this point that I began to realise what a struggle it would be to establish a studio here and that, perhaps, despite the wonderful weather, the superb scenery and the lovely homes that our place was in England.

Now it was approaching Christmas and my meagre capital was being somewhat eaten into. It was time to look around for a temporary job to help things along. I was lucky, I managed to get a job with Father Christmas photographing children. He was sitting in the window of the Hudson Bay store. There were no half measures with that store. They had removed a huge plate glass window and replaced it with a smaller window and an entrance from the sidewalk with a ramp so that parents could walk their children directly into the store from the pavement and they could sit of Father Christmas's knee and have their photographs taken by Jack Fairs who was hidden behind a reindeer.

One day a rather amusing incident occurred. Father Christmas said, "And what would you like for Christmas, little man?" The little boy said, "I would like a train set from Woodward's" a big rival department store further along the avenue. The crowd outside heard this over the loudspeaker system and roared with laughter.

Christmas over, Father Christmas returned to Lapland and Jack had to find another job. This time it was a job of many parts with Coca Cola. Guess what I drank for lunch each day – three bottles of Coke. The first week I was sweeping floors etc, in the staff room. The next few days I was removing straws from bottles as well as heaving the wooden crates around. It was quite funny really stacking the crates. They arrived in the basement by conveyor belt and I had to remove them and stack them – it was like a Charlie Chaplin movie – the belt was moving too fast even for a clever Jack. However, I was able to tell the operator that I was English and not used to hard work and certainly not experienced with conveyor belts.

The next move was on the van delivering and the driver, who had recently worked as a teller in a bank, told me that if we delivered one thousand cases, we would earn a cent for every extra case that we delivered. I told him that I was quite satisfied without the extra cash!

My next assignment was in the signs department where I was cutting out stencils for shop fascias, such as 'NELL'S KITCHEN'. I recall that I enjoyed my time with Coca Cola, I remember singing away, to myself of course – I didn't want to upset the other staff!

My lucky star was shining because one of the fellows in the basement made tea in the morning, he was English, and he made a good cup of tea at 10am, just the time I was used to at home. He also very kindly agreed to post a parcel each month to my family when I eventually returned to England. I prepared the parcels in advance which contained tins of lard, sugar etc, things that were in very short supply at home. I was very surprised when Mrs Sheepwash said that she could can the lard in tins as she had the apparatus.

I thought the business of paying your fare on the buses in Vancouver was far superior to ours back home; One entered the bus at the front by the driver and, having purchased a strip of tickets from a shop, or alternatively, having the exact money, one just slotted the coins into a glass box by the driver. he checked and then pressed a little lever dropping the cash into a container. There was no conductor like we had in England and no delay for change.

Back home in England it was clear that Bill was missing me and our little walks around the block. He had taken unto himself a young lady called Sybil and he was walking her around the block. He suggested that it was serious, which was quite a turn up for the books, the brothers Fairs were not used to being serious where girls were concerned!

Whilst I was staying with cousin Charles in Detroit he had said to me, "Do you know that you have a cousin, Dianne, in Vancouver who married a French Canadian?" So, after a couple of weeks with the Sheepwash family I phoned Dianne and it was the best thing I ever did.

Dianne and Roger were a very attractive couple. They were quite unconventional and full of fun. They lived on Grouse Mountain, a little distance from Vancouver, in a wooden house which, like many of the houses, was roofed with wooden shingles. I think it could be described as very pastoral, and if you are not too sure what that means, look at the photograph.

The house was set in woods and at the rear of it there was a forest which had the appearance of never

Roger used to go shooting for moose with a friend

having been penetrated. I was intrigued with this setting, along an unmade road, so wild and natural.

Their car was an old two-seater Ford with a dicky seat – a real vintage model. I travelled in the dicky seat, Roger and Diane and their little daughter, Sheri, sharing the front seat. Coming home one evening we passed a couple climbing up the hill and Roger asked them if they would like a lift. They said they would and Roger told them to stand on the running boards on each side of the car. Yes, running boards! Roger liked a little wine and consequently was often just a bit merry. Together with Dianne he would be singing away, sometimes 'Jacques Andrais', which was most tuneful, as we drove along. Roger was, of course, a French Canadian and I must confess I was pleased when we arrived safely at the house, his driving was just a bit erratic.

The house was somewhat unusual inasmuch as it did not have any doors except into the bathroom. The reason was that it was heated by a large stove downstairs which circulated warmth all over the house. It was most satisfactory. In the lounge they had a huge fire which took logs up to two feet in length.

Roger was a great bloke to get along with and Dianne, who was born in Rock Ferry, was attractive and nice to be with. Roger would go shooting for moose and their fridge contained many steaks. I loved visiting their home and they gave me the friendship that I missed with being away from family and friends.

The time arrived for me to leave the comfort of the Sheepwash home. I was sure a lodger would sometimes be in the way and so I moved into a small apartment. I was most fortunate because Roger had a block of four and he let me have one. He surprised me with his skill. He was wiring a couple of the apartments although his job was a hairdresser. He also did a lot of the plumbing. Another thing which surprised me over there was the availability in retail stores of just about everything you needed to build a home. They were like B&Q, it must have taken about fifty years to come over here.

I moved into Roger's apartment and I remember coming home after working the day at the Coca Cola Plant. I experienced home sickness for the first time in my life. I could describe it as a sort of hopeless loneliness. However, it didn't last long, a night's sleep and I was OK. Off to Coca Cola and singing whilst slinging wooden cases about.

My lucky star continued to shine. Dianne and Roger would call and collect me to spend the weekend at their house on Grouse Mountain. It gave me great pleasure, it was all so different, even the forest at the end of their garden appearing impenetrable and looking as though no one had ever ventured inside.

It was about this time that Bill wrote me and asked whether I thought that I was on holiday and how about coming home and doing a bit of work. He was quite right of course and I was just about to book my passage home when on a bus one evening I got into conversation with an attractive young lady who told me she was a nurse. We were chatting and getting along famously. She told me she was on night duty for a week and gave me her phone number saying that she finished at 8am. I was staying with Roger and Dianne and asked if I could invite her for breakfast. Dianne said "Sure" and Joan, the nurse, came and she even cooked the breakfast, which was very nice and during the next fortnight we walked out together.

It will be quite evident that my meeting with Roger and Dianne was a very special

Their car was an old two-seater Ford with a dicky seat – a real vintage model

right, Roger was busy chopping wood for the fire in the lounge which took two foot long logs

Roger and Dianne with Spot, their dog, and daughter Sheri, in the cart

period in my life and filled more than one patch in my patchwork quilt of my experiences.

A strange thing happened when I was taking my leave. When Roger and Dianne came to the roadside to say goodbye, Spot, their dog, came with them, a thing that he had never done before. It was as if he knew that I was going away.

I then said farewell to the Sheepwash family and thanked them for their great kindness and invited them to come for a holiday in England.

73: Back Home

Having bid farewell to Vancouver, I boarded the train with a determination not only to learn something about the journey but also something about the building of this tremendous feat of engineering. To do so, I decided to engage my fellow passengers in conversation and, with four and a half days on the train, I should have ample opportunity for acquiring knowledge.

The train ambled through the Vancouver suburbs and then travelled alongside the Fraser Canyon. Through the window I could see over precipices down into the deep waters of the river far below. The track had been cut through hard black rock and I was aware of the extreme hardships which must have been endured by the navvies who had pushed this railway through the wilderness. Every ten miles or so we passed small cemeteries and I wondered if these held the graves of some of the workers who had died in those early pioneering days.

I was lucky to be able to chat to the train conductor. I remarked about the number of tunnels and he told me that they had spent eighteen months blasting and drilling just one two mile stretch. They had brought over six thousand Chinese labourers direct from Hong Kong and hired them as cheap labour at a dollar a day.

Surprise Creek Bridge in British Columbia's Selkirk Mountains has been replaced twice. The first timber bridge was superseded by a steel structure which collapsed in 1929 under the weight of two locomotives resulting in the deaths of two engineers. It was replaced again by a much stronger steel structure over which our train passed quite safely in 1947!

The majestic Banff Springs Hotel, set against the backdrop of the mountains in Banff National Park, was the flagship of the Canadian Pacific chain where American 'aristocrats' would partake of the waters of Banff's famous sulphur springs, but not me!

During the journey we crossed ravines and gorges where the track was supported by slender steel structures such as Surprise Creek Bridge, which spans a 170 foot gulch. We were told to watch out for the wreckage from the previous bridge which had collapsed under the weight of two locomotives in 1929!

One of the passengers capped this story when he asked if we had heard of the tremendous accident that had happened earlier in the century, and he proceeded to recount the following story;

It is rare that large sections of the mountains collapse, but on 23rd April 1903 a huge section of the limestone mountain, 2000 feet high and consisting of ninety million tons of rock, fell into the valley below completely sweeping away a length of the railway track.

Approaching Banff I was surprised to see by the side of the track a number of black ravens eating the body of what appeared to be a reindeer. It was in fact an elk which had been hit by a train, the body thrown to the trackside. Apparently, in winter the snows force the elks down from the high country. Chatting with the train engineer later, he told me that as many as a hundred were killed in this way each year, and that it was, in some ways, a good thing as this natural culling prevented over-population and the possibility of starvation for many.

Our next stop was Banff. What a wonderful scene it was during the summer with its majestic Banff Springs Hotel set against the backdrop of the mountains. I had seen many pictures showing Banff in all its glory, but today it was cold and wintry – certainly not picture postcard weather.

Leaving the snowy peaks of the Rockies, although still visible in the distance, we approached Calgary and the prairies. I was quite excited as I had arranged for Ron Miller, who had emigrated with me a few months earlier, to meet me here. He had returned to be with his Canadian girl-friend. I was delighted to meet Ron again and after exchanging some of our news he told me he was working with the large Calgary Brewery. We both had a good laugh when Ron told me that his present job was pushing barrels around in the brewery basement and I told him that I had been stacking wooden cases for Coca Cola in their basement. Ron was eventually to become Personnel Manager at the Calgary Brewery. I think, perhaps, the Canadians believe in starting their employees at the bottom, because when I had told the Coca Cola people that I was returning to England the office manager suggested that they had in mind to transfer me to work in the office....

Crossing Alberta, we were passing through what was known as the 'short grass' country. We passed mile after mile of snow-covered flat countryside which, in summer, would have presented a wonderful picture of the burnished gold of endless wheat fields. Farming then gave way to ranching as we descended into Medicine Hat.

Our train changed crews at Moose Jaw and the new conductor, who lived in Moose Jaw, had no need for me to question him! Boy, was he garrulous! Did he talk! About the old days too. He told me how, when the track was first laid, because the prairies were so flat that they were ideal for laying the track and they made astounding progress laying rails at the rate of twenty miles a week. Each morning two trains would set out for the end of the track loaded with rails, ties, fishplates, sleepers and spikes, and the men would work fifteen hour shifts.....

Approaching Regina, we were pleasantly surprised to see the land a little more undulating adding a little interest. The wheat fields on each side were blanketed in snow and it was easy to see why the grain elevators had such steeply pitched roofs.

Our next station was Winnipeg. Quite a surprise here. I was so deep in conversation with some fellow passengers that it was not until the train was on the move again that I realised

above, This original Horseshoe Trestle, on the north shore of Lake Superior, was replaced with an embankment

below, Our train steamed across the Red River bridge and into Winnipeg

where we were. At the next station, Thunder Bay, I decided to walk along the train and, finding a spare seat in another compartment, I asked whether it was vacant and got into conversation with an old man who had retired from the railway and who was only too pleased to share his fund of knowledge with me.

We were passing vast forests of trees and a huge expanse of water which looked just like the sea. It was in fact, Lake Superior and very 'superior' it was. We followed alongside for much of the next two hundred miles. In fact, it was so big that the whole of England could be dropped into it – no doubt though, it would make a bit of a splash!

We were winding our way through tunnels and along ledges that had been blasted out of the granite hillsides. This incredibly hard stone had taken some moving and it had been necessary for them to build three dynamite factories each producing one ton of explosives each day. What a tremendous undertaking. I was told that as many as fifteen thousand men and four thousand horses were working on this stretch of the line and that in winter they would add three hundred dog teams.

I could write of the magnificent scenery, but I think the inclusion of these statistics will give a more accurate picture of the railway which was, in its day, the greatest engineering achievement in the world.

Three lake boats had been ordered from Scotland to transport equipment, the lake being by far the easiest way to transport goods. These boats were cut in two and transported up the St Lawrence canal system. My old friend told me that conditions for the workers were just terrible. Some of the Italian workers lived in hovels without flooring or windows and the temperature in winter dropped as low as forty degrees below freezing....

We were invited into the dining car for lunch and we chatted away saying how very fortunate we were to travel in such comfort bearing in mind the frightful conditions that the workers had been forced to endure so many years earlier.

Passengers boarding at one of the stops

We stopped at Rosport on the north shore of Lake Superior where fresh trout was taken on for the dining room. We passed a number of small towns that existed by logging, pulp and paper manufacture and fishing and hunting. From the windows we could see that the small lakes and many of the rivers were frozen. They were covered in a fresh layer of sunlit snow which made them look remarkably blue.

To sleep. Then I awoke at dawn and looked out on what I would describe as a rocky moonscape. It was the outskirts of a town called Sudbury. Then we continued on to Kingston and Montreal. Many miles further on we came across quaint cottages and dairy farms, with black and white cows grazing. I could have been home in England. Then Quebec City appeared on the skyline and from a distance I could see huge grain elevators and, in the distance, the turrets of the Chateau.

One of the huge Hudson 4-6-4 locos that pulled our train 3,000 miles across the continent

My cousin Dianne and her husband Roger, whom I had met in Vancouver, had travelled through to Quebec and so I broke my journey to stay with them for two nights. It was so long ago I can't remember why they were there, but, it was a great experience! I had never encountered temperatures of 30 degrees below, nor slept under a heated over blanket.

Back on the railway again we passed into New Brunswick where the countryside seemed quite desolate, not unlike the moors of our own Yorkshire. We passed some marshes too. It was at this juncture that I gradually lost interest in learning more about the Canadian Pacific Railway – Halifax could not come quickly enough.

Halifax was still extremely busy with many trains and ships arriving and departing each day. Not as busy, though, I was told as it had been during the war when it was the main port for departing soldiers boarding the troopships.

I was quite taken with the appearance of the houses on the outskirts. They were most picturesque, built of wood, white, light blue, grey and cream, all detached, and looking lovingly cared for.

Time was passing quickly now as thoughts of home, Mum, Dad, sister Gladys and brother Bill filled my mind. Canada had been a huge adventure and, I suppose, also a bit of a disappointment. I had hoped that we could open a studio over in Vancouver, but when it was clear that it was not a practical proposition the scenery, the people and the amazing size of everything there had kept me interested and excited. I had learned much in my short stay. The Americans and Canadians are so like us in many ways but so different in many others. It was these different attitudes that would stick in my mind and, hopefully, we would be able to approach the future and our new business with a broader outlook than if I had never made this long journey.

Crossing the Atlantic in the opposite direction the voyage was so different. Gone was the anticipation of a new and exciting land and the opportunity to start a new life. Gone were the animated conversations with fellow emigrants about their dreams, their hopes,

Halifax was extremely busy with many trains and ships arriving and departing each day, its natural harbour having been a safe anchorage for centuries

Gone, even, was my awe at the splendour of this magnificent liner. This was the First Class Smoking Room, a hangover from those glorious days of the 30s

their plans. Gone, even, was my awe at the splendour of this magnificent liner I was travelling on once again. Now it was just – please let me get home as soon as possible to my family and friends!

One sad aspect of that journey home was the number of young girls on board, many of them with very young children. I suppose many were war brides or girls who had followed their boyfriends out to Canada. I guess they were disillusioned when they discovered that their 'dream homes' as portrayed by their husbands and boyfriends during their courtships, turned out to be somewhat less attractive than anticipated. And so it was with Irene who came from Leeds originally;

She had emigrated a little earlier than me and now had a baby girl of six months. She had arrived in the village deep in the forests of Mid-Western Canada where her husband to be was working to find it little more than an outpost of a dozen or so timber cabins miles from anywhere. During the harsh winter months it was virtually cut off from the outside world and there was just one shop, the Hudson Bay Company store. Her husband was now a lumberjack and he was always away working in the forests and her life was a misery.

She had no social life, few friends and even less support when the baby was born. She missed her family and friends back home and, sadly, her relationship broke down. Now she was on her way back home, sadder but wiser. On the boat she made many friends and was flirting with members of the crew and fellow passengers. I did a bit of babysitting whilst she enjoyed herself a little. I didn't mind looking after the sweet little girl of six months, it would be good practice for the work to come in our child photography studio!

The suddenly here we were – Liverpool. The Aquitania pulled into the Mersey and eased alongside the Pier Head. I was home!

Then, suddenly here we were – Liverpool and home!

One good thing about being home was that we were able to resume our walks around the block....

One day we were walking towards Woodside Ferry when we saw a young lady in front making her way to the boat. She was carrying a suitcase. Bill recognised her. She had visited the studio on one or two occasions with her sister's children. He hurried ahead and offered to carry her case whilst I followed weighing her up.

What I saw pleased me. I thought to myself – this is the girl I would like to marry. I caught them up, not revealing my thoughts of course. But, I did arrange to take her to the theatre.

This was the start of our courtship.

I married this lovely young lady in 1950.

She is a wonderful person – my bright star is still shining!

Bill married in 1948 and like me, has had much contentment in his marriage. Bill's bright star is still shining too!

Acknowledgements

Whilst the vast majority of the photographs in this book are by the authors, Jack & Bill Fairs, they and the publisher are very grateful for permission to reproduce several other photographs and illustrations from the following sources;

Roy C Nesbit

Frank Sheepwash

Ian & Marilyn Boumphrey

Jack Archibald

Paul Lamboit

George Parry

Tom Bower

Hodder & Stroughton

Aeroplane Magazine

Wirral Champion Magazine

Bibliography

Eyes Of The RAF: Roy C Nesbit

RAF – An Illustrated History From 1918: Roy C Nesbit

Eyes In The Sky;

Railway Country: Across Canada By Train: Brian Johston & Dudley Witney

The Silver Screens of Wirral: P A Carson & C Garner

The Paperclip Conspiracy: Tom Bower

Fairs Cameras, Dacre Hill, Birkenhead today: The highly successful audio-visual and photographic business which Jack & Bill Fairs have built from the small photographic studio they had established after their demob' in 1945